Business Research Solutions Series

NEW SERIES TITLES IN PREPARATION

INTRODUCTION TO ONLINE MARKET & INDUSTRY RESEARCH
Editor and Contributor Cynthia L. Shamel

INTRODUCTION TO ONLINE COMPANY RESEARCH
Editor and Contributor Chris Dobson

INTRODUCTION TO ONLINE ACCOUNTING & FINANCIAL RESEARCH
Editor and Contributor Susan M. Klopper

INTRODUCTION TO ONLINE INVESTMENT RESEARCH
Editor and Contributor Jan Davis

INTRODUCTION TO ONLINE LEGAL, REGULATORY & INTELLECTUAL PROPERTY RESEARCH
Editor and Contributor Genie Tyburski

Produced by The Benjamin Group

EDITORIAL ADVISORY BOARD

DIRECTORY OF CONTRIBUTORS*

Mohammed Al-Waqfi
Acadia University

Melissa Barr
Cuyahoga County Public Library

Mary Ellen Bates
Bates Information Services, Inc.

Kathy Biehl
Independent Researcher

Candace Blayney
Mount Saint Vincent University

Tamsin Bolton
Acadia University

Polly D. Boruff-Jones
IUPUI University Library

Meryl Brodsky
Consultant

Helen P. Burwell
Burwell Enterprises

Edith Callaghan
Acadia University

David Campbell
ShiftCentral Inc.

Cindy Carlson
Fried, Frank, Harris, Shriver & Jacobson

Kendra Carmichael
Acadia University

Margaret Metcalf Carr
Carr Research Group

Elena Carvajal
Ernst & Young

Donna Cavallini
Kilpatrick Stockton LLP

Dudee Chiang
Amgen, Inc.

Naomi Clifford
Consultant

Lynn Ecklund
SEEK Information Services, Inc.

Wes Edens
Thunderbird School of International Management

David Ernsthausen
Kenan-Flagler Business School

Michelle Fennimore
Competitive Insights

James Galbraith
Columbia University

James Harrington
Fujitsu Network Communications

Tanja Harrison
Acadia University

Michelle Hartstrom
Columbia Financial Advisors, Inc.

Jean M. Heilig
Jones International University

Karl Kasca
Kasca & Associates

Wendy S. Katz
Factscope LLC

Hal P. Kirkwood, Jr.
Purdue University

Jan Knight
Bancroft Information Services

Jim Macaulay
Acadia University

Margery A. Mackie
Mackie Research LLC

William S. Marriott
Marriott Research and Recruitment

Matthew J. McBride
Information Consultant

Karin Mohtadi
KZM LLC

Peter Mombourquette
Mount Saint Vincent University

Kathleen Morley
Independent Researcher

Rita W. Moss
University of North Carolina at Chapel Hill

Robin Neidorf
Electric Muse

Judith M. Nixon
Purdue University

Judith Parvez
Tax Analysts

Marcy M. Phelps
Phelps Research

Vicky Platt
Willamette Management Associates

Brenda Reeb
University of Rochester

Jennifer Richard
Acadia University

Jan Rivers
Dorsey & Whitney LLP

Mary Rumsey
University of Minnesota Law School

Roger V. Skalbeck
George Mason University School of Law

Ann Spoth
A.T. Kearney

Kent A. Sutorius
Informed Solutions, Inc.

Jen Venable
Purdue University

Patricia A. Watkins
Thunderbird School of International Management

Susan F. Weiler
Weiler Information Services

Samuel Werberg
FIND/SVP, Inc.

Kim Whalen
Emory University

Morgan Wilson
Hamline University School of Law Library

* See Appendix D for more detailed biographies of most of the contributors.

An Introduction to Online Competitive Intelligence Research

SEARCH STRATEGIES, RESEARCH CASE STUDY, RESEARCH PROBLEMS, AND DATA SOURCE EVALUATIONS AND REVIEWS

Editor and Contributor Conor Vibert
Fred C. Manning School of Business
Acadia University

Produced by The Benjamin Group

THOMSON
™
TEXERE

Australia · Canada · Mexico · Singapore · Spain · United Kingdom · United States

THOMSON
™
TEXERE

An Introduction to Online Competitive Intelligence Research:
Search Strategies, Research Case Study, Research Problems, and Data
Source Evaluations and Reviews
Conor Vibert, Editor and Contributor

Vice President/
Editorial Director:
Jack Calhoun

Vice President/
Editor-in-Chief:
Dave Shaut

Acquisitions Editor:
Steve Momper

Channel Manager,
Retail:
Chris McNamee

Channel Manager,
Professional:
Mark Linton

Production Editor:
Elizabeth Lowry

Production Manager:
Tricia Matthews Boies

Manufacturing
Coordinator:
Charlene Taylor

Compositor:
GEX Publishing
Services

Printer:
Phoenix Color Corp.
Hagerstown, MD

Design Project
Manager:
Stacy Jenkins Shirley

Cover Designer:
Knapke Design
Mason, OH

Cover Photo:
Getty Images

For permission to use material from this text or product, contact us by
Tel (800) 730-2214
Fax (800) 730-2215
http://www.thomsonrights.com

For more information contact South-Western, 5191 Natorp Boulevard, Mason, Ohio 45040.
Or you can visit our Internet site at:
http://www.swlearning.com

Library of Congress Cataloging in Publication Data has been applied for.

PREFACE

If you are a graduate of a typical business school, your introduction to competitive analysis was through a textbook and perhaps a twenty-page case. Suffice it to say that for many individuals the Internet has changed this. After reading this book, we hope to convince you that a more effective path to mastering the practice of competitive analysis begins with an understanding of online information sources.

The Business Research Solutions Series is intended to make online business and legal research easier to understand and practice. Taken together, all of the volumes serve both as a training tool and a reference resource for entry-level corporate personnel, undergraduate and graduate students of business and law, corporate academic librarians, and market researchers.

Introduction to Online Competitive Intelligence specifically addresses information gathering related to understanding any industry and the marketplace within which that industry operates. For the researcher seeking the best source of information and a workable strategy to access the content of that source, this volume should provide valuable guidance.

This volume is organized in seven parts to provide background, instruction, and reference to sample solutions and key sources. The researcher should consider reading the Introduction and Chapters Two and Three together. They lay the groundwork and provide context for understanding Competitive Intelligence (CI) and search strategies, particularly as they relate to competitive analysis. Chapter Four offers a series of case examples. Chapters Five and Six work well as reference sources for understanding specific types of research questions and choosing appropriate sources.

1. INTRODUCTION: Chapter One introduces the reader to the content and organization of this volume.

2. A PRIMER ON COMPETITIVE INTELLIGENCE: Chapter Two offers readers a primer on competitive intelligence and suggests quite strongly that solid analysis lies at the heart of effective inquiry.

3. PROTECTING YOUR COMPANY FROM COMPETITIVE INTELLIGENCE: The subject of Chapter Three is defensive competitive intelligence. This chapter explores how firms can foil the CI efforts of competitors at least to some extent by decreasing their online visibility to CI monitoring efforts.

4. **CASE STUDIES:** Chapter Four presents four case studies. These offer real insight to the reader on professional research methodology and practices. They build on management insights from areas that include agency theory, resource dependence theory, population ecology, and the knowledge perspective.

5. **RESEARCH PROBLEMS AND SOLUTIONS:** This fifth chapter presents 20 detailed, worked-out research problems and their solutions. They apply to competitive analysis research with practical advice on data source selection and content. They are categorized under three headings: About Industries and Markets, About Companies, and About Issues, People, and Research.

6. **RESEARCH DATA SOURCE EVALUATIONS:** Sources in this chapter are grouped into six categories: Competitive Intelligence Business Portals, Industry Analysis/Company Information, News/Alerts/Literature, Consumer Information, Data and Statistics, and Employer Insights.

7. **APPENDIX:** The four-part appendix contains valuable reference material that will be useful to any researcher. Included is a data source directory with contact names plus the combined results of data source evaluations and ratings for the 119 business research sources that are (or will be) reviewed in this seven-volume series.

The topics, problems, solutions, and sources featured in this book were identified through the editor's experience, through the business literature, through the input and guidance of other series editors, and through the wise contributors who rely on their professional research, skills, and experiences every day to meet their customers' information needs.

I would like to thank David Campbell, Tanja Harrison, Jennifer Richard, Carolyn Vella, and John McGonagle for their chapter contributions. A special thanks is due to Steve Momper of Thomson South-Western for bringing this opportunity to my attention. I am also indebted to Bill Benjamin for his confidence in me, and to Helene Segal for her patience and guidance. A final note of thanks to my wife, Sonia, and our children, Colin, Brendan, Jennifer, and Sean, who are my true inspiration.

In the near future, all of the content for all of the books in the series will appear online as well as in print with the fervent hope that more and more useful material (as well as revisions) will be made available on a continual basis. A number of additional volumes are also planned for inclusion in this series so as to eventually address all special aspects (and vertical applications) of business research that cover international as well as domestic practices.

The Benjamin Group of Santa Barbara, California, developed the concept of this series with considerable help from the volume editors and the advisory board. We will appreciate any and all suggestions for improvement in future editions and, of course, regret any shortcomings in the present content for which we are responsible.

Conor Vibert
Editor

The Editor

Dr. Conor Vibert is an associate professor of business strategy at the Fred C. Manning School of Business of Acadia University in Wolfville, Nova Scotia. He obtained a Ph.D. in organizational analysis from the University of Alberta in 1996. At Acadia University, he teaches business strategy and organization theory, and his current research interests focus on the application of the Internet to contemporary business issues. He is the author of *Web Based Analysis for Competitive Intelligence, Theorizing on Macro-organizational Behavior: A Handbook of Ideas and Explanations*, and *Competitive Intelligence: A Framework for Web-based Analysis & Decision-Making*. Conor has published in *Competitive Intelligence Review, Education and Information Technology*, and the *Journal of Competitive Strategy*. He is also a recipient of the 2002 Outstanding Teacher Award for Acadia's Faculty of Professional Studies as well as a recipient of the 2000 Acadia University President's Award for Innovation.

TABLE OF CONTENTS

Introduction

The term *competitive intelligence* conjures up an image of industrial espionage: electronic listening devices on European jetliners, satellite photos of industrial manufacturing facilities, minivans equipped with high-resolution cameras and dark curtains, trained interrogators posing as trade show employees, or the arrest of shady characters in Dumpsters. For many, the topic has a cloak-and-dagger aspect to it.

As it happens, these romantic activities have nothing at all to do with competitive intelligence (CI). Increasingly, executives are realizing that just as money laundering is not considered a legitimate pursuit by your typical chartered accountant, and spin doctoring is unacceptable to serious journalists, illegal and unethical conduct is not condoned by professional CI practitioners. CI is about analysis and processes for understanding the competitive environment.

AN EXPERT'S VIEW OF COMPETITIVE INTELLIGENCE PROCESSES

I asked Sundar Kadayam, chief technology officer of Intelliseek, to take a few moments to ponder the present and the future of competitive intelligence. Particularly, I asked him why online CI matters and where it is headed. Here is what he had to say.

> Before the Internet, companies held all the power—they created and controlled the flow of information about their products, services, and corporations to consumers, and most of the communication was one-way. But the Internet changed all that. Information now emanates from multiple sources, flows freely from consumers back to companies, and most importantly, now circulates among consumers—without company filters—and often with far more influence.

Why is online competitive intelligence important?
Well, there are lots of reasons. Two in particular are most poignant. First, it offers the potential for unique insight to analysts not previously available prior to the advent of the popularization of the Internet. A telling example can be found in the auto industry. Historically, the cycle time for feedback from consumers to be incorporated into new car- or truck-model development has been two years. The use of the Internet for gathering consumer feedback and the analysis of this online information has cut this cycle time in half to one year or less.

Second, it has altered how much of the practice of marketing is conducted. Traditionally, companies had two means to influence buyer behavior—advertising and public relations efforts. Research now suggests that buyer behavior is most influenced by a different factor—word of mouth from trusted parties. Indeed, consumer feedback is currently perceived to be far more influential than messages from sponsoring companies. Buyer or choice behavior is now being influenced online through the sharing of people's experiences.

Where is online competitive intelligence headed?
CI has evolved from a practice that originally focused on identifying issues related to competition and competitors to one with a much broader vision. The practice of online CI will soon encompass all forms of information intelligence that will help a company succeed. Indeed, there will be a massive impetus toward obtaining intelligence from multiple perspectives or all stakeholders who can impact the company in one way or another—consumers, media, marketers, sales, competitors, analysts, social issues, government regulators, etc. And not only do I mean gathering and analyzing information but also building a flexible capacity to do so, as needed. Those companies that do not make the jump to this paradigm will be left behind.

The Web is the world's largest repository of information. Its sheer size offers both opportunity and chaos. Consider that the Internet now encompasses more than a hundred thousand Usenet groups, more than a hundred thousand discussion boards, upwards of four million Web logs, and tens of thousands of Web sites. Collectively or individually, these sources offer information about consumers or can influence consumers. In their pure form, they represent the chaotic side of the equation. Yet, sophisticated analytical tools, using text-mining techniques, are now becoming available to make sense of this chaos. A good example can be found in the case of

Oxyclean, whose launch took the market by surprise a couple of years ago and left the big traditional consumer product manufacturers shaking in their boots. Interestingly, a multiple-perspective approach to data collection and analysis would have allowed its competitors to predict its launch and its successes ahead of time. The Internet is particularly influential in key industries—auto, electronics, entertainment/ gaming, retailing, etc.

Among the most powerful of new tools available to CI practitioners is the analysis of online consumer-generated content. Interestingly, the issue of "consumer behavior" is just a small slice of what CI practitioners, marketers, and other online analysts can and will address with new technologies. Their previous reliance on internal data for strategic and tactical decisions will be supplanted by holistic intelligence that combines internal data with externally generated information and intelligence. Now, finally, they have the benefit of the 360-degree view.[1]

Along with Kadayam's thoughts, this book will help you understand why online CI matters. It will also help position you for the future. It mixes the theoretical with the practical, the timely with the timeless, skills enhancement with mental models, and the Internet with paper and pen. Our readers are academics, business analysts, corporate trainers, students, online researchers, and the curious. Upon completion, you will note an increase in your abilities to offer critical insight and make sense of the competitive and environmental complexity facing organizations as you grapple with the realities of operating in an Internet-enabled world. This book offers tools and ideas that will help you use both the free and fee-based information resources of the World Wide Web to improve your ability to reason. Its major contribution is the presentation of a series of innovative Web-enhanced analytical approaches useful for students, researchers, and professional analysts in their day-to-day activities. It does not, however, replace the human qualities that support decision making. At best, it lays a foundation stone in the lifelong quest for knowledge.

---

1. Kadayam, S. 2003. Notes from personal conversation with Conor Vibert, accessed December 14, 2003.

CURRENT COMPETITIVE INTELLIGENCE PRACTICES

Throughout this book, reference will be made to the *practice* of CI. The assumption underlying this term is that competitive intelligence is something that organizations or individuals do. How they do it often differs by individual or entity. Larger corporations may practice CI with sophisticated intranets, highly cultivated networks of experts, fee-based online information services such as Lexis-Nexis or Infomart Dialog, and customized reports from companies such as Forrester Research or Yankee Group.[2] They may also make use of carefully chosen teams of highly skilled analysts who are formally embedded in the corporate hierarchy to allow decision makers quick access to information.[3]

Currently, many analysts and researchers do not have access to such specialized services. Instead, they may make use of free, public resources available on the World Wide Web. Interestingly, these resources are often similar to those used by their multinational counterparts, such as corporate regulatory filings from the U.S. Securities and Exchange Commission Web site, industry reports from Strategis, patent summaries from the U.S. Patent and Trademark office, share price trends from BigCharts, and company profiles from Corporate Information.

To organize their data, these practitioners may use the bookmarking feature of their browser along with folders available in Microsoft Outlook messaging software or IBM Lotus Notes messaging and collaboration software. They may also cultivate a network of experts that may include university librarians and academics, fellow industry association members (such as those of the Society of Competitive Intelligence Professionals), members of government support organizations, university alumni, stockbrokers, and others.[4]

Whether they work with many or few resources, CI professionals and researchers have come to recognize the important role that an ever-changing Internet may play in their efforts to understand the competitive environment and the behavior of large-scale

---

2. Metayer, E. 1999. Demystifying competitive intelligence. *Ivey Business Journal* 64 (2): 70–74.

3. Ibid.

4. Vibert, C. 2001. Staying smart: Competitive intelligence isn't just for the high and mighty anymore. *Atlantic Progress* 8 (8): 190–195.

organizations. Harnessing the power of the Internet is itself a challenge. Many academics are in the forefront of helping users make sense of this vast library of information.

CONTENT OVERVIEW

This book offers a set of chapters that suggests how researchers, CI practitioners, managers, analysts, academics, and students may combine personal insight and knowledge with the online resources of the Internet to improve business analysis. Its main argument is as follows: CI is really an alternative style of research. It is a process that is enhanced by access to online information sources. Informed personal insight, developed through years of experience, formal education, and professional accreditation, represents content. Exposure to this combination of content and process results in improved analysis. CI professionals and researchers who practice Web-based CI and who incorporate personal insight will gain a competitive advantage over their peers. That's CI in a nutshell.

Divided into six chapters, this volume explores the practice of competitive intelligence in an online world. Topics covered by these chapters include the role of competitive intelligence, strategies for protecting organizations from Web-based CI, case studies, problems and solutions, and finally, an overview of online data sources.

In Chapter Two, David Campbell, vice president for research and CI services with ShiftCentral (*www.shiftcentral.com*), offers readers a primer on competitive intelligence and suggests quite strongly that solid analysis lies at the heart of effective inquiry. Even with an awareness of how to search the Web effectively and an ability to distinguish good information from bad, researchers often fail to distinguish a context because of the vast quantity of information available. Interestingly, large entities are also challenged by the awesome power of the Internet. With no shortage of information and often hundreds, or occasionally, thousands of exceptional analysts in their employ, large corporations are increasingly faced with the difficult task of making sense of large volumes of information and making it available in a manner meaningful to decision makers. These issues are in the domain of CI, a practice that seeks to aid analysts and their employers in their quest to make sense of the competitive environment and its attendant information.

For many organizations, easy online access to information has become a double-edged sword. Although the Internet has helped to build an awareness among customers and stakeholders of available products and services, in many instances it has also opened an unwanted flow of information to competitors. The relative newness of online information access poses a challenge to most organizations. How much information should be made available to the public, and how should that information be presented? In Chapter Three, John McGonagle and Carolyn Vella, partners in The Helicon Group, discuss how companies can protect themselves against Web-based CI.

Chapter Four offers four case studies termed research missions. Research missions demonstrate how the information resources of the Internet can be used to apply established management insight to contemporary situations. Research missions are search processes that include a statement of context, a mission statement, guides for online searching, suggested online information sources, and a customized rationale for the use and display of the information. Effective use of research missions assumes that the reader possesses a basic knowledge of how to efficiently search the Internet and identify relevant information. The missions highlighted in this chapter illustrate the role that four different management perspectives may play in improving analytical insight. The first case study examines the online music distributor MP3.com, and the latter three case studies use the diversified media industry as a setting.

Chapter Five presents a series of shorter problems, including worked-out solutions, to provide even more professional insight into the online research process associated with competitive intelligence. Each of the problems and solutions in this chapter is organized according to the following sequence: (1) the research background, (2) the research budget, (3) the strategy employed, (4) the search results, and (5) a summary of the solution. Sidebars provide useful research tips directly related to the search questions.

Effective practice of CI assumes a basic understanding of online information sources and their origins. The importance of this assumption becomes even more apparent if we take into account the continued and phenomenal pace of growth of the Internet. Although the Web offers countless opportunities for organizations to gain competitive intelligence, strategy and logic are needed to tap it and use it to its full potential.

Part of any personal research strategy is knowledge of specific information sources. Chapter Six serves as a reference for undertaking effective research. Its authors are research librarians Tanja Harrison and Jennifer Richard. The chapter offers detailed critical evaluations of some of the more important online business data sources. Sources explored include both those available for a fee and those that are gratis. They also include sources best described as "general" as well as those of a more targeted or specialized nature.

2

A Primer on Competitive Intelligence

Competitive intelligence (CI) is the formalized process of monitoring the competitive environment. The Society of Competitive Intelligence Professionals (SCIP) defines CI as "a continuous process involving the legal and ethical collection of information, analysis that doesn't avoid unwelcome conclusions, and controlled dissemination of actionable intelligence to decision makers."[1] Unlike the ad hoc nature of traditional market research (as you need it), competitive intelligence involves establishing a systematic program for collecting, analyzing, and disseminating key competitor and market information at regular intervals. Most industry practitioners now believe that in the current context of rapidly evolving markets, developing a real-time or on-the-fly approach to CI is the only way to effectively cope and keep ahead of the competition. In addition, CI is at its greatest value when it is tied to and feeds strategy.

Although the CI process is multifaceted, a robust CI methodology encompasses at least these five key components:

1. **Design and setup.** This initial phase of the CI process is arguably the most critical. It involves determining the requirements for intelligence within the organization. In the past, CI was considered a strategic activity, and the results were shared only among senior management and key staff. The emerging mindset around CI is that it can be used by all levels of the organization to enhance competitive advantage. This point was emphasized by Tom Peters as early as 1986, when he admonished corporations to "get everyone involved—educate the factory team, the MIS bunch, the product designers and sales

---

1. SCIP. 2003. What Is CI? Retrieved August 25, 2003, at *http://www.scip.org/*.

persons about the best competitors' ways of doing things."[2]

2. **Information collection.** After determining the requirements, an effective CI program establishes a methodology around the collection and archiving of key information. This market and competitor information is collected in a legal and ethical manner.

3. **Analysis.** The real value of CI is in the strategic analysis of key informational variables. A good system will compile and archive information, but a vital next step is transforming that raw data into strategic knowledge, including benchmarking, product/service reengineering, trend identification, strategic positioning, and so on. In fact, a recent study found that the success of a competitive intelligence program within an organization is tied to its role in developing and implementing strategy.[3]

4. **Dissemination.** Highly tailored analysis is then presented to decision makers throughout the organization based on their individual requirements.

5. **Feedback/system reset.** The Internet has opened up whole new models for CI collection, analysis, dissemination, and archiving. With any CI program, it is important to constantly monitor the environment for CI itself to adopt leading industry methods and tools. It is also critical to integrate any feedback on the CI program from staff, because they are the ultimate users. A recent report by Best Practices, LLC, found that company-wide support for the competitive intelligence function is critical to its success.[4]

THE ROLE OF COMPETITIVE INTELLIGENCE

Competitive intelligence methodologies provide the bridge between the vast amount of unstructured, but potentially important, information and empowered business strategies and action. Figure 2-1[5] illustrates how CI is used to turn unstructured information (content) into business action, particularly in light of emerging Web-based research tools.

---

2. Peters, T. 1986. Getting to know your competitor. Retrieved March 2002, at *http://www.tompeters.com/*.

3. Best Practices, LLC. 2002. *Managing the competition: Turning competitive intelligence into strategy.* Chapel Hill, NC.

4. Ibid.

5. ShiftCentral Inc. 2002. Retrieved March 2002, at *http://www.shiftcentral.com/*.

The first phase, *content generation,* involves the creation of primary information that may or may not be relevant in a particular competitive intelligence context. The sources of this content range from magazines and trade journals to company Web sites to high-end analyst reports and market research. They can also include chat rooms, message boards, and other informal information sources, especially when the goal is to better understand consumer markets.

Better-known primary content generators would include census agencies such as Statistics Canada, magazines such as *Time* and *Newsweek,* newswire services such as PR Newswire and Business Wire, and newspapers such as the *New York Times* and *USA TODAY.* Many of these sources have much (if not all) of their content available on the Web and can be searched either directly at the source or through a major search engine such as Google, AltaVista, or HotBot. For the most part, the content-generation industry is mature; however, the Web has revolutionized how this created content reaches users by opening up whole new cost-effective distribution channels and methods.

The second phase, *information aggregation,* is the process of compiling primary information (content) in various formats. Information aggregation is becoming a major industry in and of itself. Outsell, Inc., estimates the total content aggregation and distribution market's worth at some $8 billion U.S..[6] Factiva, a joint venture between Dow Jones and Reuters, is a good example of an information aggregator. The company compiles information from more than eight thousand global information sources ranging from newspapers to magazines to technical information databases. Factiva then provides custom content in various formats (e-mail, PDAs, and so on) to users based on their individual preferences.

There can be an overlap between content generation and information aggregation. This occurs when an organization creates its own primary information but also aggregates information from other sources. News portals such as CNN.com are good examples of this category.

---

6. Outsell, Inc. 2001. *Information About Information Briefing* 4 (40).

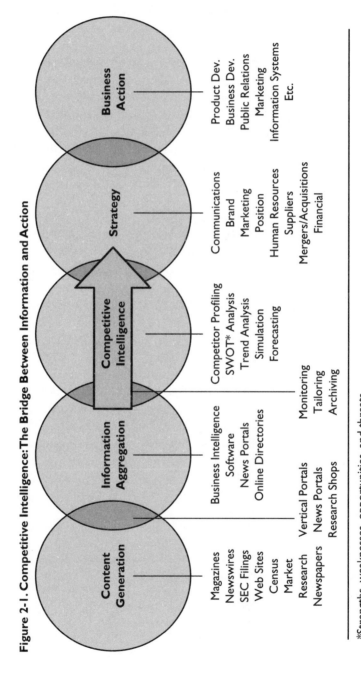

Figure 2-1. Competitive Intelligence: The Bridge Between Information and Action

Content Generation
- Magazines
- Newswires
- SEC Filings
- Web Sites
- Census
- Market Research
- Newspapers

Information Aggregation
- Business Intelligence Software
- News Portals
- Online Directories
- Vertical Portals
- News Portals
- Research Shops
- Monitoring
- Tailoring
- Archiving

Competitive Intelligence
- Competitor Profiling
- SWOT* Analysis
- Trend Analysis
- Simulation
- Forecasting

Strategy
- Communications
- Brand
- Marketing
- Position
- Human Resources
- Suppliers
- Mergers/Acquisitions
- Financial

Business Action
- Product Dev.
- Business Dev.
- Public Relations
- Marketing
- Information Systems
- Etc.

*Strengths, weaknesses, opportunities, and threats

From ShiftCentral Inc. 2002 (*http://www.shiftcentral.com*)

The third phase, *competitive intelligence,* uses information from primary content sources and information aggregators to develop a comprehensive monitoring system. The CI analyst then employs tools to tailor, analyze, and archive the intelligence (detailed below). There can be overlap between information aggregation and competitive intelligence, and in fact, many of the information aggregators (such as Factiva, NewsEdge, and LexisNexis) are starting to provide more value-added services rather than just content, realizing that the real value is not embedded in the primary information per se but in its analysis.

The fourth phase, *strategy,* involves turning the gathering and analysis of competitive intelligence into strategies that are based firmly on the competitive landscape in which an organization is positioned. The final phase, *business action,* occurs when the organization turns good strategy into empowered business action.

CATEGORIES OF COMPETITIVE INTELLIGENCE

A popular misconception of competitive intelligence is that it is actually "competitor" intelligence and involves only the detailed analysis of direct competitor moves. In reality, a strong competitive intelligence program includes monitoring and analysis of all information that can affect a company's strategic positioning within its market. There are at least five broad categories of CI:

1. **Market intelligence** includes industry-level information on trends, government regulation, geopolitical issues, and so on.
2. **Partner intelligence** involves monitoring the activities of a company's major suppliers and strategic partners. This keeps the company abreast of any trends that may negatively affect it down the road—and allows it to take action.
3. **Competitor intelligence** involves detailed monitoring and analysis of key competitors, high-level scans of other competitors, and the ongoing identification of new entrants into the market.
4. **Technical intelligence** is emerging as a major component of a robust CI program. Technical intelligence involves monitoring advancements of a technical nature that may affect a company's business model (internal and external).
5. **Customer/prospect intelligence** is an especially important tool for products and services that have a longer and more intensive sales cycle. It involves determining and monitoring key internal influences, budget cycles, key focus areas, and the like.

USES OF COMPETITIVE INTELLIGENCE

To Facilitate Strategic Direction

This is the traditional use of CI. By tabulating and analyzing key competitor and market information, senior management can make well-informed and rapid decisions. CI can be used to benchmark a product or service, assist in the identification of a merger and acquisition candidate, and stimulate wholesale changes to management direction. One article in *Fast Company*[7] outlined the view of CEOs on why companies fail: (1) They have the right information but can't get it to the right place, (2) they get information to the right place but don't take the appropriate action, and (3) they don't act quickly enough. A robust CI program can help companies avoid these three pitfalls.

For New Product/Service Development

By effectively monitoring its competitors' product development activities, patent databases, and trade journals, a company can determine the best-of-breed components of a variety of competitors and build those functionalities into its product or service.

Within the Sales Process

Increasingly, having a strong CI program for the frontline sales team is becoming a key strategic advantage. Traditionally, the sales force is closest to the market and typically has a fairly good read on it. However, in a time of many new entrants, mergers/ consolidation, foreign competition, and wholesale technological advancements, even frontline staff cannot keep up.

To Assist with Marketing/Communications/Public Relations

There is no more important role for competitive intelligence than in the development and conveyance of the corporate brand and image in the marketplace. The link between these functions and competitive intelligence is becoming more visible. In 2001, there were at least seven partnerships between major marketing/PR agencies and competitive intelligence providers, culminating in

---

7. Fuller, M. B. 1993. Business as war. *Fast Company* 1 (1): 44–50.

the partnership between Fleishman-Hillard, one of the largest public relations firms, and Fuld & Company, a leading provider of CI services. Under their agreement, Fleishman-Hillard offers its clients access to Fuld & Company's competitive intelligence services, and Fuld provides its clients access to Fleishman-Hillard's communications services.[8]

For HR and Recruitment

Using Internet-based CI, companies can monitor the job descriptions and in many cases the pay scales of their competition. In addition, U.S. Securities and Exchange Commission (SEC) filings and other public-disclosure documents provide insight into senior management and executive-level salaries as well as benefits such as stock options.

SOURCES OF COMPETITIVE INTELLIGENCE

Just a few short years ago, collecting a wide range of market and competitor information was a very expensive and laborious process. However, the advent of the Internet has opened up a wealth of information sources that can be exploited for competitive intelligence purposes. Upward of ninety percent of relevant competitive information is in the public domain. Some examples of sources include the following:

Corporate Web Sites

The Web sites of the competition tend to be an excellent source of information about a company's products and services and its approach to brands and marketing. Company Web sites also typically include financial information if the company is publicly traded. Most companies tend to brag about their major clients, providing valuable information for CI analysis. On a cautionary note, corporate Web sites tend to have a marketing focus and not to reveal any direct weaknesses.

---

8. F-H expands competitive intelligence offering via alliance. 2001. The Holmes Report. November 14, 2001. Retrieved November 2001, at *http://www.holmesreport.com.*

News Aggregators

A relatively new phenomenon, these are companies that aggregate information in real time from thousands of different sources, including newswires, newspapers, trade journals, general interest magazines, industry portals, and more. The information can then be searched by keyword or by category. In most cases the companies have free and premium service offerings. A list of major news aggregators appears in Figure 2-2.

Figure 2-2. Major News Aggregators

COMPANY/SERVICE	URL
bizjournals.com	*http://www.bizjournals.com*
FT.com	*http://news.ft.com*
Hoover's Online	*http://www.hoovers.com*
NewsHub	*http://www.newshub.com*
NewsNow	*http://www.newsnow.co.uk*
RocketNews	*http://www.rocketnews.com*
Yahoo! Finance	*http://finance.yahoo.com*

Public Company Disclosure Information

All publicly traded companies in the United States and Canada (and a number of other countries) are required to make detailed information about the company's financial situation and future plans available so that shareholders can have a clear picture of the company they are investing in. This information, submitted to the SEC, is invaluable to the CI analyst. However, plowing through hundred-page filings with a fine-tooth comb can be cumbersome. Fortunately, there are tools available to help analyze these documents.

Vertical Portals

In recent years, Web sites have emerged that provide detailed information on a specific industry called vertical portals. These sites can be advertising- or subscription-based and include a wide variety of industry-specific information. Typically, industry directories, research reports, and industry-specific news and analysis can be found within vertical portals.

Analyst Reports

Most of the major investment management companies provide detailed analysis of specific companies and industries. This information tends to be well-thought-out and valuable to the CI process. However, since the dot.com meltdown, these analysts have come under increased scrutiny, as their so-called unbiased analysis has tended to favor companies they have invested in.

Newsgroups and Chat Forums

Newsgroups and chat forums have become a convenient way to interact with various industry experts and glean valuable intelligence. In many cases, first contact with an expert can be facilitated through an online discussion group, but deeper analysis will come at a price.

Surveys and Interviews

This old-fashioned CI collection method continues to be an important way to extract competitive information. This is not misrepresentation or interviewing under false pretenses: it involves interviewing legitimate sources with intentions stated up front.

INFORMATION OVERLOAD: THE IMPORTANCE OF A STRUCTURED COMPETITIVE INTELLIGENCE PROGRAM

At least 2.1 billion unique URLs (Internet pages) are publicly available through the Internet.[9] In addition, millions of new pages are added on a daily basis. For example, it is estimated that some ten thousand global newspapers post content on the Internet.[10] There is also an emerging trend toward premium content sources that are not indexed by the major search engines (the hidden Internet) and are accessible only through a fee-based service.

To provide a sense of scope, Figure 2-3 displays the results of a simple search on various keywords related to the telecommunications industry. The search was completed using the HotBot/Lycos

---

9. Google's total indexed sites. April 12, 2001. Retrieved March 2002, at *http://www.fuld.com/softwareguidetest.*

10. Campbell, D. 2002. Estimate made from review of online newspapers, at *http://www.onlinenewspapers.com/.* Unpublished raw data.

search engine, which date-codes new URLs as they are added to its database, allowing for date-sensitive searching. In the two-week period preceding this search, HotBot had indexed 34,900 new URLs in which the word *telecommunications* appeared. Over the past three months, more than 1.3 million new URLs were added with the word *telecommunications* included somewhere on the page. The sources of these URLs include magazine articles, research reports, press releases, corporate Web sites, and others.

Figure 2-3. URLs Added to a Search Engine

SEARCH TERM	URLS ADDED LAST 2 WEEKS	URLS ADDED PAST 3 MONTHS
telecommunications	34,900	1,300,000
Nortel	5,100	190,500
virtual private network (VPN)	3,200	216,400
Lucent	5,000	250,200
broadband	17,200	848,500
satellite	31,500	1,200,000

HotBot®/Lycos®. Search run on April 8, 2002.

For any particular competitive intelligence program, only a very small fraction of the information is required. It is vitally important, then, for the CI analyst to put in place a robust and targeted monitoring, gathering, analysis, and archiving program that will scan the widest possible array of information sources but will pull back highly targeted results.

THE WEB-BASED TOOLS OF COMPETITIVE INTELLIGENCE

Given the vastness of the information on the Web and its exponential growth, a variety of tools and services have been developed to assist companies in the monitoring, gathering, analysis, and archiving of intelligence. Some examples include the following:

Web Search and Meta-Search Engines

Web search engines are essential for today's competitive intelligence professional. Essentially, Web search engines act as the indexing system for the Web. They operate by sending out automated search agents that prowl around the Web and index all the Web pages they find. Most search engines then categorize the information in some fashion to assist users in targeting their searches.

Because of the sheer volume of information and multiple formats available on the Web, this indexing process faces significant challenges. For example, most of these engines claim to re-index the Web every three to six months. However, independent studies have found significant gaps in this process.[11] Generally speaking, given the monumental task, many of the major search engines have done a reasonably good job, and there are other methods (detailed below) to capture information not indexed in the major search engines.

There are dozens of major search engines. The most used are shown in Figure 2-4.[12] Most of these search engines offer unique functions such as date-sensitive searching and on-the-fly language translation. The example of Google, the most-used Internet searching tool, is detailed in this chapter.

Figure 2-4. Major Web Search Engines

SEARCH ENGINE	URL
AlltheWeb.com	http://www.alltheweb.com
AltaVista	http://www.altavista.com
AOL Search	http://search.aol.com
Ask Jeeves	http://www.ask.com
Google	http://www.google.com
HotBot	http://www.hotbot.com
Inktomi	http://www.inktomi.com
iWon	http://home.iwon.com
LookSmart	http://www.looksmart.com
Lycos	http://www.lycos.com
MSN Search	http://search.msn.com
Netscape Search	http://channels.netscape.com/ns/search
Open Directory Project	http://dmoz.org
Teoma	http://www.teoma.com
Yahoo!	http://www.yahoo.com

Search Engine Watch 2002 (http://www.searchenginewatch.com)

---

11. Brantford Educational Services. 2001. Understanding search engines. Retrieved March 2002, at *http://www.kerrvance.com/html/lesson36.htm.*
12. Search Engine Watch. Retrieved March 2002, at *http://www.searchenginewatch.com/.*

Web Surveillance Software

These are software agents that can be given specific tasks and set up to monitor various Internet URLs at preset intervals. Although there are dozens on the market, very few are powerful enough to overcome specific challenges around different databases, platforms, and content management tools.

Alerts

A number of companies now offer alerts. With these systems, people enter in URLs and keywords to be monitored. When there is a change, they are notified in real time. Like Web surveillance software, alerts have some technical hurdles to overcome, and the best services are pay-for-use.

Third-Party Monitoring Services

Despite the advancements in technology, there is still no substitute for human intervention. A new group of CI companies is emerging that offers a blended solution encompassing the best of Web surveillance techniques. With these services, human analysts pore over the raw data to tailor it to the needs of a specific client.

Analysis Software

A recent survey conducted by Fuld & Company found that the lack of good CI analysis software is a major issue among CI practitioners.[13] Although attempts have been made to develop software that will perform some CI functions within the system (such as trend identification and scenario development), the results have been less than spectacular. As more and more raw data become available, the ability to have an intelligent tool to analyze and make expert decisions will become increasingly important.

ADVANCED WEB SEARCHING: THE GOOGLE EXAMPLE

As noted earlier in the chapter, the vast amount of information available via the Internet and the volume of new information regularly added make the task of pinpointing relevant sources and

---

13. Fuld & Company. 2000. Intelligence software report 2000. Retrieved March 2002, at *http://www.fuld.com/*.

information very challenging. Google, the most widely used search engine, has been adding new features periodically to assist in this process. Google's advanced search capabilities include the following:

- **Phrase searches.** The user can search for specific phrases and concepts instead of only keywords. In addition, the user can conduct either/or searches (retrieving pages containing either or both of two terms) as well as keyword exclusions, which return search results without specific words or phrases.
- **Specific language searches.** Google allows users to restrict a search to one of more than thirty different languages. Google also has a robust translation tool (see the discussion of multi-lingual CI later in the chapter).
- **Specific country searches.** Google indexes URLs based on their country of origin, allowing users to limit a search to specific geographic regions.
- **Multiformat searches.** In addition to standard Web formats such as Hypertext Markup Language (HTML) and Active Server Page (ASP), Google also indexes Adobe Acrobat (.pdf), Adobe PostScript (.ps), Rich Text Format (.rtf), Microsoft Word (.doc), Microsoft PowerPoint presentation graphics program (.ppt), and Microsoft Excel (.xls) formats.
- **Date-sensitive searches.** Google allows the user to search Web pages added to its index.
- **Occurrence in the page.** Users can restrict searches to specific areas of the Web page such as the title, URL, and main body.
- **Domain search.** Google allows the user to search only in specific domains. Doing a Google search on a specific domain is some-times more effective than using the search engine employed by the actual Web site. For example, many people find that Strat-egis, Industry Canada's business portal, does not have an overly effective search tool built into its site. By using Google's advanced functions and specifying, for Domain, "strategis.ic.gc.ca," the user can do highly targeted searches not available via Strategis's internal search tool. This method has two drawbacks. First, there is no way of knowing when Google last indexed Strategis (although within the last three months is a good estimate), and second, there is no way of knowing the extent of Google's index of Strategis's database.
- **News search.** Google has added a news search function that searches various news media it has indexed. Google indexes news sites on a daily basis, allowing access to up-to-date information.

- **Image search.** One of the more interesting search functions Google has introduced is the Image search. Google indexes graphics files found on the Web, and users can search for specific images. This function is particularly useful to the CI analyst who is looking for charts, graphs, and tables. For example, a search on "GDP growth" yields more than a thousand charts, graphs, and tables that the CI analyst can plow through for relevant information.
- **Groups search.** Google also allows users to search through Usenet newsgroup postings that are updated daily. This is particularly helpful if the CI analyst is looking to evaluate public opinion or find any informal scuttlebutt about a specific topic of interest.

MULTILINGUAL COMPETITIVE INTELLIGENCE

CI professionals are no longer constrained by language in their competitive intelligence-gathering activities. New online language translation tools allow researchers to translate documents quickly and easily between multiple languages, and in most cases, this service is free (see Figure 2-5).

Figure 2-5. Online Translation Tools

TOOL	URL
AltaVista's Babel Fish	http://babelfish.altavista.com
Dictionary.com/Translator	http://translator.dictionary.com
FreeTranslation	http://www.freetranslation.com
Google	http://www.google.com (choose Language Tools)

Google, for example, translates Web pages from English to German, Spanish, French, Italian, and Portuguese, as well as from some of these languages to others. Google will also translate on the fly, meaning that when it detects that a search term in a Web page is not in the user's preferred language, it provides a "translate" option that the user can click to translate immediately. Google then continues to translate pages as the user clicks through the Web site. The AltaVista search engine offers an even more expansive list of languages, including Japanese, Korean, and Chinese.

On a cautionary note, these language tools are still not very advanced and tend to conduct literal, word-for-word translations. Therefore, the translated text is to be used with caution but typically can provide the essence of what the researcher is looking for.

COMPETITIVE INTELLIGENCE ON PUBLICLY TRADED COMPANIES

Since the Securities Act of 1933, U.S.-based publicly traded companies have been required to disclose detailed information on their financial situation to their shareholders. Specifically, the act "require[s] that investors receive financial and other significant information concerning securities being offered for public sale; and prohibit[s] deceit, misrepresentations, and other fraud in the sale of securities."[14]

The Securities and Exchange Commission is the governing agency for all U.S. securities regulation. All companies publicly traded on U.S.-based stock exchanges are required to file company documents with the SEC, and since 1995, the commission has provided this information to the public at no charge via its Web site, *http://www.sec.gov*.

Of specific interest to the CI researcher are the 10-K and 10-Q filings, which are the annual and quarterly filings to the SEC, respectively. In the filings is a wealth of intelligence, including the following:

- Detailed financial information
- A review of product and service offerings
- Mergers and acquisitions
- Geographic markets
- Any outstanding legal proceedings against the company
- The company's market risk factors

In addition, the CI researcher can use these SEC filings and others for a number of specific CI functions, including identifying power holders in an organization; performing a social responsibility audit on an organization; and completing a due diligence process for a potential merger, acquisition, or new partner.[15]

---

14. The laws that govern the securities industry. June 27, 2003. Retrieved July 30, 2003, at *http://www.sec.gov/*.
15. Vibert, C. 2000. *Web-based analysis for competitive intelligence.* Westport, CT: Quorum Books.

Other countries have different legislation, policies, and procedures governing disclosure of public company information. Many European countries, for example, do not require disclosure at anywhere near the level that the SEC mandates. Other countries, such as Canada, have similar reporting requirements. SEDAR is the public filings Web site for the Canadian Depository for Securities, the agency governing publicly traded companies in Canada.

There are two potentially significant challenges facing CI analysts with the use of public company SEC filings. First, if the company they are analyzing is not publicly traded (or is foreign), access to this information is much more difficult. However, it has been shown that most of the information required to properly analyze a company from a CI perspective (that is, competitive threat) can be found in public information sources. Second, a number of high-profile companies recently have not followed the spirit of the Securities Act of 1933 and have filed false or misleading information. Therefore, CI analysts must examine information from a variety of sources to uncover anomalies that may not be evident from using just one information source.

THE COMPETITIVE INTELLIGENCE PRACTITIONER

Who performs the CI function? Typically, a good CI professional has a strong business background with one or more specific industry strengths. The person also has strong research skills and a good understanding of technology.

Finally, and of vital importance, the best CI practitioners have very strong analysis and writing/communication skills. The graph in Figure 2-6 shows a breakdown of CI professionals by area of expertise, based on the membership of the Society of Competitive Intelligence Professionals.[16] CI practitioners can be found in a variety of areas within organizations.

---

16. Membership survey, Society of Competitive Intelligence Professionals. 2001. Retrieved March 2002, at *http://www.scip.org/*.

Figure 2-6. CI Practitioners' Job Functions and Areas of Work

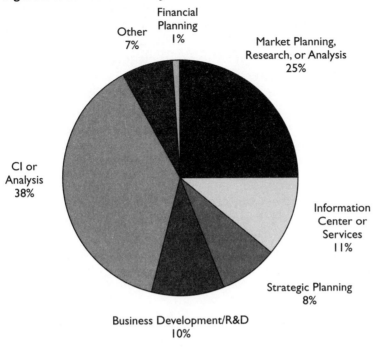

Membership Survey, SCIP 2001 (*http://www.scip.org*)

AN EXAMPLE OF USING COMPETITIVE INTELLIGENCE METHODS TO COLLECT AND ANALYZE COMPETITOR FINANCIAL DATA

At the time of this writing, there had been a lot of discussion about the firing of Ford's CEO and the financial troubles that faced the company. Implementing a formalized and systematic approach to analyzing the competition's financial position in a relative fashion can be a valuable tool in developing and maintaining a competitive advantage.

Figure 2-7 provides a financial snapshot of Ford against three of its major competitors right before the CEO was fired. Set within a proper CI program, senior management would review these figures on at least a quarterly basis.

For Ford, the numbers reveal some interesting facts. Although their employee-to-revenue ratio and gross profit margins are as good as, or better, than those of their competition, bottom-line profits and the profit trend are noticeably down relative to at least two of their competitors. In addition, their leverage and debt-to-equity ratios are out of line, which indicates that the company has too much debt, undermining its ability to grow. The current and quick ratios are both significantly lower than their competitors' and indicate real structural problems within the company.

Closely monitoring and analyzing financial performance is a key feature of a robust competitive intelligence program.

Figure 2-7. Competitive Landscape Review

	FORD	DAIMLER-CHRYSLER	GENERAL MOTORS	TOYOTA
Annual Sales ($ mil.)	170,064	152,446	184,632	106,030
Employees	345,991	416,501	386,000	215,648
Market Value ($ mil.)	29,369	36,841	61,187	92,954
Profitability				
Gross Profit Margin	24.4%	24.3%	27.6%	24.9%
Pretax Profit Margin	2.2%	-1.4%	1.6%	9.2%
Net Profit Margin	0.4%	-0.9%	0.9%	5.1%
Return on Equity	5.0%	--	5.5%	9.5%
Return on Assets	0.2%	-0.7%	0.5%	4.0%
Return on Invested Capital	0.4%	-1.1%	1.0%	6.6%
Operations				
Days of Sales Outstanding	10.7	--	266.9	89.4
Inventory Turnover	18.4	6.7	11.3	11.0
Days COGS in Inventory	20.0	--	32.0	33.0
Asset Turnover	0.6	0.8	0.6	0.7
Effective Tax Rate	34.5%	--	42.2%	43.3%
Financial				
Current Ratio	0.88	2.77	3.26	1.24
Quick Ratio	0.50	2.30	2.40	0.90
Leverage Ratio	21.05	5.37	10.24	2.40
Total Debt/Equity	12.66	2.38	4.86	0.74

Figure 2-7. Competitive Landscape Review (*cont.*)

	FORD	DAIMLER-CHRYSLER	GENERAL MOTORS	TOYOTA
Interest Coverage	1.30	(15.20)	1.30	30.30
Growth				
12-Month Revenue Growth	-4.7%	-1.7%	0.1%	-11.4%
12-Month Net Income Growth	-83.5%	-100.0%	-70.6%	20.0%
12-Month EPS Growth	-89.5%	-100.0%	-72.9%	20.7%
12-Month Dividend Growth	-40.0%	-6.3%	8.1%	32.4%

Media General Financial Services, SEC filings, annual reports

COMPETITIVE INTELLIGENCE IN GOVERNMENT

Traditionally, techniques for competitive intelligence-gathering and analysis have been employed primarily in the private sector, particularly in highly competitive markets or markets with a high rate of technical change. In recent years, however, governments and other public sector and quasi-public sector organizations have begun to understand the importance of competitive intelligence. Although government departments or agencies may not be competing in a traditional sense, they are competing in many other ways, including the following:

- With other jurisdictions and countries
- With other government departments and functions for increasingly scarce public funds
- For public support of their activities
- To attract and retain key staff

A good CI program can provide critical information to assist in fulfilling a government mandate. Because most government functions do not have a profit motive or other market drivers, the value of their services has become increasingly subjective in the minds of elected officials and the public at large. Competitive intelligence can provide insight on a variety of themes, such as the following:

- Best practices in government service delivery
- Developing public policy in the context of a global economy
- Developing legislation and regulation

- Best practices and methods for global economic development
- Taxation issues
- Environmental issues

EXAMPLES OF COMPETITIVE INTELLIGENCE USE IN THE PUBLIC SECTOR

In recent years the competition for new business investments among states, provinces, and even countries has reached a fevered pitch, as governments have realized the economic effect that this activity can have in their jurisdictions. High-profile expansions such as the Mercedes-Benz plant in Alabama and the BMW plant in South Carolina have forced governments to hone their value proposition, marketing techniques, and approach to financial incentives. The Michigan Economic Development Corporation (MEDC) is using innovative competitive intelligence techniques to assist with lead generation activities for investment attraction.[17] MEDC developed a comprehensive database of companies head-quartered outside Michigan and uses competitive intelligence techniques to determine linkages with the state that will help it target its business development activities. MEDC's assumption is that if a company has a solid linkage to the Michigan economy, it is more likely to establish a business function in the state. Using CI, MEDC ranks companies within the database in the following ways:

- **Products**—are they made with a Michigan resource?
- **Present location**—do they have a need for additional capacity in the U.S. Midwest region?
- **Customers**—do they have major customers in Michigan?
- **Growth projection**—will they have to expand anytime soon?
- **Proximity needs**—would it be advantageous to be near a major supplier based in Michigan?

---

17. Blake, K. J. 2002. Targeting for success: How the Michigan Economic Development Corporation targets companies to attract investment. In Proceedings of Strategic Intelligence & Knowledge Management for Growth and Competitiveness, Competia Public Service Symposium. Retrieved March 2002, at *http://www.competia.com/symposium/ottawa/home.html.*

By using a systematic and formalized CI model, MEDC is able to target companies that have a higher probability of locating in Michigan. As a result, it can be much more focused in its business development activities. Does this approach work? Michigan was among the top ten U.S. states for new and expanded facilities during 1997–2000.

Another government example is the Alberta Agriculture, Food and Rural Development Department.[18] In 1996, the department established a competitive intelligence unit mandated to collect and analyze critical market information that would help Alberta-based farmers and agri-food producers compete in the global marketplace. The CI unit compiles and analyzes information on a variety of topics, including food safety systems, other countries' agriculture biotechnologies development strategies, investment attraction, and the competitiveness of Alberta's industry. It also provides training on competitive intelligence to players within Alberta's agriculture and agri-food industries.

COMPETITIVE INTELLIGENCE IN A GLOBAL ECONOMY

The Internet has opened up tremendous opportunity for the collection of important market and competitor information in the global context. Although the requirements for public disclosure of relevant information are highest in the United States, other countries are beginning to demand more accountability from publicly held companies. In addition, the Web has opened up international newswire services, magazines, trade journals, portals, and corporate databases, all of which can provide valuable information on international companies and markets.

THE VALUE OF ANALYSIS

We have outlined the process of good competitive intelligence-gathering and have provided a few examples of how CI has been implemented in organizations. The true value of CI is in the analysis of data and action on that analysis, not in the process of

---

18. Blake, K. J. 2002. Targeting for success: How the Michigan Economic Development Corporation targets companies to attract investment. In Proceedings of Strategic Intelligence & Knowledge Management for Growth and Competitiveness, Competia Public Service Symposium. Retrieved March 2002, at *http://www.competia.com/symposium/ottawa/home.html.*

collection and reading. This section of the chapter provides a summary of some of the specific tools that CI practitioners use to analyze data and then develop accompanying strategies.

Competitor/Company Profiling

Developing detailed information on specific competitors can be valuable to an organization as it creates strategies for everything from product development to marketing to executive compensation. Constructing detailed profiles of potential clients is equally important, especially in markets offering higher-value goods and services. Understanding a potential client's business model will assist a company in structuring the most appropriate business development process for that individual client.

SWOT Analysis

CI can be useful when developing a traditional "strengths, weaknesses, opportunities, and threats" (SWOT) analysis for an organization. The research gleaned from the competitive landscape will allow the CI analyst to develop these four quadrants effectively. For example, the strengths and weaknesses of a company can be assessed in the context of a solid analysis of an organization's major competitors. Opportunities can be determined by reviewing industry-level data such as reports and white papers and scanning the general competitive landscape for clues to what might be on the horizon. Threats to an organization can come from multiple sources, including competitors, suppliers, large customers, and governments. Pulling information from a well-structured CI program can help a company formulate strategies to limit risks.

Trend Analysis

One of the great advantages of implementing a formalized CI program is the long-term capture and archiving of key competitive intelligence. Over time, an organization can map out trends among its competitors, trends in the industry at large, changing consumer preferences, changing cost structures, and more. Instead of starting the research process from scratch each time, archived intelligence makes developing trends a fairly simple process.

Simulation/War Gaming

Simulation uses computer-based tools that enable a company to engineer a strategic game plan and test it in a risk-free environment. Simulation helps ensure that the planning process yields realistic, achievable strategic plans. It assists managers in determining the dynamics of their competitive landscape by allowing them to experiment within a safe environment. Users make decisions, watch indicators, and view competitor actions and reactions as they would in real life. But because of the speed of game play, users can try many different strategies and view many different outcomes—all without risk. The ongoing CI program feeds the simulation process with the required market- and competitor-level intelligence.

A recent white paper on the subject of simulation puts it this way: "[The] safe practice environment levels political tensions, builds consensus among your management team and aligns them with the resulting strategic decision. It also helps define the action plan required to implement the strategic decision. This process builds confidence in the decision since it is based on real industry information and explicit assumptions."[19]

Forecasting

Related to both simulation and SWOT analysis, a good CI program will provide the information required to forecast sales, the need for new product enhancements, changes in the competitive landscape, and so forth.

ETHICS IN COMPETITIVE INTELLIGENCE

The perception of competitive intelligence as a mix of illegal and unethical practices to extract internal, private corporate information continues to be a problem for the industry. The association of CI with military intelligence-gathering is most likely a major cause of this reputation. In military intelligence practice, activities such as monitoring private communications, infiltrating governments, and spreading misinformation could be considered legitimate (depending on the context). However, in normal business markets, these practices are not only unethical but, in most cases,

---

19. Monitor Company/Decision Architects. 1998. Monitor Company/Decision Architects: Competitive simulation white paper. Retrieved May 10, 2001, at *http://www.decisionarc.com/ cs_wpaper.PDF.*

illegal. A better analogy would depict savvy (and ethical) journalists who are able to ferret out public information that for whatever reason is being deliberately hidden from the public.

The following are some examples of unethical (and, many times, illegal) industrial espionage:

- Hacking into a competitor's Web site to extract confidential information
- "Dumpster diving"—sifting through memos and other confidential documentation (either physical or electronic) to gain access to private intelligence
- Misrepresenting oneself as a potential customer to extract pricing information or other information that the company intends to keep private
- Interviewing (and paying) ex-employees of the competition to extract information when the former employees are bound by a nondisclosure agreement
- Deliberately spreading misinformation about a competitor (or even one's own company), especially in the age of the Internet and day trading

In 1999, John Pepper, then chairman of Procter & Gamble, remarked when speaking to the Society of Competitive Intelligence Professionals: "I can't imagine a time in history when the competencies, skills and knowledge of the men and women in competitive intelligence are more needed and more relevant to a company being able to design a winning strategy and act on it. I can't imagine a company not realizing the fundamental need for this today."[20]

In August 2001, Pepper confessed that P&G managers had implemented an elaborate and unethical spying campaign against a major competitor, Unilever. Procter & Gamble's operation to glean competitive information on its rival's hair-care strategies to protect its own important brands of Pantene and Head & Shoulders lasted eight months, cost about $3 million, and involved a CI consultancy.[21] The lesson of this case is that not even the most respected global corporations or CI industry experts are above crossing the line.

---

20. Miller, S. 2001. Competitive intelligence: An overview. Society of Competitive Intelligence Professionals. Retrieved May 8, 2001, at *http://www.scip.org/*.
21. P&G brushes with infamy in spy case. 2001. *Brand Strategy*. November 2, 2001. Retrieved March 2002, at *http://www.hoovers.com/*.

Organizations such as the Society of Competitive Intelligence Professionals have taken a strong stance on the ethics of the CI industry. SCIP has developed a detailed code of ethics.[22] All members must be in compliance with this code to maintain membership.

Interestingly, most CI practitioners would say that approximately eighty to ninety percent of all useful information is in the public domain anyway and that proper extraction and "filling in the blanks" would yield the same results, in most cases, as gathering the information through unethical and/or illegal activities. Resisting the temptation to cross the line will continue to be a major challenge facing the industry as it moves forward.

DOES IT WORK?

Although the process of CI seems intuitively valid, research into the tangible, long-term benefits has been limited. One study, however, completed in 1995 at the University of North Texas, found that businesses that used formal CI programs generally outperformed those that did not in three areas: sales, market share, and earnings per share. The study suggested that "there is a positive relationship between emphasis on CI and successful financial performance."[23]

STRATEGIC CONSIDERATIONS

There are a number of strategic issues facing the CI industry over the next few years:

Outsourcing versus In-house Competitive Intelligence Activities

Increasingly, the expertise associated with the CI function itself has become a core competency, and a number of companies are building that expertise and offering it as a service. Because the skill sets, methodologies, and technologies required to develop a

---

22. SCIP. SCIP code of ethics for CI professionals. 2002. Retrieved March 2002, at *http://www.scip.org/*.
23. Cappel, J. J., and Boone, J. P. 1995. A look at the link between competitive intelligence and performance. *Competitive Intelligence Review* 6 (2): 15–23.

strong CI function are quite complex, a blended solution of CI partner(s) complementing a strong internal analysis competency may be the optimal configuration.

Synergies with Other Business Functions

There is a definite overlap between CI and a variety of other business functions such as marketing/communications, traditional research and development, financial analysis, and industry consulting. There will most likely be some merging of those functions over the next few years (for example, CI as a service of marketing firms or within the Big Five's suite of services).

CONCLUSION

The case for implementing CI within organizations has never been stronger. With the emergence of the Internet and Web-based CI tools, the cost of deploying a robust CI program is within the reach of SMEs (small- to medium-sized enterprises) as well as large corporations. A recent survey conducted by The Futures Group found that some 80 percent of large U.S.-based organizations had a formal in-house CI department.[24] It also found that 60 percent of companies, in general, used some CI functions to assist in the development of their business models.[25]

However, just establishing a CI function per se is no guarantee of success in the market. What organizations do with CI (that is, turning market knowledge into strategic action) is ultimately the true test of its utility as a competitive advantage. An example of problems that can arise when formalizing a competitive information-gathering, analyzing, and dissemination program, and not acting on the results, is demonstrated by the telecom equipment manufacturing industry. The major players (Nortel, Cisco, Alcatel, Lucent Technologies, and others) were growing at a tremendous rate (primarily through acquisition) and jockeying for position within what was perceived to be an industry with unlimited growth potential. However, from the time that John Roth (former CEO of Nortel) first warned that the company's quarterly revenues would be off significantly, the entire collapse of

---

24. Corporate CI "eagles." 1998. *Competitive Intelligence Magazine.* January 1998. Retrieved March 2002, at *http://www.scip.org/*.
25. Miller, S. 2001. Competitive intelligence: An overview. Society of Competitive Intelligence Professionals. Retrieved May 8, 2001, at *http://www.scip.org/*.

the sector occurred in less than six months. The industry had shed almost fifty percent of its revenues and employees and had shown record quarterly losses. Paradoxically, the telecom sector had been one of the largest proponents of competitive intelligence, and many of the companies that fell the hardest had been applauded for their competitive intelligence activities.[26]

The inability of CI professionals within the telecom equipment manufacturing industry to adequately forecast its meltdown only strengthens the argument that an effective CI program must have more than just a lateral view—that is, it should not be absorbed by analyzing only the competition. An effective CI program must look upstream at its suppliers to monitor their competitive environment, cost pressures, and legislative issues, and it must look downstream at its customers and keep abreast of their movements. It must also monitor general trends in geopolitics, government regulation, trade policy, and public attitudes, all in the context of a specific business model. Ultimately, it could be argued that it was the telecom equipment manufacturers' preoccupation with each other while ignoring downstream and general economic trends that caused such a hard landing.

Over the next few years, competitive intelligence activities will become even more mainstream, as the unit cost of competitive information access continues to fall, and the software tools to aggregate, disseminate, analyze, and archive strategic intelligence continue to improve. The emphasis going forward will shift from information-gathering models and knowledge management to effective analysis and the resultant strategic action. Successful organizations will be those that have the best knowledge of a broad set of competitive intelligence criteria and that are relentlessly integrating that knowledge into product/service development, marketing/sales, and strategic positioning activities.

---

26. Ibid.

3

Protecting Your Company from Competitive Intelligence[1]

Businesses and other institutions are becoming increasingly reliant on the Internet to conduct their activities at all levels. Already we see a wide variety of reasons for using the Internet, and the quantity and quality of attractive features and services available online will only increase. The following are several examples of how businesses use the Net:

- To set up a Web site to serve as an electronic billboard that tells anyone who reads it about themselves, their capabilities, their personnel, and their experience
- To establish a Web site for the use of customers or others with whom the business connects, providing them with directories of locations, downloadable forms, online catalogs, and ways to track orders
- To develop sites to assist in the effort to recruit new employees or even to subtly advertise that the business is for sale—to the right buyer
- To launch separate Web sites for new projects or for existing subsidiaries and affiliates in an effort to show how large they are while still making themselves accessible

Whatever the reason firms use the Internet, the placement of data in cyberspace also creates a new area of vulnerability for businesses. That vulnerability is to the competitive intelligence (CI) efforts of their competitors.

---

1. Some of the case material of this chapter was originally developed for an in-class study at Acadia University by undergraduate students Heather Ongo and Erin Burke. I owe them a debt of gratitude.

As a new-frontier data depository, the Internet is already being studied by experts seeking to predict what kinds of data will most likely be posted[2] and what that means in competitive terms.[3] That, in turn, has led to increasing efforts by CI professionals to explore and then exploit information on the Web for CI purposes ;[4] .[5] As with so much else in business, these actions have resulted in a reaction. That reaction is the application of defensive CI techniques to the Internet.

HOW IS COMPETITIVE INTELLIGENCE EXPLOITING THE INTERNET TODAY?

Perhaps the easiest way to show how CI is exploiting the Internet today is by relating the following series of examples, all of which are based on real work we have done:

Unindexed Materials

Businesses put materials on their home page assuming they cannot be found if the firm has not indexed them or listed them on the site map. However, trained CI Web searchers use a technique borrowed from headhunters called X-raying to discover this hidden information.[6] X-raying involves using one of several search engines and tying the search to the company's name with commands such as *host:* or *url:* followed by the company's home page address and key search terms.

In one case, as we worked our way through a target's complex of multiple home pages, we were able to locate a hidden link to a test site the target had set up. That site was actually the final test of a new set of Web pages to be released in connection with the launch of a new service. The hidden link easily led us to this page,

2. Weiss, A., and England, S. 2000. Internet intelligence—Analysing web-sites for competitive intelligence. *Free Pint* 65. June 22, 2000. Retrieved March 2002, at *http://www.freepint.com/issues.*

3. Vibert, C. 2000. *Web-based analysis for competitive intelligence.* Westport, CT: Quorum Books.

4. Kassel, A. 2001. *Super searchers on Wall Street: Top investment professionals share their online research secrets.* Medford, NJ: CyberAge Books.

5. Lang, E. A., and Tudor, J. D. 2001. *Best Websites for financial professionals, business appraisers, and accountants.* New York: John Wiley & Sons.

6. Silverman, R. E. 2002. *Internet recruiters' tricks of the trade: A how-to manual for headhunting online.* Retrieved March 2002, at *http://www.careerjournal.com/recruiters.*

the existence of which we had previously identified through a search for Web sites using terms reserved by the target for what appeared to be a new marketing initiative.

Hidden Anchors and Notes

Some Web page designers use key terms to help them keep track of Web pages as they are developed and updated. These terms, although not a part of the actual text of the page, can sometimes be accessible to skilled searchers. We have found situations in which key terms were used as if they were page markers, leading us to new sites with new data.

In one case, we looked for a hidden link in a Web page. We suspected it was there because the target had reserved a number of domain names that seemed to be indicative of a new marketing initiative. We eventually found it by searching for a new Web site using the domain names themselves. One of them turned out to be a new Web site, ready for launch, complete with biographies of executives assigned to the project and its marketing materials. From that site, we could go back to the home page and thus confirm the location of the secret link.

Inbound Logistics

Inbound links are those that connect independent sites to a company's site but of which it may not be aware. Inbound links can be located using advanced features in search engines such as AltaVista or HotBot. They often disclose sites that host current or former employees' résumés and that include a link from their own page to the company's pages.

Such pages can be a gold mine to CI professionals seeking someone to interview. In addition, they can often hold otherwise unavailable details about a firm. Using this technique in one case of ours, we located a résumé for an IT specialist who had been a consultant to our target. Not only did this give us a name to pursue for a potential interview, but the résumé itself was also a real find. In describing his experiences at the target organization, the IT specialist provided a list of every firm that had been involved with the company in a major Web-based marketing project.

Job Advertisements

In another case, a chain retailer was aware that its most aggressive competitor was probably expanding. The retailer needed to know how many new stores and distribution centers were in the works, as well as how much the competitor was planning to spend on its expanded logistics needs.

Starting with the premise that these new stores would need staff, we began by searching through job clearinghouses at sites such as HotJobs and Monster. There we found advertisements for the kinds of personnel that would be needed to staff these new units and functions. That alone served to confirm the expansion process. However, the advertisements, as a part of selling to potential new hires, also indicated where the expansion was to take place and included brief notes on the probable supply chain and related software and warehousing issues. This information, combined with other research, including zoning applications and calls to securities analysts, helped us to model the competitor's expansion process as well as its logistics spending.

HOW DO YOU STOP THIS?

As CI develops, businesses eventually come to realize that "if we can get this on them, they can get this on us." To defend against Web-based CI efforts aimed at your firm, you must first understand that you can foil the CI efforts of competitors at least to some extent. You can accomplish this by making yourself virtually invisible to CI monitoring efforts. And doing so successfully is, above all, based on understanding the ways you can be tracked. Once you have that understanding, strategies and tactics to minimize or avoid detection in the future can easily be developed. Essentially, you and your firm will be practicing *defensive competitive intelligence*.

WHAT IS DEFENSIVE COMPETITIVE INTELLIGENCE?

Initially, many people called these attempts to blunt active CI efforts counterintelligence. Although this term seems to accurately describe what is being done (that is, countering competitive intelligence), it has fallen into disfavor. As a term taken from the world of governmental and military intelligence and including within its scope so-called direct action, *counterintelligence* carries connotative baggage with it into the business world. Implicit within *direct action* is the notion that opposing intelligence personnel and physical assets can be removed, that is, destroyed, as a part of the counterintelligence process.[7]

Given the distasteful overtones of this term, CI professionals have been striving for a new label. Although *protecting against competitive intelligence* accurately describes the process, other terms such as *protecting a competitive advantage* are being used to encompass this concept in a world that likes short terms and parallelism of expression. Among them, the most accurate label is probably *defensive competitive intelligence.*

Regardless of what term or phrase is used, what should be kept in mind is that when professionals talk of defensive CI, they are not talking about something that is a mere annex to existing corporate security programs or an adjunct to staff functions that serve to enforce current legal protections of certain classes of data. They are talking about CI that supplements other information protection regimens, while not actually being part of them.

WHAT ABOUT CORPORATE SECURITY AND LEGAL PROTECTION PROGRAMS?

CI is the collection of public data by legal and ethical means and the conversion of that data into intelligence through the use of analysis. Various legal stratagems, such as trade secret protection and confidentiality and nondisclosure agreements, aim to protect critical categories of information assets by making those who violate certain patterns of behavior subject to legal, usually civil, penalties. Someone who collects competitive data by inducing a former employee of a competitor to violate a nondisclosure agreement, for example, is involved in illegal conduct because such activity violates civil law.

Similarly, if someone goes through a business's trash in a jurisdiction where that is not against the law or poses as a student to try to interview a product manager, his or her conduct is not illegal, because it does not involve the actual commission of a crime. Rather, it is unethical. It is the job of your legal staff and those working with them to deal with enforcing the civil protections available for certain classes of business data. It is the role of both

---

7. McGonagle, J. J., and Vella, C. M. 1998. *Protecting your company against competitive intelligence.* Westport, CT: Greenwood Group.

businesses and trade groups such as the Society of Competitive Intelligence Professionals (SCIP) to establish standards of ethical behavior when collecting data for CI.

Ways in which competitively sensitive data might be collected can, of course, involve criminal activities. The criminal activity may arise from how data are collected, such as in a burglary, or from the effort to gather protected data, such as by violating the Economic Espionage Act of 1996. It is traditionally the role of corporate security, working with the law enforcement community, to protect a business against these efforts.[8]

HOW DO YOU DEVELOP A DEFENSIVE COMPETITIVE INTELLIGENCE STRATEGY?

To develop a defensive competitive intelligence strategy, you should first try to determine what areas of your activities are of greatest interest to competitors. You can then focus your efforts on protecting those areas. However, since you cannot know with any real certainty what your competitors are focusing on, you should approach this task in a disciplined manner. We have found that there are seven key points in identifying the data you should protect:

1. Protect the information that would be most difficult for your competitor to develop. Of greatest importance is to protect data that would require your tacit or active cooperation to develop or obtain. Most often, you will find that this information relates to subjects such as intentions and goals.
2. Remember that competitive information has a half-life. The half-life of data is the period of time for which raw data retain at least 50 percent of their accuracy and/or relevance. This varies widely with the type of data. So, protect competitively sensitive information only for as long as is necessary.
3. Protect the competitive data that are crucial to completing a profile on your firm. For example, if your firm is increasing its market share, there is no reason to tell your competitors (through press releases or attached graphs) exactly how fast you are growing.
4. Protect data that are already partially protected in some other way. In particular, focus your protection efforts on the subject matter of information already being protected as trade secrets. For example, if your marketing plan is a trade secret, protect

---

8. —. 1999. *The Internet age of competitive intelligence.* Westport, CT: Greenwood Group.

information from which someone could derive critical elements of that plan.

5. Identify the information that is critical to your operation as a business. This varies from case to case. The information may be identified in terms of how intimately related it is to the immediate success or failure of your firm. Focus first on protecting this core before moving to protect other data that are not associated with your essential activities.

6. Review the CI you are already collecting on your competitors. From that, determine what pieces of raw data are critical to efforts to produce your CI analysis. Next, determine what pieces of data on competitors have been difficult or impossible for you to locate. Then, look at the data about your firm that can be easily accessed. What types of information are you surprised to see on your own Web site? Move to protect all of that data.

7. Identify the data analysis techniques most likely to be used in your industry or market. Protect those key bits of information vital to completing that type of analysis.

WHAT IS INVOLVED IN IMPLEMENTING A DEFENSIVE COMPETITIVE INTELLIGENCE PROGRAM?

Once the data, or classes of data, in need of protection are identified, those running a defensive competitive intelligence program must provide guidance on what to do next. The use of an easily understood set of rules can make that relatively simple to do.

We have developed a set of nine such precepts, using the familiar model of reporters: who, what, where, when, and why. In our model, the *when* is as soon as possible, and the *who* is everyone.[9] These key precepts fall into three separate categories: what to do, how to proceed, and where to act.

(1) What to Do:

- Precept 1: Seek to control only critical, not all, information.
- Precept 2: Do not tell everyone everything.
- Precept 3: Continually watch for sources of CI on your firm.

---

9. —. 1998. *Protecting your company against competitive intelligence.* Westport, CT: Greenwood Group.

(2) How to Proceed:

- Precept 4: Preventing disclosure is preferable to impeding it.
- Precept 5: Do not ignore simple solutions.
- Precept 6: Pay attention to details.

(3) Where to Act:

- Precept 7: If you cannot prevent disclosure, conceal some information.
- Precept 8: If you cannot conceal it, make it harder or more costly to acquire.
- Precept 9: The top may be harder to control than the bottom.

A PROGRAM FOR PROTECTING YOUR COMPANY FROM INTERNET COMPETITIVE INTELLIGENCE INITIATIVES

The best way to protect your firm from the loss of competitively valuable data is to conduct a onetime review of your vulnerabilities and then to engage in regular reviews after that. The precepts we have provided will help you determine where best to focus your review activities as well as your initial audit. However, you may find that it is easier to sell a defensive CI program after you identify the vulnerabilities that exist now. To help you in that effort, what follows is a broad-scale program indicating where and how to review your Internet-based vulnerabilities.

Your Web Site

Start by visiting your own Web site. Go through every page. Note which pages of the site are old. How far back do press releases and announcement files go? If Dave Smith left the company and was replaced by Sharon Brown as vice president of sales, did anyone go back and remove Dave's biography from the Web site?

Find out whether there is any formal, enforced policy on removing materials from the Web site. You may be surprised to find that although there is a policy on adding materials, there is often none on removing them.

Now look for mistakes on your Web site. Are there pages or slides that were mounted in error? In one classic case, we found that a firm had put up the draft version of a quarterly press release. It still showed the deletions and additions that were made in producing the final version. Being able to read such edits can offer very telling insights into what has really been happening at a company. In this particular case, key phrases such as *continuing growth in sales to key customers* were clearly marked to be deleted. What obviously had happened was that when the final edit was done, the page was saved still showing changes and then put up in that form. No one in the firm checked to see what it looked like on the Web.

Next, look at the pages themselves, one by one. What kinds of data do you see on them? Does the personnel page include an unnecessary table of organization? Does the technical center's flashy page include catchphrases that describe important internal initiatives? Do your e-mail and mailing lists for press releases and other materials ask recipients to identify who they are, whom they work for, and why they are asking for materials? If not, ask yourself why not.

Now, sit back and look at your pages as a Web designer might. For what purpose are they intended? Are your lists of regional offices designed to showcase how many you have or to drive customers to use them? Who is the primary audience of your Web site—customers, shareholders, or suppliers? Do you want that sort of information visible to your competitors?

Next, determine what is on your Web site but is not indexed. You may well be surprised to see that it supports "temporary" lists of people attending upcoming meetings, test pages not ready for release, draft materials, versions of pages never used, previous versions of current pages, and materials removed from the index but not from the site. Never assume that these materials cannot be found and read. They can—and they will be.

All major Internet browsers allow their users to read certain things about your pages, variously called code and source data. These are usually just bits of information on when the page was mounted and by whom, when it was last changed, and what software was used. Most of the time the contents are innocuous and of no competitive value, but sometimes designers put additional notes to themselves in them or add searchable terms to the headers to be activated later. Take them out.

The Invisible Web

Now, move to the way the Web relates to your home page. Start by checking into the pages of related organizations, your subsidiaries, and your affiliates. What do they say? To what sections of your home page are they linked?

Sometimes, links on outside pages can accidentally allow people unplanned, or even unauthorized, access to pages on your site. In one case we worked on, we were trying to find an open-source article on a change in certain rules. One search engine gave us what was evidently the home page of a practitioner in that area. We did not have a complete copy of the final draft of the revised rule and noted that this home page had a link to the proposed changes. We clicked on the link and voilà! We found that we had been transported into the members-only archives of a professional association that had this text. That was not evident, at first, but was soon obvious, when we simply went from that page to "Home." What this practitioner obviously had done was copy the address of the page that contained these changes while online in the members-only section. In so doing, he actually added his own password and thus provided a back door into the organization's pages. Do any of your affiliates do that?

Also, check the Web sites of your affiliates and subsidiaries for specific details. Are they providing sketches from your facilities to show their expertise? Are these sketches too revealing?

Move now to the companies that do business with you: your suppliers, your consultants, your distributors, and so on. You can go to their Web sites, if they are few in number, and search for your firm's name. What are they saying?

In addition, for suppliers or consultants who have worked on particularly important projects, such as building plants with new capabilities, look for an anonymous case study on their pages that is used to demonstrate their expertise. Is that case study you? What does it tell your competitors that you prefer they not know? You will sometimes see descriptions, plans, and even photographs about how they redesigned your plant and what it can do now.

External Sites You Use

Now, move to the external sites your company uses, such as job listings and association directories. What are you, or they, saying about your firm? Does a review of past job listings show a pattern that is helpful to a competitor? For example, do you always advertise on Monster when you are opening a new office?

Alter links that create these listings of unnecessary content. Rather than noting how many new facilities you are opening and when, why not say you are "aggressively expanding"? If you need to provide specific data to entice the best applicants for your job openings, consider reserving some of the data for those who actually apply and providing it after (rather than before) you speak to them. That way you can warn the applicants first about keeping confidential what you are about to tell them.

Also check external sites to see what you do *not* have to protect. For example, if your senior managers always serve on association committees and the association always posts a current biography of these key members, why should you worry about keeping these same biographies off your own home page?

Links Back Home

Next, check into inbound links, those that link back to your home page. What do they show? Don't forget to check inbound links to your subsidiaries and affiliates. The most common link of importance you will find is to résumés of former (and sometimes even current) employees and consultants. How much detail are they disclosing about what they did and, most important, about what you are still doing? If it is too much, contact them and ask them to make changes.

Follow up links that start from colleges and universities. Increasingly, colleges and universities are using their Web sites to promote the activities of their faculty. Do they also discuss the consulting contract you gave one of their professors?

Many of these schools use the Web to provide information about courses and research projects being undertaken by the faculty. You may be surprised to find that one of your midlevel managers, going part-time for an advanced degree, has just had his or her paper published on the Web. Is that a problem? Let us give you one example of such a case.

In searching for information on the marketing strategy of a target, we found a recent paper done by a student in a fairly arcane area of mathematical modeling. It was clear that the subject of the study was the target. The paper involved efforts to determine how to allocate costs across several markets as well as across different groups of customers.

When we presented our findings to the client, it saw the same thing we did. The client's CI manager then located someone in the company who was familiar with this area. She took one look at the outline of the paper and observed that it was a way of calculating costs across state lines for large customers. The discovery was an intelligence breakthrough for our client, who had suspected that the target was moving in that direction. The paper was the first hard evidence that the target was doing the computer modeling necessary to calculate costs in this way. Harmless? No. Harmful!

The Regular Review

Obviously, you cannot track down every link to your Web site and every link to those links. If you did, you would be searching the Web forever. Approach regular defensive Internet reviews as a competitor would. Do not waste your time checking everything. Rather, focus your efforts on the subject matter and areas that are currently most sensitive. Search under your firm's name as well as under its nicknames and under new, even unused, domain names. Take several of the following approaches to help ensure the security of your data, and train others to do the same:[10]

- Never use the same search engines again and again. If you use Google this time, switch to HotBot or Ask Jeeves next time, and so on. No engine or crawler covers even half the Web.
- Educate those who maintain your Web page, as well as those who provide content, to review what they post before they post it and then to look at it once it is on the Web, preferably not on their own computers. Also remind these workers to remove materials in a timely manner.
- Find out how long different items are kept on your Web site. For example, some public firms keep analyst briefings, including audio-casts and overheads, mounted for years. Others remove them after three months or less. Although many firms have a complete press release library, others, perhaps with an eye

---

10. Ibid.

toward defensive issues, keep only the most recent press releases online.

- Review descriptions of your firm at commercial sites that provide industry- or company-specific data for a fee. Do not limit your review to Dun & Bradstreet. Look for broad-ranging sites such as 1Jump: as well. Most of the data there, and at similar sites, are captured from public, often published, sources. So, if they are listing all your officers and shareholders, for example, and you are a private firm, you can elect either (1) not to give such data to these companies in the future or (2) to keep the data off your own site.
- Make sure that outsiders designing or redesigning Web sites do not use internal terms of art or catchphrases they have heard from your employees. In doing so, they have given your competitors more to start with than they deserve.
- For new Web-based initiatives, make sure they are not mounted on, or even linked to or from, your home page, until they are ready to become operational.
- Look for Web page designs that are helpful to consumers, not competitors. For example, if you want to make available to customers a list of all seventy-five of your sales offices, wouldn't they find it easier to use if they could be given the address of the one closest to their ZIP code? Not only is that more customer-friendly, it is competitor-hostile, for it makes a competitor seeking that list ask for locations possibly hundreds of times.
- Consider design options that make it more difficult for a competitor to save an entire page. Some frames, JavaScript elements, and other options have this often unintended consequence.
- Feel free to ask why things are put up. Speeches and presentations by your executives may be interesting, but are they too revealing of overall strategy? To what articles or interviews are you providing your own links? Not every interview with every employee deserves to be given its own link. In fact, there are some interviews, usually with your very top officers, that you are better off not drawing attention to. They can provide a great deal of assistance in profiling.[11]
- Caution your contractors and consultants that they can, inadvertently, become a window into matters that are competitively sensitive. Ask them to hold off publicizing what they are doing in any detail for several months.
- Save time and money while protecting your company by linking to sources of data on your firm. More and more public firms in

---

11. —. 2000. Profiling in competitive analysis. *Competitive Intelligence Review* 11 (2): 20–30.

the United States are directing those wanting to review documents filed with the U.S. Securities and Exchange Commission (SEC) to the SEC's own Web site, rather than posting documents on the company Web site. Then competitors are at the mercy of the limitations of EDGAR when trying to review such filings. You may want to do the same with articles on your firm.

- Consider subscribing to or using software that monitors changes in targeted home pages. Then use it on your own.
- Regularly check what new domain names your own firm has filed for. Do not assume that your emerging Internet strategy is hidden. Skilled CI professionals can turn to services that allow them to see what domain names you have reserved and when. Looking at these lists can help them determine where your strategy is going. Should your firm be filing for other domain names to mask the intent of the new names? The reservation of multiple names makes it that much harder for your competitors to keep you in their sights.

Should your new domain names be reserved by a subsidiary that does not carry the parent name? Some firms use such relatively anonymous entities to hold all of their patents, trademarks, and other intellectual property assets.

In your efforts to protect your firm, always remember that you cannot possibly protect everything. If you try to protect all your information, you may impair or destroy your firm's ability to communicate with important stakeholders and run the risk that the business may not survive in a competitive environment. Instead, shield your intelligence—develop and implement a defensive CI program.

4

Online Competitive
Information Case Studies

Although many competitive intelligence (CI) professionals do not have access to the same level of resources found in large corporations, the playing field for solid analysis may actually be quite level when a talented researcher has at his or her fingertips the online resources of the Internet. Consultant Susan Hollett (*http://www.hollettandsons.ca*), who works in Shoal Harbour, Newfoundland, offers an example of how independent analysts may effectively practice CI despite being away from major urban centers and employers:

> A recent project involved a multi-media company that was looking to enter the educational CD ROM market in the Northeastern United States. They wanted to identify competitors, understand their behavior, and track their activities. Using the Internet and the Canadian Commercial Trade Commissioners' research, we were able to come up with a preliminary list. Armed with this, we "dug in" and searched the online business, local and sector press; the industry and professional association Web sites; and the conference and trade show circuit for relevant information. We offered the client a multi-dimensional picture of the competition on the other side of the continent. In addition, we provided research tools and co-developed strategies that would enable them to stay abreast of changes. These strategies included the use of alert services, automatic notification of changes to "product" Web pages, and identification of the business and sector press most likely to track pertinent market niches in specific geographic areas.

Along with understanding online information sources, professionals such as Hollett also realize the importance of tried-and-true analytical frameworks for grasping the significance of specific business activity. In the following pages, a number of abbreviated case examples illustrate how theory can be effectively integrated with online information to inform the practice of CI.

Specifically, in this chapter, we suggest a series of *online research missions* to help observers make sense of the behavior of our major institutions. Individually, each couples insight with real-time information in a manner that improves analysis. Building on the work of Dodge,[1] each mission displays a number of common features. First, an opening remark, termed a *mission overview,* sets the context for the online activity. Second, a *mission statement* is presented that defines the mission to be undertaken. Third, a series of *mission guides,* or context-specific questions, direct the online analyst toward queries that fit the parameters of the underlying ideas being applied. Fourth, *mission sources* or Web sites hosting relevant online information useful for responding to the mission statement are suggested. Fifth, a *mission source rationale* is presented that outlines how the online information might be retrieved and used in the context of the mission and the theory under examination. The first example explores the case of online music distributor MP3.com,[2] and the latter three cases address the media industry.

CASE EXAMPLE ONE: MP3 AND THE CEO'S PAYCHECK

Doubt. Among the most important implications of the dot.com era and the scandals associated with companies such as Worldcom, Enron, and Andersen Consulting is a healthy dose of doubt among analysts, business observers, and CI practitioners. No longer taken for granted are corporate press releases long on promise but short on evidence. Gone are the days when speeches by high-profile executives offering rosy industry forecasts are unquestioned. A business environment characterized by doubt, in turn, has its own implications for executives. In the realm of the publicly traded corporation, an increasingly endangered species is the heavy-handed CEO with a longer-term tenure to protect. Demands by investors for enhanced information disclosure along with increasingly proactive regulatory agencies have resulted in a wealth of information being available to researchers interested in under-

---

1. Dodge, B. 1999. The WebQuest page. Accessed August 22, 2003, at *http://webquest. sdsu.edu.*
2. Vibert, C. 2001. Mixing theory with real-time analysis: A look at an online music distributor. *Competitive Intelligence Review* 12 (3): 10–20.

standing the behavior of these large institutions and their managers. Of interest to many CI practitioners is the issue of performance. Aside from the normal hype associated with corporate Web sites, public relations efforts, and much of the business media, often left unsaid is the relative performance of executives relative to their peers. How does one assess the true performance of a CEO or an associated executive team when an industry as a whole is in a downturn? This topic is addressed in the following paragraphs.

Mission Overview

This abbreviated case study explores the means by which shareholders protect their interests from corporate managers, using the online music distributor MP3.com as an example.

Mission Statement

Did MP3.com's CEO act in the best interests of shareholders during 1999?

Mission Guides

In 1999, was the compensation package or formula of MP3.com's CEO primarily outcome-based or behaviorally oriented? Based on its share value during 1999 and relative to that of its three major competitors, was this individual's compensation in the best interests of shareholders?

Mission Sources

The mission sources for this endeavor are primarily regulatory documents filed with the Securities and Exchange Commission (SEC) but gleaned through 10k Wizard, company profiles made available through Hoover's Online, and an employment contract listed on the FindLaw Web site.

Mission Source Rationale

Integral to this discussion is the identification of the CEO and any important issues that might be worrisome to shareholders. One source for this information is MP3.com's 2000 DEF 14A Proxy

Statement filed with the SEC. It identifies Michael Robertson as the CEO and offers the following background details:

> Michael L. Robertson founded MP3.com and has served as our Chief Executive Officer and Chairman of the Board since March 1998. From September 1995 to March 1998, Mr. Robertson operated several Web sites that focused on merging search technologies with commerce. From September 1995 to September 1996, Mr. Robertson was President and Chief Executive Officer of Mounds, Inc., a developer of digital picture software. From January 1994 to August 1995, Mr. Robertson was President and Chief Executive Officer of Much Software, a developer of networking and security tools. Mr. Robertson received his Bachelor of Arts from the University of North Carolina.[3]

Noteworthy is that, in 2000, Michael Robertson also owned thirty-seven percent of the outstanding common stock of MP3.com.[4]

During 1999 and 2000, MP3.com was a somewhat controversial entity. The following excerpt from a May 1999 regulatory filing suggests why shareholders were probably paying close attention to the performance of the company and its CEO:

> Our model for conducting business and generating revenues is new and unproven. Our business model depends upon our ability to generate revenue streams from multiple sources through our Web site, including:
> * Web site advertising fees from third parties;
> * online sales of CDs and music-related merchandise;
> * promotional activity fees; and
> * leveraging our aggregated artist and consumer information.[5]

This was followed up two months later with another statement by MP3.com to regulators:

> It is uncertain whether a music-based Web site that relies on attracting people to learn about, listen to and download music, mostly from lesser-known artists, can generate sufficient revenues to survive. We cannot assure you that this business model

---

3. MP3.com Form DEF 14A. 2000, April 28 filing. U.S. Securities and Exchange Commission. Retrieved July 2000, at *http://www.sec.gov*.

4. Company capsule for MP3.com. n.d. Retrieved November 20, 2000, at *http://www.hoovers.com*.

5. MP3.com Form S-1/A. 1999, May 24 filing. U.S. Securities and Exchange Commission. Retrieved May 5, 2001, at *http://www.10kwizard.com*.

will succeed or will be sustainable as our business grows. . . . We provide many of our products and services without charge, and we may not be able to generate sufficient revenue to pay for these products and services. Accordingly, we are not certain that our business model will be successful or that we can sustain revenue growth or be profitable.[6]

The inherent risk of MP3.com's 1999 business model suggested a role for the ideas that underlie agency theory. Does outcome or behavioral best describe the contract that linked Michael Robertson to MP3.com in 1999? An MP3.com employment contract found at FindLaw.com suggests an outcome descriptor:

- 1.3 Executive shall do and perform all services, acts or things necessary or advisable to manage and conduct the business of the Company and which are normally associated with the position of Chief Executive Officer, consistent with the Bylaws of the Company and as required by the Company's Board of Directors.
- 3.1 The Company shall pay Executive a base salary of $150,000 per year (the "Base Salary"), payable in semi-monthly payments in accordance with Company policy. Such salary shall be prorated for any partial year of employment on the basis of a 365-day fiscal year.
- 3.2 Executive's compensation may be changed from time to time by mutual agreement of Executive and the Company.
- 3.3 Executive shall be eligible for an annual performance bonus of up to $50,000 payable at the sole discretion of the Company's Board of Directors.
- 9 . . . This Agreement does not supersede or alter in any way the terms and conditions of the Founder Stock Agreement dated March 18, 1998.[7]

How well was MP3.com's CEO paid in 1999? Very fairly, if its regulatory filings are any indication. A search using the keywords *executive compensation* on 10k Wizard indicated that, in 1999, Robertson received $158,626 in salary, $148,500 in bonus payments, and $4,850 toward a car lease. This was an increase from a salary of $70,833. How did his compensation compare with that of other CEOs? Using the CEOs of two main competitors, ARTISTdirect,

---

6. MP3.com Form 424B4. 1999, June 21 filing. U.S. Securities and Exchange Commission. Retrieved July 2000, at *http://www.10kwizard.com*.

7. Employment agreement by and between MP3.com and Michael L. Robertson. 1999. May 13, 1999. Retrieved November 20, 2000, at *http://www.findlaw.com*.

Inc., and Launch Media, Inc. (now LAUNCH, the music destination on Yahoo!), for comparison,[8] this salary appears reasonable. The better compensated of these latter two received $162,500 in base salary as well as stock options during 1999.

How did MP3.com perform? In an absolute sense, not well. On 1999 revenues of $22 million, it lost $42.5 million. Relative to competitors, however, it fared adequately. ARTISTdirect, Inc., and Launch Media, Inc., lost $57.8 million and $37.5 million on sales of $10.3 million and $16.6 million, respectively[9,10] In terms of share price performance[11] the results were also not outstanding. From an initial public offering (IPO) priced above $60 per share, stockholders ended 1999 with shares worth half that amount. This was in line with the performance of MP3.com's major competitor, whose initial price of $35 per share melted away to $20 per share at year-end.

Mission Display

In this instance, a textual display offers as much insight as findings portrayed in matrix form. How might these results be interpreted in light of agency theory?

MP3.com shareholders chose to use an outcome-based contract to retain the services of Michael Robertson, who owned thirt-seven percent of the company's shares. Performance in the first year as a publicly traded company was not outstanding. Indeed, shareholders saw their equity decrease significantly. However, the salary and benefits of the CEO were not excessive in light of this performance; in fact, relative to those of other chief executive officers, they were quite low. Although share price did decrease, Michael Robertson certainly did not benefit from this bad news and indeed shared the pain. Thus, at least in terms of

8. Company capsule for MP3.com. n.d. Retrieved November 20, 2000, at *http://www. hoovers.com.*

9. Company capsule for ARTISTdirect, Inc. n.d. Retrieved November 20, 2000, at *http:// www.hoovers.com/.*

10. Company capsule for Launch Media, Inc. n.d. Retrieved November 20, 2000, at *http://www.hoovers.com.*

11. Stock chart for MP3.com and competitors. n.d. Retrieved November 20, 2000, at *http://www.bigcharts.com.*

salary and benefits paid to their CEO, the interests of shareholders were protected fairly effectively.

CASE EXAMPLE TWO: WHO CONTROLS THE MEDIA INDUSTRY?

Similarity. Researchers have long recognized the importance of this idea when seeking to understand patterns of behavior within and among corporate entities. In our professional lives we become similar to others through our pursuit of professional designations or university degrees, our attendance at specific universities, our employment in certain organizations, or our decisions to move to specific locales. Spend some time in Tokyo. If you are an American, you may find yourself developing friendships with other expatriate Americans. If you are British, it would probably not surprise you if many of your friends were British. If you have attended Harvard University, you know the importance to your career of being associated with Harvard. Further consider professionals who have spent time with McKinsey and Co. or PricewaterhouseCoopers. Both of these organizations have extensive networks of alumni. Finally, consider your attainment of a professional designation. As a lawyer, engineer, accountant, or scientist, you share knowledge and experience specific to others in the same discipline. You are probably also aware of the opportunities presented as a result of these similarities. Decision makers dislike uncertainty. CEOs tasked with putting together a senior management team are no different. Most will attempt to build operating teams of individuals they understand. This understanding often results from similarities in backgrounds and training. Analysts seeing to understand the makeup of an executive team, present or future, should look for similarities among executives.

The same logic can also play a role in understanding why decisions are made as they are in specific industries. It may be because the membership of the different boards are all alike. The following case explores the origins and similarities of boards with the intent of helping analysts discover where the true power lies in each industry.

Mission Overview

This abbreviated case study explores important relationships of dependence in the context of the media industry. It compares the profiles of The Walt Disney Company's board of directors and executive management team with those of two of its top competitors, Time Warner and Viacom Inc.

Mission Statement

Identify those companies upon which your firm is dependent.

Mission Guides

Are any particular industries overcompensated for on the boards of firms participating in this industry? In the case of the company under study, is there any pattern to the origins of the top management team?

Mission Sources

The mission sources for this endeavor are primarily regulatory documents filed with the SEC and executive profiles made available through Hoover's Online.

Mission Source Rationale

Regulatory filings were reviewed for The Walt Disney Company,[12] AOL Time Warner,[13] and Viacom Inc.[14] to identify the industry affiliations for each director. The results are presented in Figure 4-1.

Company affiliations for each board member were identified via officer profiles found using Hoover's Online. By searching with the Industry Keyword option selected, we identified the industry sector for each affiliated company.

---

12. The Walt Disney Company Form DEF 14A. 2001 filing. U.S. Securities and Exchange Commission. Retrieved February 2002, at *http://www.sec.gov.*
13. AOL Time Warner Form DEF 14A. 2001 filing. U.S. Securities and Exchange Commission. Retrieved February 2002, at *http://www.sec.gov.*
14. Viacom Inc. Form DEF 14A. 2001 filing. U.S. Securities and Exchange Commission. Retrieved February 2002, at *http://www.sec.gov.*

As expected, it was found that directors from the media, finance, telecommunications, and legal industries were well represented on corporate boards in the media sector. The results also suggest heavy participation in charity and political organizations by board members. One explanation for this is the presence in the industry of the Federal Communications Commission as a regulator. Effective lobbying necessitates the involvement of well-connected individuals who are also normally well placed in charity circles.

In all three cases, a large number of directors either are lawyers or have a background in financial services. The concentration in financial services is mostly linked to venture capital firms and investment companies. We expected a higher concentration in banking; however, given the influence that new technologies have on the media industry, it stands to reason that the firms would have a heavy interest in venture capital. All three companies view the Internet as being an important part of their future. Each has board members affiliated with the telecommunications sector. Each board also has at least one director linked to the real estate industry.

Directors with links to the political arena present an interesting cross section of talent. For instance, it appears that the Walt Disney Company is strategically placed in Washington by having George Mitchell, a former U.S. senator and majority leader, on its board. Mr. Mitchell was also chairman of the Ethics Committee of the U.S. Olympic Committee. Time Warner has a former U.S. trade representative (Carla Hills), and Viacom has George Abrams, former general counsel and staff director of the Senate Judiciary Subcommittee on Refugees; William H. Gray, a former U.S. representative; Ken Miller, a member of the board of directors of the United Nations Association of the United States of America; and William Schwartz, who was chairman of the Boston Mayor's Special Commission on Police Procedures.

Figure 4-1. Director Affiliations in the Media Industry

INDUSTRY SECTOR	THE WALT DISNEY COMPANY	TIME WARNER	VIACOM INC.	TOTAL
Media	4	1	13	18
Charities	6	0	11	17
Education	6	0	7	13
Finance	2	3	8	13

Figure 4-1. Director Affiliations in the Media Industry (*cont.*)

INDUSTRY SECTOR	THE WALT DISNEY COMPANY	TIME WARNER	VIACOM INC.	TOTAL
Lawyers	1	3	7	11
Real Estate	4	5	1	10
Telecommunications	3	3	4	10
Investments	2	7	0	9
Political	3	1	4	8
Computer	2	22	2	6
Leisure	1	3	2	6
Transportation	3	2	1	6
Consumer Products	0	3	1	4
Drugs	0	1	3	4
Health Services	2	1	1	4
Retail	1	1	2	4
Diversified Services	1	1	1	3
Food/Tobacco	0	1	2	3
Insurance	1	1	1	3
Construction	1	0	1	2
Specialty Retail	0	0	2	2
Technology	0	0	2	2
Defense/Aero	1	0	0	1
Manufacturing	0	0	1	1
Metals and Mining	0	0	1	1
Utilities	1	0	0	1

The influence of interlocking ownership structures is also evident when executive roles and backgrounds are examined. In the case of Time Warner, the chief operating officer position has been split into co-chairs, one being the president of AOL, the other the president of Time Warner. All the top corporate executives have expertise in the media industry. For example, Mel Karmazin, Viacom president and chief operating officer,[15] was the president and CEO of CBS before the merger. Robert Iger was president and chairman of ABC before the merger with Disney. Michael Eisner, CEO of The Walt Disney Company, has a strong media background, which has taken him from ABC to Paramount

---

15. Viacom Inc. Form DEF 14A. 2001 filing. U.S. Securities and Exchange Commission. Retrieved February 2002, at *http://www.sec.gov.*

Pictures.[16] Richard J. Bressler, senior executive vice president and chief financial officer of Viacom Inc., came from Time Warner. *Dependence* is a term that aptly fits this industry. Executives appear to be chosen not only for their industry background but also for their influence in a tightly knit industry.

CASE EXAMPLE THREE: AN ECOLOGICAL TAKE ON INDUSTRY ATTRACTIVENESS

Survival. For many companies, this often takes priority, more so than profits, in the early years of their existence. If you disagree, consider looking back only a few years ago to the dot.com frenzy. How many sure bets failed? What percentage of venture-capital-backed companies remain? The answers to these questions are not really that important. What is crucial is understanding some of the factors that might make it easier for newer companies to survive today. Among the most important of these is the level of industry-wide resources available to the aspiring Microsofts, IBMs, and British Airways of the world. CI practitioners and online researchers can help their clients and employers by learning how to spot industries that are resource rich and those that are resource poor. The result can be better advice regarding which industries or markets to enter and which to stay away from.

Mission Overview

This abbreviated case study explores the role of ecology in assessing the attractiveness of an industry for new entrants. It addresses issues related to the birth and death of companies in the context of the Media industry.

Mission Statement

Is the Media industry attractive to new organizational forms?

---

16. The Walt Disney Company Form DEF 14A. 2001 filing. U.S. Securities and Exchange Commission. Retrieved February 2002, at *http://www.sec.gov.*

Mission Guides

Is this industry attractive to new companies? What new entities are being born into a particular industry? Does the industry provide adequate resources that might favor the survival of a new organizational form?

Mission Sources

The mission sources for this endeavor are primarily regulatory documents filed with the SEC and gleaned through 10k Wizard, industry profiles obtained from Hoover's Online, and professional association Web sites linked to and from Business.com.

Mission Source Rationale

To assess the attractiveness of the media industry for new organizational forms, we identified the relevant industry and conducted a count of recent IPOs in the category.

According to Hoover's Online, The Walt Disney Company participates in the Media industry.[17] A search for IPO offerings in this industry category from 1994 to 2002 using 10k Wizard discovered only one occurrence. 10k Wizard's categories differ slightly in terms of titles. "Media—Major Diversified" is the heading used by its search tool. Further examination suggests that a Fox Family Network S-1 filed in the 1998–1999 time range dealt with a sale of common stock in an attempt to restructure and reorganize News Corporation.[18] This was confirmed by a search using the Hoover's Online IPO Central portal. These findings indicate that there have been no new organizational forms born in the media category since at least 1994.

However, when related categories are examined, the picture becomes somewhat different. Not surprisingly, the year 2000 saw the greatest number of new public offerings, with twelve companies achieving this form of success. Analyzing the various media

---

17. Company capsule for The Walt Disney Company. 2002. Retrieved February 2002, at *http://www.hoovers.com.*
18. Fox Family Network Form S-1. 1998 filing. U.S. Securities and Exchange Commission. Retrieved February 2002, at *http://www.sec.gov.*

segments listed on the 10k Wizard Web site (as illustrated in Figure 4-2), we determined that the only subcategory that experienced IPO growth in the media industry in 2001 was Internet & Online Providers.

Figure 4-2. IPO Activity in the Media Industry, 1996–2002

	1996	1997	1998	1999	2000	2001	2002
Major Diversified	0	0	1	0	0	0	0
Motion Pictures	1	1	1	0	2	0	0
Theatres	0	0	1	0	0	0	0
TV & Music	3	1	2	0	2	0	0
Radio	0	1	0	1	2	0	0
TV Production & Programming	0	0	0	2	3	0	0
TV Broadcasting	0	0	0	1	1	0	0
Internet & Online Providers	0	0	0	0	2	2	0

This suggests that players in the media category are well established. Even with the surge of investment dollars available during the period surrounding the new millennium, new organizational forms attempting to enter this category may not have been able to compete effectively with the larger established conglomerates. Therefore, they entered the industry in a support capacity.

The companies that made their IPOs in 2001 in the Internet & Online Providers segment are developing new technologies to support established players such as The Walt Disney Company and Time Warner. For example, InfoSpace, Inc., provides commerce, information, and communication infrastructure services for wireless devices.[19] Many pundits suggest that the future direction of media delivery will likely be toward wireless handheld devices. Indeed, InfoSpace, Inc., is developing technology that will allow organizations such as The Walt Disney Company to broadcast their programming.

Are resources available to support new entities seeking to enter the Media industry? To answer this question, a search was conducted using Competia.com's Express feature. Unfortunately, "media" is not one of the major industry groups covered by this

19. InfoSpace, Inc., Form S-1. 2001 filing. U.S. Securities and Exchange Commission. Retrieved February 2002, at *http://www.sec.gov.*

service provider. It did note a number of organizations, publications, and associations dedicated to the Multimedia industry. Business.com's online resources were then explored. These offer a Media & Entertainment industry category, where links to the following associations that support the subindustry of Broadcasting were found:

- The National Academy of Television Arts and Sciences
- Writers' Guild of America
- Motion Picture Association of America
- The U.S. National Association of Broadcasters (NAB), a full-service trade association that promotes and protects the interests of radio and television broadcasters in Washington and around the world[20]

Connected to the issue of resource availability is the state of the industry itself. Is it growing, contracting, stagnating, or remaining the same? According to a Hoover's Online Industry Snapshot obtained in 2002, the industry categorized as Media had already matured. The result was that the birthrate for new organizational forms had tapered off. A "survival of the fittest" struggle appeared to be ongoing as the major players acquired smaller companies that would give them a competitive advantage.[21]

Aside from resources and industry-competitive dynamics, another issue to be addressed is the role of government. Does government encourage new entrants? The breadth of the industry or sector labeled Media suggests that any answer will at best be incomplete. Filmmaking and broadcasting are just two of many important areas. Unfortunately, regulators that govern one area may not have jurisdiction over another. In broad terms, the FCC regulates the media industry in the United States. It controls the number of major players in the industry through the management of broadcasting licenses to prevent monopolies from forming. Currently, the Media industry is "working toward a government-imposed 2006 deadline to provide High Definition Television (HDTV) for viewers."[22]

---

20. Multimedia industry. n.d. Retrieved February 2002, at *http://www.competia.com/express.*
21. Company capsule: "Media" Industry Snapshot. 2002. Retrieved February 2002, at *http://www.hoovers.com.*
22. Company capsule: "Media" Industry Snapshot. 2002. Retrieved February 2002, at *http://www.hoovers.com.*

Even when a firm is successful in entering an industry such as this, competitors may play a role in reducing its chances of survival. One example is EchoStar's efforts to remove Disney's ABC Family channel from its satellite service. EchoStar later settled a lawsuit with Disney and continues to carry all Disney services.[23] Although The Walt Disney Company can hardly be described as a new entrant or representing a new organizational form, the case illustrates what can happen when one corporation attempts to take resources (viewers) away from another entity. The case and the FCC's role in developing an HDTV alternative suggest that although entry into and exit from some subindustries is possible, entry into others is quite difficult.

Attractive industries draw new companies. Aside from a significant body of S-1 filings, another indicator is worth noting. Given the importance of IPOs as exit strategies for venture capitalists, attractive industries should also be awash in venture capital at all stages. Unfortunately, during this time, as noted above, there were no IPOs in the media category. Investors apparently knew what most others realized—the industry was mature, and barriers to entry were high. Thus, they directed their money elsewhere.

CASE EXAMPLE FOUR: THE PROTECTION OF INTELLECTUAL PROPERTY BY THE MEDIA INDUSTRY

Knowledge. Some might suggest that to survive and prosper, firms must be able to capture, protect, and harness the knowledge of their employees and access that of their network partners. The idea, though promising, still somewhat resembles the quest for the Holy Grail. Although conceptually simply, this process of acquiring, protecting, and using knowledge remains one characterized by great uncertainty. It does, however, offer promise to online researchers and business analysts. Efforts by companies to protect their knowledge provide signals of what is and what is not important to their operations as well as the extent to which they will go to protect it. This alone is useful to any CI practitioner. It is the subject of the following paragraphs.

---

23. EchoStar chided by FCC, settles with Disney. 2002. *Denver Business Journal.* April 5, 2002. Retrieved September 4, 2003, at *http://denver.bizjournals.com/denver/*.

Mission Overview

This abbreviated case study explores the role and importance of knowledge in the context of the media industry.

Mission Statement

How is intellectual property protected in the media industry?

Mission Guides

How do firms in this industry use patents, trademarks, or copyrights to protect their intellectual property? What role is played by the use of trade secrets? For one company and three of its competitors, count the number of patents registered per year for the last four years. Is a patent race under way? If so, who is in the lead? For the same company and its competitors, count the number of trademarks registered per year for the last four years. What does this mean? In its regulatory filings or press releases or through its Web site, does the company identify its most important patents, trademarks, or copyrights? If so, what are they? What would this company consider to be a trade secret?

Mission Sources

The mission sources for this endeavor are primarily regulatory documents filed with the U.S. Patent and Trademark Office, as well as the Web site of The Walt Disney Company.

Mission Source Rationale

A patent search using the United States Patent and Trademark Office Web site, as illustrated in Figure 4-3, suggests that Yahoo! and Time Warner are the most prolific patent filers in recent years in this industry. Indeed, in its annual report for 2000, Yahoo! stresses the importance of patents: "We rely upon trademark, patent and copyright law, trade secret protection and confidentiality of license agreements to protect our proprietary rights."[24] Time Warner and Yahoo! are currently competing for top spot in

---

24. Yahoo! Form 10-K. 2000 filing. U.S. Securities and Exchange Commission. Retrieved February 2002, at *http://www.sec.gov.*

the Internet and broadband communications industry. Both companies are securing their competitive advantage by protecting their innovations, using the patent system.

Figure 4-3. Patent Activity in the Media Industry

COMPANY	2001	2000	1999	1998
Time Warner	12	12	13	27
Viacom Inc.	0	1	1	0
The Walt Disney Company	0	1	2	5
Yahoo!	23	20	23	14

On the other hand, using the same database, Viacom Inc. is leading the trademark race, as illustrated in Figure 4-4. Viacom is currently ranked third in the media industry and therefore needs to compete more aggressively to sustain its market share and obtain the level of competitive advantage that The Walt Disney Company enjoys.

Figure 4-4. Trademark Activity in the Media Industry

COMPANY	2001	2000	1999	1998	TOTAL FILED
Time Warner	132	166	358	223	1,889
Viacom Inc.	257	381	349	213	2,523
The Walt Disney Company	112	62	109	120	890
Yahoo!	14	19	21	8	107

Disney and Time Warner's intellectual property was at risk during the late 1990s, when the copyright on some of their most valuable assets was set to expire. It was one of those rare occasions when Disney and Time Warner combined forces to lobby Congress to extend copyright protections. The companies were successful in persuading Congress to pass HR 2589. The resulting law gives the media industry twenty more years of copyright protection.

Why would a major media conglomerate such as Disney be concerned with protecting its copyrights? Mickey Mouse has huge symbolic value and still has a lot of commercial value. The Disney characters and brands have considerable earning potential, and they can be licensed and merchandised in so many ways. Mickey Mouse and friends are billion-dollar brands. Disney has said that

Winnie the Pooh and the Hundred Acre Wood characters generate a third of its licensing revenue. Indeed, in the late 1990s, Pooh generated $2 billion a year for Disney and its licensees.[25]

Firms such as The Walt Disney Company do not promote their trade secrets for obvious reasons, and they are serious about protecting them. For instance, in an ongoing court case that pits Disney against the Slesinger family regarding their royalty rights to Winnie the Pooh, the issue of information disclosure has arisen. "The next hearing in the case is expected to be about whether documents Disney has managed so far to keep sealed should remain so. [Daniel] Petrocelli [Disney's lawyer] has argued that the documents contain trade secrets and other proprietary information that could harm Disney's business if disclosed."[26]

25. Weinstein, H. 2002. Studios may have the most to lose. *Los Angeles Times*. February 21, 2002. Retrieved March 15, 2002, at *http://www.latimes.com*.
26. Wagner, H. J. 2002. Disney pooh-poohs family's claim. January 25, 2002. Retrieved March 15, 2002, at *http://www.hive4media.com*.

5

Competitive Intelligence Research Problems and Solutions

Competitive research and analysis is not a new activity, yet the practice remains both intriguing and fashionable. When thought of in commercial or management terms, it is hard to conceive of any industrial or professional markets where it is not practiced. Indeed, the performance of online competitive analysis is not limited by disciplinary boundaries. This chapter offers a wide variety of problems and solutions, or examples that demonstrate the breadth of this applicability. It suggests how readers can become more effective competitive analysts using online information sources.

Unfortunately, the breadth of the many practical examples also presents a problem for an editor seeking to meaningfully categorize the inherent ideas. In many instances, problems and solutions that are supported by online information sources and are written for a general audience may be viewed by readers as having specific applicability to particular products or market niches. Examples that are specific to particular products may, on the other hand, be thought of by readers as being generalizable across industries and markets. This concern is addressed by categorizing the problems and solutions in this chapter under three headings: *About Industries and Markets; About Companies;* and *About Issues, People, and Research.*

ABOUT INDUSTRIES AND MARKETS. Six problems and solutions are presented in this set. These offer the reader insight into how he or she might quickly construct an industry overview, identify risks facing new entrants, and highlight cultural traits common to industry players. Also offered are problems and solutions that demonstrate how industry trends, marketing practices, suppliers, and market size can be identified for the cell culture laboratory market. As well, readers will learn how to identify competitors in the voice recognition software industry and how to map the competitive landscape for Web-based customer services in the financial services sector. Researchers who developed these examples include Robin Neidorf of Electric Muse, Jan Knight of Bancroft Information Services, Conor Vibert, Mohammed Al-Waqfi, and Tamsin Bolton, all of Acadia University.

ABOUT COMPANIES. The problems and solutions categorized under this set will help readers to do the following more effectively: benchmark financial company–specific data, build competitor profiles, make use of alternative means to identify specific competitors, identify key decision makers employed by an acquisition target, and obtain information about private companies. Authors of these examples include Michelle Fennimore of Competitive Insights, David Ernsthausen of the Kenan-Flagler Business School, and Conor Vibert.

ABOUT ISSUES, PEOPLE, AND RESEARCH. Under this heading are found examples that suggest the future direction of computer display technology, how a manager can use patents to identify human resource talent, and how patents can be used to find inventions associated with a specific scientist. Readers will also learn how to identify toxic chemical releases that affect the environment, how a business operator might assess the effect of a public health crisis on its competitors, and how a researcher might explore product quality issues among consumer goods manufacturers. Also of interest to readers may be problems and solutions that demonstrate how a hotel operator might implement an environmental plan, how an analyst might assess the feasibility of opening a bookstore, and how nontext competitive intelligence can be found and captured. Authors of these examples include Kent Sutorius of Informed Solutions; Kendra Carmichael, Conor Vibert, Edith Callaghan, and Jim Macaulay of Acadia University; Roger Skalbeck of George Mason University School of Law; David Campbell of ShiftCentral; Candace Blayney; and Peter Mombourquette from Mount Saint Vincent University.

PROBLEM NUMBER 1: HOW CAN AN INDUSTRY OVERVIEW BE BUILT IN THIRTY MINUTES?

RESEARCH BACKGROUND: With the advent of the Internet and dramatic improvements to communication technologies, business opportunities can arise at any point. When given a few minutes to pull together insight on a specific industry, numerous options are available to the agile researcher. Which options are important depends, of course, on the reason behind the request for industry information. Thus, of use is a series of sources that offers different forms of insight about the industry in question.

In this particular instance, a client of an investment broker has called and expressed interest in directing some of her funds toward the oil and gas sector. The client is not knowledgeable about this industry and would like to quickly get herself up to speed with a general overview of how the industry functions. The investment broker would like to capitalize on this business opportunity and understands the importance of responding quickly to her request.

RESEARCH BUDGET: The online information used to put together this industry overview is free.

RESEARCH STRATEGY EMPLOYED: A number of information sources are useful for developing a quick industry overview. These include, but are not necessarily limited to, the Securities and Exchange Commission (SEC), the Department of Energy (DOE), Investopedia, Wetfeet.com, and the Web site of the industry association for this industry. Each 10-K annual report filed by a firm operating in the industry should offer a brief overview of the industry from the perspective of that firm. The U.S. Bureau of Labor Statistics (*http://www.bls.gov*) summarizes key industries from a labor perspective, and Wetfeet.com (*http://www.wetfeet.com*) does so from a human resource angle. The U.S. Department of Energy (*http://www.doe.gov*) highlights issues from the perspective of a government regulator. The industry association Web site offers a perspective common to industry participants, while highlighting issues being brought to the attention of regulators. This can be accessed through the Gateway to Associations portal of the American Society of Association Executives Web site (*http://www.asaenet. org*). Investopedia (*http://www.investopedia.com*) will describe the industry in a manner useful to investors.

RESEARCH RESULTS: The search began at Investopedia (*http://www.investopedia.com*). On the home page, the broker clicked on the Tutorials button and then was offered numerous options. The correct option in this instance was to click on the button labeled The Industry Handbook. This led to different industry options, including Oil and Gas Exploration and Equipment. Under this heading a broad description of the industry was offered. Of particular emphasis were the areas of oil drilling and refining and oilfield services. It also included a number of useful features such as an analysis of the industry, using the Porter 5-Forces model, links to industry specific resources, definitions of key buzzwords, and different techniques for valuing companies.

The next step was to access information at the Wetfeet.com Web site (*http://www.wetfeet.com*). On its home page is a heading termed Career Research. Under that heading is a subheading, Industry Profiles. A click on this subheading leads to a choice of industries. Of interest, in this instance, is the one with the title *Energy and Utilities*. This overview offers readers a high-level picture of both of these industries from the point of view of a job seeker. It offers a lengthy description of the industry, an overview of the major trends, a descriptive breakdown of the industry into different subindustries and geographical regions, descriptions of what current and former employees love and hate about working in the industry, and a listing of the major players along with their revenues, profits, and employee numbers.

Using this list of major players, the broker visited the U.S. Securities and Exchange Commission Web site (*http://www.sec.gov*). Under Filings and Forms (EDGAR), the Search for Company Filings button was clicked. Under General Purpose Search, the link titled Companies and Other Filers was then clicked. On the next page, the name of the company of interest was typed in the search box. Following this procedure for each company, the broker accessed regulatory filings. For each company, after scrolling down the page, the most recent 10-K filing was retrieved with a click. Within the most recent 10-K annual report of each company, a subsection titled Overview within the Management's Discussion and Analysis of Financial Conditions and Results of Operations section proved most helpful. It offered a quick overview of the challenges that each of the companies faced during the previous year. A quick pass-through of the filings of a number of companies allowed trends to become obvious.

Relevant industry associations were identified using the ASAEnet.org Web site. Clicking on the link titled Finding People, Associations and Businesses led to another choice of links. From this group was chosen Gateway to Associations. This, in turn, led to a search tool allowing associations to be queried based on keyword or by alphabetical order. Using the latter option, the broker clicked on the Petroleum link. This offered links to the home pages of a number of related associations and organizations. The link to the American Petroleum Institute (*http://api-ec.api.org*) was chosen. This association, representing the views of companies operating in the industry, offers insight into the policy issues that it is lobbying for in Washington, industry statistics, a description of the oil and gas industry, and an overview of the environmental initiatives of its members.

For a different perspective, the broker then accessed the U.S. Department of Energy Web site (*http://www.doe.gov*). On its home page, the researcher noticed a link titled Energy Prices and Trends. Clicking on this link led our researcher to a number of important sources, including a series of Country Analysis Briefs and Short Term Energy Outlook papers. The former documents offer detailed analysis of the U.S. energy market and those of other countries. The latter document is a forward-looking eighteen-month forecast of the U.S. energy market.

SUMMARY OF SOLUTION: Using a mixture of information from commercial Web sites such as Investopedia and Wetfeet.com, regulatory agencies such as the SEC and the Department of Energy, and an industry association Web site, the American Petroleum Institute, the broker was able to quickly put together an overview of the oil and gas industry for a valued client.

CONTRIBUTOR NAME: Conor Vibert
AFFILIATION: Acadia University

USEFUL TIPS

- Among the simplest means of finding a quick industry overview is to glance at the 10-K annual reports and S1 Forms of firms operating in the industry.
- Wetfeet.com offers a unique Human Resource slant on industries. For selected industries it also offers a list of trends.

PROBLEM NUMBER 2: HOW CAN AN ONLINE RESEARCHER IDENTIFY RISKS FACING NEW INDUSTRY ENTRANTS?

RESEARCH BACKGROUND: *Initial Public Offering* (IPO) is a term used to describe the process that companies follow when they seek to trade their shares publicly on stock markets for the first time. To do so, they must issue a prospectus or business plan that outlines to potential share purchasers how they plan to use their money. This document is called Form S1. Companies that wish to go public must electronically file an S1 form with the Securities and Exchange Commission (SEC). Industries that are characterized by firms going through, or having recently gone through, the IPO process represent a wealth of information for analysts. Completed S1 forms normally outline the risks faced by a firm as it strives to succeed in that particular industry. Because these firms are faced with the task of persuading savvy investors to part with their money, the information they offer about their operations and their environment must be relevant and current. Thus, an effective means for an analyst to understand the risks faced by firms in a specific industry is to summarize the information found in S1 forms of new entrants to that industry.

In this instance, our researcher, on contract to a group of university professors, is interested in learning more about the risks faced by firms operating in the drug development or pharmaceutical preparation industry.

RESEARCH BUDGET: If company representatives are willing to do their own research, the information can be accessed for free.

RESEARCH STRATEGY EMPLOYED: The search was begun by using PWC Global's EdgarScan (*http://www.edgarscan.pwcglobal.com*). The first step was to click on the Initial Public Offerings button and then search by Industry. Under the heading of Pharmaceutical Preparations, indicators were found that suggested a number of S1 filings during the fall of 2003. Once the companies were identified in this manner, the actual S1 forms were accessed through the Securities and Exchange Commission Web site (*http://www.sec. gov*). Within each company filing, a keyword search was undertaken for the words *risk factors.*

RESEARCH RESULTS: The EdgarScan search revealed that Idenix Pharmaceuticals Inc. and Incara Pharmaceuticals Corp. issued S1 forms during December 2003.

Highlights of Incara's S1 filing, accessed at the SEC Web site (*http://www.sec.gov*), suggest a small company with cash flow concerns and a dependence on third parties for the manufacturing and marketing of any drugs that it might develop. Because of its status as a research-and-development outfit, the document also suggests that any future revenues are dependent upon successful efforts in its lab. These, of course, are uncertain. Given its size, the loss of key personnel, product liability claims, or the loss of trade secrets could cause it immense harm. Further, its stock is currently illiquid and not traded on the Nasdaq.

The S1 Form for Idenix, accessed by the same manner, reveals that it is a larger R&D company that also is experiencing ongoing losses from operations. It is also dependent upon third parties for its survival, in this instance, Novartis, which markets its products. Loss of intellectual property, key personnel, and product liability claims are also concerns to this company. Most important, investors should be aware that the future success of this company and its revenues rests on the progress of its drugs in the Food and Drug Administration's (FDA) clinical trials.

SUMMARY OF SOLUTION: Idenix and Incara are two typical drug research firms that have gone the IPO route to obtain the financing necessary to sustain their operations over time. They both are at risk of losing key individuals, and need to guard their intellectual property and trade secrets very carefully. Until they have been successful at developing an FDA-approved drug and marketing it, they will experience financial losses. Thus, future cash flows are inextricably linked to R&D activity and third-party support for technology and product marketing. This is but a summary of a wealth of information regarding the risks facing these two companies and others similar to them, information that is available on their S1 forms.

CONTRIBUTOR NAME: Conor Vibert

AFFILIATION: Acadia University

USEFUL TIPS

- 10k Wizard or EdgarScan serve as useful starting points for quickly finding out which companies issued IPOs in any particular year.

Although numerous online tools exist to help sort through Securities and Exchange Commission filings, it is always useful to go to the original source, the EDGAR database, through the SEC Web site, *http://www.sec.gov.*

PROBLEM NUMBER 3: CAN ONLINE INFORMATION SOURCES BE USED TO IDENTIFY COMMON INDUSTRY CULTURAL TRAITS?

RESEARCH BACKGROUND: Nortel Networks has faced tremendous challenges during the past three years. Its troubles are synonymous with the crash of the telecommunications industry that precluded the general market downturn commencing in the early fall of 2000. Its stock price reached a high of more than $80 in 2000 and now hovers around the $4 mark. A massive downsizing and restructuring effort over the last three years resulted in a workforce reduction from more than 95,000 in 2000 to around 36,000 today, with more than $18 billion lost to special charges related to restructuring and write-downs of assets and goodwill.

Although the cost cutting and refocusing of the business continues, the effect of this massive downsizing on the morale of retained employees has not gone unnoticed. To achieve sustainable benefits from the restructuring process, some observers might suggest a need for a reassessment and re-creation of the organizational culture to adapt to the changing business environment.

As part of the ongoing restructuring process, you have been hired as a consultant to help assess the relationship of Nortel's organizational culture to its performance. Working with a committee of senior managers from different sections of the company, your task is to identify areas where changes in the current organizational culture may be required. The outcomes of the committee's work are expected to help reposition the company ahead of its competitors in an increasingly competitive and unstable business environment.

Aspects of working cultures are often shared industry-wide. Thus, a starting point is to explore similarities among Nortel and its competitors. Key competitors in Nortel's core business include Cisco Systems, Lucent Technologies, and Juniper Networks. Cisco is the major player in the networking equipment industry as estimated by sales and capital valuation. In recent years, Lucent has been following a similar restructuring process, which has led to a spin-off of the company's microelectronics business (Agere Systems Inc.) and enterprise-networks business (Avaya Inc.). Lucent is now focusing on optical, data, and wireless networking, competing directly with Nortel. Juniper Networks was chosen for analysis because it is a younger and smaller company known for its innovation and success in competing for market share with the major players in the industry.

RESEARCH BUDGET: Given the exploratory nature of this stage of the research, data is being collected from free online information sources.

RESEARCH STRATEGY EMPLOYED: Several online sources can be used to learn more about corporate cultures in this industry. The first is the Web site of Nortel Networks and each of its three competitors. In particular, the careers, company information, and investor relations sections normally offer information about the company's mission, values, and other aspects of its culture. Further, insight was also gleaned from the annual reports of the four companies. Annual reports were downloaded from the investor relations sections of the Web sites.

Another source used to collect information is *http://www.vault. com,* which is an online business providing company information and career management services. Vault is described by Fortune magazine as "the best place on the Web to prepare for a job search." The Web site provides a rich collection of information about various companies under three main categories: *company snapshot, employee message board,* and *workplace surveys.* The company snapshot describes the working environment at the company and an "Uppers and Downers" section listing the most positive and most negative aspects of working for the company. The employee message boards present a forum for current and former employees to anonymously discuss various aspects of their experiences while working for the company and to answer questions about the company from job seekers. The workplace surveys provide detailed accounts by current and former employees of various companies, describing the corporate culture, opportunities for advancement, the interviewing process, and pay.

A distinguishing feature of Vault.com is its offering of insider perspectives on the company culture from the point of view of both current and former employees as well as outside commentators. The information posted on the Vault Web site can be contrasted with official corporate perspectives posted on the corporate Web site. This contrast can reveal the degree to which a company has been successful in creating a work system and environment conducive to its intended organizational values and behaviors.

Another online source useful for this task is Wetfeet.com (*http://www.wetfeet.com*). WetFeet Inc. is a recruitment solutions company providing services to recruiters and job seekers. The Web site includes information on various companies and industries for potential job seekers. Of particular interest are company profiles, company interviews, insider guides, and industry profiles. The company-specific information on this site varies from one company to the other. In the industry profile section there is an item titled "Love-Hate" that describes the major positive and negative aspects of working in the particular industry. This information includes references to certain aspects of the corporate cultures prevailing in the industry and within the major players.

Another useful Web site is that of Network World Fusion (*http://www.nwfusion.com*). This Web site provides a wealth of knowledge about the networking industry, including news, feature articles, white papers, and forums. The material on this Web site is mainly technical, but some of the articles may give insights into the corporate cultures of various companies in the networking industry.

RESEARCH RESULTS: Using information obtained from the various sources identified above, a report was compiled describing each company's culture as indicated by the core values and principles declared by the company as well as various artifacts, including company systems, rules, policies, and observable behavior of members. The report included comparisons between the four companies and an analysis of their ability to translate the declared values into real behaviors and practices. It also included the following contents: (1) overview of the industry and business environment with reference to its implications for effective organizational culture; (2) core corporate values; (3) company systems, policies, and standards of behavior; (4) living up to the company values: an assessment of the company's effectiveness in translating values into practice; and (5) conclusions and implications.

Information about the networking equipment industry was collected from Yahoo! Finance at *http://finance.yahoo.com* and the *http://www.nwfusion.com*. The core values of each of the four companies were found on the company Web sites. The following table describes the core values of each of the four companies:

Table 5-1. Company Core Values

NORTEL NETWORKS	CISCO SYSTEMS	LUCENT TECHNOLOGIES	JUNIPER NETWORKS
Nortel's core values are: 1. Customers are the driving force; 2. People are our strength; 3. Quality is in every aspect; 4. Innovation fuels our future; 5. Accountability brings clarity; and 6. Integrity underpins everything **Nortel's people:** 1. Best talent in the business 2. Culture of innovation and collaboration 3. Focus on creating customer value[i]	**Cisco was founded on, and still thrives today on the principles of:** 1. Open communication; 2. Empowerment; 3. Trust; and 4. Integrity **Cisco's values are expressed through:** 1. Ethical workplace practices; 2. Philanthropic, community, and social initiatives; and 3. The quality of Cisco's people[ii]	**Lucent's core values are:** 1. A total focus on customers; 2. A commitment to business excellence, demonstrated by a focus on results, innovation, quality, speed, and the highest standard of business ethics; 3. A deep respect for the contributions of each person to the team; and 4. A strong sense of social responsibility[iii]	**Juniper's core values are:** 1. Integrity; 2. Respect; 3. Trust; 4. Humility; and 5. Technical excellence. **We share responsibility for fostering a culture that promotes:** 1. Open communication; 2. Survival-of-the-fittest ideas; 3. Decisive action; 4. Team commitment; and 5. Focus and execution[iv]

Sources: i, *http://www.nortelnetworks.com*; ii, *http://www.cisco.com*; iii, *http://www.lucent.com*; iv, *http://www.juniper.com*.

Information on the company systems and policies was found on each company's Web sites under different titles such as Code of Business Conduct, Business Guideposts, and Standards of Business Conduct. These documents provide detailed accounts of company policies and standards of behavior expected from company members in various situations while conducting the company's business. These documents were used to examine how each company translates its core values into standards of business behavior. Comparisons between the four companies' codes of conduct were made and conclusions drawn.

SUMMARY OF SOLUTION: The consultant was able to identify several online sources to collect information about the organizational cultures of Nortel Networks and a few of its major competitors. The Web site of each company was used to collect information about the company's core values and various artifacts reflecting the corporate culture, including company regulations, policies, and standards of behavior required from its members. A comparative analysis between the corporate cultures of Nortel and its competitors was conducted. The consultant found that values, principles, and corporate culture advocated and intended by the company's executives may not be identical to the actual culture of the organization as perceived by its employees, customers, and the outside world. Therefore, it is important that perceptions of employees, customers, and outside business analysts are taken into consideration when assessing the effectiveness of the organization's culture in its performance and when deciding whether certain changes in the current culture should be initiated.

CONTRIBUTOR NAME: Mohammed Al-Waqfi
AFFILIATION: Acadia University

USEFUL TIPS

- Information about the company's culture can be found on most companies' Web sites. The careers, company information, and investor relations sections, in particular, may contain useful information to help understand the organizational culture.
- Although some information may be obtained from the Web for free, certain Web sites require subscription fees to allow use of their information. Some sites such as Vault.com offer valuable information about various companies. Paying the required fees to obtain access to these sites is recommended.
- To understand the core values and culture of a particular company, it is important to seek information not only from the company sources but also from other sources that may give insights about the company, including the perspectives of current and previous employees and various other outside observers.

PROBLEM NUMBER 4: REACHING POTENTIAL CUSTOMERS: MARKET SIZE, SUPPLIERS, MARKETING PRACTICES, AND INDUSTRY TRENDS FOR THE CELL CULTURE LABORATORY MARKET

RESEARCH BACKGROUND: LabWorks, a technology company, has created a new product to be used in a very specific type of laboratory: its product will be marketed and sold to laboratories that perform "cell culture" work, the biotechnological process of growing cells outside of living organisms. To revise its business and marketing plan to incorporate this new product, LabWorks is looking for information on this relatively small niche within the pharmaceutical industry. The marketing manager already knows that there are a limited number of cell culture laboratories in existence in the United States and that numerous vendors sell other products to this market. He wants a researcher to determine (1) approximate potential market size, (2) key suppliers to this market, (3) how these laboratories purchase these products, and (4) any trends that are being discussed in this industry.

RESEARCH BUDGET: The marketing manager does not have access to any fee-based databases and does not want to take the time to perform his own Internet research. He is willing to hire an independent researcher to spend 10 to 15 hours researching and writing up the findings as well as to pay for database fees ranging from $150 to $175.

RESEARCH STRATEGY EMPLOYED: The researcher knows that cell culture work takes place primarily within the pharmaceutical (drug) industry, and that it also exists within other biotechnology areas such as genetic and chemical engineering. To expand his limited understanding of the industry, he first conducts a simple Internet search using the phrase *cell culture* in Google (*http://www. google.com*). This allows him to identify pertinent industries, basic information on the potential market size, and a selection of companies that are already selling to this market. Additional searches take place using the search phrase *cell culture* combined with other search terms such as *suppliers; buyers guides; vendors; market size; pharmaceutical industry;* and *drug industry.* The Web sites of the vendors are reviewed for information on how their marketing and sales operations are set up as well as for hints on any strategic company news that might help to identify trends.

The researcher uses a "reverse lookup" of suppliers' Web sites to identify potential strategic partners as well as to locate additional resources and buyers' guides where LabWorks might advertise. There are a number of ways to do this, but the easiest is to use the following search term in a search engine: *Link: www.companyname.com* (with "companyname" referring to the company's Web site address). This search retrieves a list of Web sites that links to the site entered in the search. For example, to search for companies that link to Invitrogen's Web site, simply enter the search term *link:www.invitrogen.com.* The results include a listing described as "Laboratory Suppliers," an example of a buyer's guide.

A subsequent search to find out more about marketing to this niche industry is then performed using a combination of terms, such as *marketing OR advertising AND "life scientists."* This latter term was chosen after reviewing various Web sites of companies that sell to cell culture laboratories and after determining that a major group of customers are academic researchers who are often referred to as "life scientists."

In addition to searching the Internet via a search engine, the researcher reviews another site, MarketResearch.com, to see if any market research studies on the cell culture industry are available for a fee. Although the budget doesn't allow for the purchase of market research reports, reviewing what is available can often provide an idea of just how much study there has been in a particular area or industry. It is often possible to review the table of contents of such reports and to purchase small sections "by the slice."

To determine what is being reported about the industry as a whole, the researcher then conducts an article search of newspapers, magazines, and trade journals. He chooses this strategy rather than turning to an industry search in an online database because he knows that cell culture is a small niche within a larger industry, and that this subject would be too small for most commercial databases that provide information by industry topic. Such predefined industry searches typically focus on larger industries such as "pharmaceuticals" or "engineering."

The search for articles takes place within the two subscription databases of Dow Jones Interactive and Hoover's. In Dow Jones, the researcher turns to the Publications Library, where he conducts keyword searches, including the aforementioned terms, along with the addition of the keyword *trends.* In Hoover's, it is first necessary to search by company name for each of the identified suppliers. If articles are available for the company selected, they can then be found under the section "Current Stories Mentioning Company X" within the News & Commentary section.

RESEARCH RESULTS: The searches described above are useful for identifying potential LabWorks customers (cell culture laboratories), vendors who sell to these laboratories, and examples of how these vendors market and sell their products. It has also provided some background information on potential market size and trends. The results are summarized below:

- *Names of Other Suppliers.* The initial Internet search and review of buyers' guides provides names of major suppliers to the cell culture market: Invitrogen, Irvine Scientific, Hyclone, Bio Whittaker, and Cambrex. This is not an exhaustive list of suppliers, but from reviewing the resources, the researcher concludes that it includes the key players. The reverse lookup of links in the suppliers' Web sites provides additional examples of buyers' guides.

- *Selling and Marketing.* The annual reports and Web sites of these identified suppliers provide information on their customer base, typically both academic and private laboratories, and further review finds information on specific methods used for selling and marketing their products and services. The search using *"life scientists" AND marketing* immediately provides information on a company called BioInformatics, which describes itself as "an innovative market research and consulting firm supporting marketing and sales executives in the life science, medical device and pharmaceutical industries" (*http://www. gene2drug.com*). The BioInformatics Web site provides executive summaries of surveys, such as "Marketing to Life Scientists: Keys to Success," "Marketing to Life Scientists: A Comparison of the Industrial and Academic Segments," "Advertising to Life Scientists," and "Support and Service for Life Science Products: Creating Loyal Customers." Other surveys listed on the Web site reveal additional information. The search in Dow Jones also provided a citation for a 2002 article in a journal called *Chemical Week*: "Suppliers to the Drug Industry Are Trying to Stay Ahead of Competitors, Customers, and Technologies." This article provides additional general information on the suppliers, their concerns, and their methods of marketing.

- *Trends.* The Dow Jones and Hoover's article searches provide a number of citations for review. Two articles from the journal *Genetic Engineering News* are highlighted to report on. One is titled "Current Trends and Innovations in Cell Culture" and the other is "Survey of Market Trends for Cell Culture Media." Both are written in 2001 and outline a number of trends and events in the cell culture industry.

- *Market Size.* Initial searches discovered a 1997 study from PhorTech International, a company that conducts marketing research and technology assessment for life science research companies. The data are probably not current enough, and subsequent searches did not produce newer statistics on the same subject. However, the PhorTech Web site also provides a more recent 2002 study on "Global Laboratory Product Usage," which includes some useful information that, combined with the older data, satisfies LabWork's need for information about the potential market size.

SUMMARY OF SOLUTION: The researcher reviews the Web sites and, in some cases, the annual reports of the suppliers he has identified, looking for specific information on marketing, selling, and advertising methods. The review shows that a combination of direct mail, trade show attendance, articles, and print advertising in trade journals and Web sites are some of the key methods used by suppliers to reach this specific market.

The BioInformatics reports include a wealth of information on the purchasing preferences of scientists, including information about how they learn about vendors, products, and services and make purchasing decisions. The reports also show that good customer service is critical in scientists' choice of suppliers. Much more information along these same lines is available from the executive summaries of the studies, and the researcher does not suggest that LabWorks purchase the full studies.

The potential market size (number of cell culture laboratories) does not seem to be readily available, but the 1997 study by PhorTech cites that "Over 60,000 U.S. life science researchers are currently involved with cell and tissue culture, spending approximately $100 million annually on instrumentation and media." Providing a more global context, the Global Laboratory Product Usage study says that "the estimation of total population of life scientists is 356,000 worldwide, of whom 281,250 are working in the laboratory." Additional data in this study report "61.14% of these life scientists are involved in cell culture." These numbers are provided to the client, and LabWorks determines that the numbers will suffice for current planning.

CONTRIBUTOR NAME: Jan Knight
AFFILIATION: Bancroft Information Services

USEFUL TIPS

- Reviewing what is available from large market research/survey companies is a good first step to determine the potential availability of information.
- Online buying guides are often a good place to find an initial list of competitors.

- The reverse lookup on a company Web site (link:www.
  companyname.com) helps to find strategic partnerships and potential advertising/marketing vehicles.

PROBLEM NUMBER 5: WHO ARE THE COMPETITORS AND RESEARCHERS IN THE VOICE RECOGNITION SOFTWARE INDUSTRY?

RESEARCH BACKGROUND: The client, a medium-sized computer software company, has been looking to expand and add voice recognition software to its growing list of products. Voice recognition software has not had a strong success rate in the past, but technological advances have enhanced the reliability of the software; the client believes that this industry has room for development and competition. Before jumping into the voice recognition software market, the client wants to compile information on the industry leaders and on those researching new uses for the software. This will allow the company to assess the competition and prepare for future industry developments.

RESEARCH BUDGET: $1,500. Much of the information will require the use of online subscription databases. The client does not have in-house access to subscription databases and has chosen to hire the services of an information research firm. It has been estimated that the research will take a week to complete. The research firm fee and the online database fees should remain less than $1,500.

RESEARCH STRATEGY EMPLOYED: If one has access to online subscription databases, they can provide a much better research alternative to the "free Web." These databases offer access to a range of reliable information, often far more in depth than any freely available Web resources. Factiva (*http://www.factiva.com*) is one such database. It provides access to worldwide newspapers, magazines, and scholarly journals, as well as company and industry information and analysis. One feature of Factiva is "Company Screening." This allows the researcher to retrieve lists of companies that match the criteria required. In this case, the search requires a list of companies operating in the voice recognition software industry. No search terms are required in Company Screening. All the information is retrieved by narrowing predetermined categories until the proper information is arrived at. Voice recognition software falls under several other broader industry headings: Computers—Computing—Software—Application Software. By highlighting Voice Recognition Software, Factiva will display a list of companies for which this is the primary industry. Each listing will come with a full company analysis, including an overview, financial details, company news, and press releases.

Another online subscription database is the article index *Web of Science.* This database differs greatly from Factiva in type of content, yet is invaluable in gaining an insight into those researching in the area of voice recognition software. In most cases, *Web of Science* provides access to citations and abstracts of scholarly articles and conference papers in a multitude of areas. Often authors of these scholarly articles are associated with companies in the respective industry. Analyzing these articles can provide an insight into those companies that are researching the industry and enhancing the product. In *Web of Science,* a "topic" search was employed using the strategy "speech recognition software" OR "voice recognition software." This search allows both *speech* and *voice* to be retrieved as a keyword. Since these two different terms can be used to describe the product, it is best to use them both in the search, so as not to miss anything. When conducting a search, it is always important to analyze the results. If they are too narrow, too broad, or unrelated to the topic, the terms should be adjusted and the search performed again. All databases differ, and similar search terms will not always return similar results across the board.

RESEARCH RESULTS: The Company Screening search in Factiva retrieved six companies, all of which are U.S.-based and list voice recognition software as their primary industry. Detailed financial and stock information, current and archived news, and press releases were included for each of the six companies. Enough information could be found on each company to do a proper assessment of their situation. Factiva also has a feature that allows for comparison reports to be created, contrasting any of the six companies to the industry as a whole.

The search in *Web of Science* returned thirty-three documents. The results indicate that a lot of research is being done in the field of voice recognition software but primarily by university-affiliated researchers. However, several results did have corporate involvement. For example, an article titled "Voice recognition: Software solutions in real-time ATC workstations" has the involvement of researchers from Lockheed Martin. The paper "Voice recognition software for GC-OLFACTOMETRY" comes from a researcher at the scientific equipment company Mass Evolution,

Inc. An interesting aspect of *Web of Science* is the "Cited References" and "Times Cited" feature. This allows the user not only to view the references for a certain article but also to view how many times that article has been cited by others. This allows for a very good analysis of all the research done on a certain topic over the years.

SUMMARY OF SOLUTION: When looking for detailed company and research-related information about an industry such as voice recognition software, it is helpful to have access to one of the many subscription databases, such as Factiva and *Web of Science,* which offer this kind of data. Some free Web resources, such as Hoovers.com, can offer somewhat similar data but without the same depth and coverage.

CONTRIBUTOR NAME: Tamsin Bolton
AFFILIATION: Acadia University

USEFUL TIPS

- Check article indexes, such as *Web of Science,* to locate current industry research.
- Use a variety of search terms and strategies to locate relevant information; the first search does not always yield the best information.
- Company information can be accessed through a variety of sources. But if you have access to subscription databases, they are often much more comprehensive.

PROBLEM NUMBER 6: FINANCIAL SERVICES COMPETITIVE INTELLIGENCE: HOW CAN THE COMPETITIVE LANDSCAPE FOR WEB-BASED CUSTOMER SERVICE BE MAPPED?

RESEARCH BACKGROUND: MaxMoney, a financial services company, is planning to roll out an extensive new Web-based service platform for providing customers with information, account access, new account applications, tax preparation, advice, and more. The financial services industry is a highly competitive, customer-oriented industry, and many companies are leaping into Web-based customer contact and services. To stake its claim in cyberspace, MaxMoney needs to know exactly what its competitors are doing—and are planning to do—on the Web, as well as initiatives they have abandoned. With this information, the company will be best able to position its own offerings and garner market share.

RESEARCH BUDGET: Many high-quality market research firms offer expensive reports detailing activity in the financial services sector. But MaxMoney is not willing to spend the $10,000, or more, per report that these firms charge. To minimize the costs of research, MaxMoney plans to identify and purchase discrete pieces of longer reports as well as use free sources, including filings to the Securities and Exchange Commission (SEC), industry news journals, and the competitors' own Web sites. The company sets an overall budget of $3,000 for any information purchases it deems necessary.

RESEARCH STRATEGY EMPLOYED: Because each competitor has a Web site, information-gathering begins "at home," with these sites; supplementary searches on the Wayback Machine (an archive of Web sites going back to 1996) enable a comparison of current strategy with past strategy. Searches of most recent 10-Ks (annual reports) with the SEC are also collected for each competitor. Trade magazines and journals are searched for relevant references to competitors, as well as references to proprietary research that might be available for review or purchase. Finally, MaxMoney also checks research-oriented portals for industry overviews and company-specific information; some relevant reports are available on a "by the page" basis, and in some cases, free summaries (abstracts, executive summaries or even press releases) provide enough insight to fill in the picture.

With this portfolio of information, the company will be able to identify and maximize its unique selling proposition in the Web-based marketplace.

RESEARCH RESULTS: Many overlapping resources are employed for this project. Results are best considered one resource at a time, and then in aggregate as per the following four examples:

1. *Competitor Web sites.* Each competitor's Web site offers a wealth of information, including
   - Tag lines, images, colors, and other marketing/ communications cues indicating the marketing approach of the company
   - Customer service interfaces, showing which services and information customers can access via the Web

- Press releases on initiatives, partnerships, structural changes, and earnings reports
- A "contact us" page. Viewing this page offers unexpected rewards in the form of information on the competitor's marketing efforts. The form asks visitors to indicate, "How did you hear about us?" and provides a series of check boxes showing different places the competitor advertises or is otherwise visible.
- An "about us" page. Careful review of the information on this page helps draw a more detailed picture of the way the competitor is positioning itself in the marketplace. Since part of the research effort is to learn what has changed for competitors, the company also searches each competitor's files on the Wayback Machine (*http://www.archive.org*). Entering the competitor's URL into the Wayback Machine's search interface pulls up copies of the way the site looked on dates going back over eight years. This search allows review and analysis of changes in product offerings, strategy, pricing, and target audience.

2. *SEC Filings.* Since all of the competitors under scrutiny are publicly traded companies, they all must file reports with the SEC. The most detailed and relevant report for our intelligence purposes is the 10-K, the annual report. The 10-K includes sections that describe the business, market, competition, and strategy of the subject company and serves as an excellent source of detailed competitive information.

Some companies make their SEC filings available directly from their Web sites, often in an "investor relations" section. However, all SEC filings are easily retrieved directly from the SEC through the EDGAR database (*http://www.sec.gov/edgar/searchedgar/Webusers.htm*). A simple Web-based form allows entry of a company name, index, state of incorporation, and SIC; because this project involves specific companies, the company names are entered one by one in the search box, and a complete list of filings is pulled up. From this list, the 10-K is selected and downloaded. To simplify use of the 10-K, which is a lengthy document, the relevant sections are cut and pasted into a word processing document. This minimizes the size of the document and allows keyword searching through the word processing program. Thus, the company's statements about Web-based customer service and the competitive marketplace are easily extracted from these filings.

3. ***Trade and Industry Publications.*** Databases of business publications are searched for articles dealing with Web-based service offerings of financial services companies, as well as overview of market trends and proprietary research released in the past twelve months. Gale Group's Business & Industry Database, accessible through the public library, is a key source, as are ProQuest and InfoTrac. Searches are conducted on combinations of terms, including competitor names and terms such as *Web services, electronic business, e-business, trends, research, competition,* and *outlook.* These searches yield a wide range of articles, including the following:
   - Company profiles
   - Articles comparing lead players in the industry
   - Press releases and feature stories describing recent analyst reports on the sector
   - Reviews of Web-based service offerings
   - Surveys of customer experiences on financial services Web sites
   - Estimates of the size of the current and future market for Web-based services

4. ***Proprietary Reports.*** Several articles mention reports published by three different industry analyst groups—a professional association for financial services companies, and two market research firms. A visit to the Web site of the professional association reveals that a PDF version of the research report is available simply by registering on the site. Although this report does not have the most recent or cutting-edge information, it does provide more depth than the news articles, as well as a helpful overview of factors affecting the market.

The two market research firms each have a large report on financial services trends, in general, as well as shorter reports on e-commerce and e-business trends in the sector. The large reports cost between $8,000 and $10,000, whereas the shorter reports cost $5,000 each. The firms both indicate that the only way to get this information is to purchase the full report.

However, a visit to a research portal proves otherwise: a search at MarketResearch.com (*http://www.marketresearch.com*) reveals that one firm's reports are available on a "by the slice" basis. Five relevant pages from the overall industry report and four chapters from the specific report on Web-based services are identified and purchased through the portal. The pages from the industry report cost $175 apiece, and each chapter from the Web-based services report costs $450, resulting in a cost of $2,675. The other firm's reports are not available anywhere on a per-page or per-chapter basis.

SUMMARY OF SOLUTION: Each competitor has been studied thoroughly for its current and proposed Web-based service offerings, abandoned initiatives, market standing, and outlook. MaxMoney learns how its competitors are slicing and dicing the marketplace, where the market is stronger or weaker, and what specific factors affect consumer decisions about Web-based service and information offerings.

Using a combination of competitor communications materials, SEC filings, historical Web site information, trade journal coverage, and proprietary research, MaxMoney has created a detailed map of the competitive landscape in Web-based financial service offerings. Because so much information was gleaned through publicly available sources, and because the company was strategic about where and when to purchase information, the budget of $3,000 was maintained.

MaxMoney is now prepared to map out its own strategy for rolling out Web-based services.

CONTRIBUTOR NAME: Robin Neidorf

AFFILIATION: Electric Muse

USEFUL TIPS

- Competitive intelligence can start with the competitor. Visit a competitor's Web site, read public filings (if available), and analyze the language you find there. How does the competitor present itself? What words and concepts appear frequently? How would you describe the competitor's market and unique selling proposition, based on the language the competitor uses?
- It's not "all or nothing." If a costly report has information you need, look for a source that might offer pieces of the report. Some research portals offer reports by the page or by the chapter. Additionally, news coverage announcing the publication of the report or quoting the authors of the report sometimes provides insight into the detailed data. If you can't afford "all," it doesn't mean you have to settle for "nothing."

PROBLEM NUMBER 7: HOW MIGHT COMPANY FINANCIAL DATA BE BENCHMARKED?

RESEARCH BACKGROUND: The vice president of finance for a public company is anticipating tough questions at the next meeting with Wall Street analysts and wants financial data to show that the company's performance is not that different from what others in the industry are achieving.

RESEARCH BUDGET: The budget for this research is zero dollars, and the vice president would like the information by the end of the day tomorrow. The researchers do not have access to any fee-based online resources such as LexisNexis or Hoover's.

RESEARCH STRATEGY EMPLOYED: The researcher will need to answer two basic questions: Who is the company competing against? And what financial and/or performance figures will accurately describe each company's performance over the appropriate time period? Figures for sales, net income, earnings per share, and the like will probably be useful. For a U.S. public company, these figures can be found using the income statements and balance sheets that can be found in the company's 10-K and 10-Q reports that publicly traded companies are required to file with the Securities and Exchange Commission (SEC). The SEC has a Web site that lets users find this information, but other Internet sites provide the same information in a format that is a little easier to use. One of the best of the alternate Internet sites is Pricewaterhouse-Coopers' EdgarScan.

RESEARCH RESULTS: The following steps are used to find financial statement information for a public U.S. company using the Edgar-Scan Web site by PricewaterhouseCoopers:

Step One. At the EdgarScan Web site (*http://edgarscan.pwcglobal. com/servlets/edgarscan*), the researcher clicks on the Benchmarking Assistant link and then enters the company name (one could also enter part of the company name). He then clicks on the Search button; a list of U.S. public companies containing the term entered is displayed. He selects the name of the company from the list, and it shifts to the Selected box.

Step Two. The researcher clicks on the Find Peers button, and a list of companies that have the same Standard Industrial Classification code (SIC code) as the selected company is returned. He then clicks on company names for comparison, and the company names also move to the Selected box. (This is where some judgment is necessary. It is possible that not all the companies in the list of peers are really competitors of the company. See Useful Tips.)

Step Three. The researcher now clicks on the Graphs tab and selects the desired financial or performance measures from the pull-down menu. He then clicks on the Excel Graph button, and a graph and a spreadsheet of the data are returned (for examples, see Figure 5-1).

Step Four. The researcher then saves the graph and spreadsheet to his computer using the Save As function of his Internet browser. For multiple measures, he repeats this process for each desired measure from Step Three.

SUMMARY OF SOLUTION: Using the Benchmarking Assistant at the EdgarScan Web site provides a quick comparison of a company's financial performance against other companies that have been assigned the same SIC code.

CONTRIBUTOR NAME: David Ernsthausen

AFFILIATION: Kenan-Flagler Business School

USEFUL TIPS

- Remember that SIC codes and the number of SIC codes assigned to a company are decided by the publisher of the resource, so it is possible that a company may be assigned a slightly different set of SIC codes, depending on the resource used. EdgarScan assigns only one SIC code per company; other sources may assign multiple SIC codes to the same company. For this reason, constructing a complete competitor list may be difficult. Ask for a list of competitors from your company, or make your own list.
- Remember that many companies may participate in several industries and therefore could be assigned several SIC codes. This can make comparing companies' financial performance difficult because the companies may compete against each other only in one or two areas. There is no good way around this.
- Many university and public libraries pay for access to electronic databases and print resources that contain company financial information and/or listings of companies in an industry and industry averages information. If you are close to a library, go visit its online databases.

Figure 5-1. Graphic Representation of Financial Data Found in EdgarScan

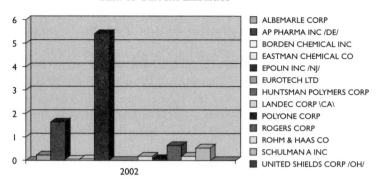

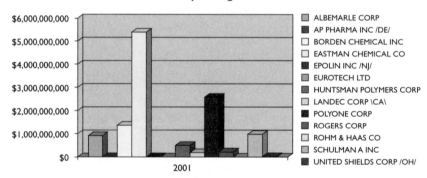

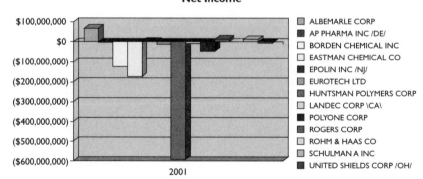

Reprinted with the permission of PricewaterhouseCoopers LLP.

- There are no free online resources for finding detailed financial information for segments of a company's business, a company's subsidiaries, or for private companies.

PROBLEM NUMBER 8: HOW MIGHT COMPETITOR PROFILES BE BUILT FROM ONLINE INFORMATION SOURCES?

RESEARCH BACKGROUND: The Internet can be a valuable tool to compile and analyze competitor information. For most publicly traded companies, comprehensive competitor profiles can be constructed from Web-based sources. However, some sources are better than others, and some information is more reliable than others. This vignette outlines the methods and sources that can be used to compile robust and reliable competitor profiles that include the following information:

- Company summary and organizational structure
- Key management and employment
- Product/service overview
- Financial overview
- Market share
- Corporate strategy

RESEARCH BUDGET: Many companies prepare customized competitor profiles for clients. The price for this service can range anywhere from $500 to $10,000 per profile, depending on the depth of research and analysis required. If a company needs to develop profiles on a number of competitors, the cost can be onerous. However, by using the methods described below, the cost will be limited to a few basic subscription fees and the internal cost of developing the profiles.

RESEARCH STRATEGY EMPLOYED: To build a comprehensive competitor profile a variety of sources should be used. General company information can be obtained from sources such as Hoover's (*http://www.hoovers.com*) and OneSource (*http://www.onesource.com*), which provide good summary data on a company's organizational structure, products/services, geographic markets, and financial information. For U.S.-based companies and foreign companies with substantial business in the United States, the Securities and Exchange Commission (SEC) requires quarterly and annual filings (10-K and 10-Q) as well as ad hoc filings for specific events such as a merger or an acquisition (*http://www.sec.gov/edgar.shtml*). These filings must include geographic market information, the company's financial situation, corporate strategy, and what the company perceives to be risk factors in executing its business plan. The philosophy behind these public filings (which are made available for free) is that investors in public companies have the right to comprehensive information to make informed investment decisions.

The best sources of information on company management and governance are the corporate Web site and SEC filings. The company's own Web site typically offers the most up-to-date data on key management and directors. The company's SEC filings contain pertinent information related to salaries and other compensation. A general Web search using Google (*http://www.google.com*) or AlltheWeb.com (*http://www.alltheweb.com*) will usually turn up interesting information on the background and affiliations of a competitor's management team.

For most companies, a competitor's Web site is also a good source of information on its products and/or services. SEC filings require a review of products and services, and in many cases companies break down revenue and margins by major product category. Other good sources of product-related information are online industry magazines, product review Web sites, and newsgroups/chat rooms where consumers share their observations about a particular product or service.

The best source of financial information on publicly traded companies are the SEC filings (10-K and 10-Q), which require a detailed accounting of revenue by source (product/geography), cost structure, and profit/loss, as well as shares outstanding. Secondary information providers such as Hoover's, OneSource, and Yahoo! Finance (*http://finance.yahoo.com*) provide good comparative data on most publicly traded companies.

To determine a company's position in the market (or market share) can be a more complicated process. If competitors are pleased with their market share, or it is increasing, they will tend to promote it in their public filings and other public information. However, if it is decreasing, they won't. Most industries have trade publications or specialized research companies that calculate market share by company. IDC (*http://www.idc.com*), for example, calculates market share data for a wide variety of information-technology-related sectors. Plunkett Research (*http://www. plunkettresearch.com*) provides a detailed analysis of more than 300 companies in the automobile sector. Another way to estimate market share is to evaluate a competitor's revenue (by product/ service line) against the total market size for that product or service. The total market size by the North American Industrial Classification System (NAICS) category is published by the Bureau of Economic Analysis (*http://www.bea.gov*) in the United States and Statistics Canada (*http://www.statscan.ca*) in Canada.

Obtaining an accurate read on a company's overall strategy and corporate direction can be challenging. SEC filings require information on this topic, but it tends to be more generic in nature. Other public information such as executive presentations can provide clues to future strategy but is also sanitized, providing only as much as the company wants to reveal. One of the better sources of strategy information can be stock market analysts. Morningstar (*http://www.morningstar.com*), for example, prepares detailed reports on more than 3,000 publicly traded companies. Others such as W. R. Hambrecht (*http://www.wrhambrecht.com*) specialize in specific industries or categories of companies. These reports tend to include insight on a company's strategy and direction, because that will have a direct effect on its share price. However, this information also needs to be viewed carefully. In recent years, analysts have come under fire for being biased in their research.

A number of sources can be used to determine the marketing activities and strategies of a competitor. The company's Web site will, in most cases, provide information on marketing activities as well as annual reports and other public documents. There are also a number of marketing-related online publications that can be accessed for references to a specific competitor's marketing activity. Some companies archive advertisements (text and video) and offer it in a fee-based environment. One such service is Eloda (*http://www.eloda.com*), which contains an archive of advertisements from Canadian television stations. Eloda archives these advertisements in a digital format, and users download the ones they want from a specific time frame and market.

When developing a competitor profile using Web-based information, it is important to conduct a general search in addition to the specific methods mentioned above. A general search can uncover interesting trends and other information that will be helpful in developing a complete picture of a competitor's activities. A general news search using engines such as Google (*http://news.google.ca*) or Hoover's (*http://www.hoovers.com*) provides recent news on a competitor's activities. A broader search using GooFresh (*http://www.buzztoolbox.com/archives/000009.shtml*) can provide recent information on a competitor (GooFresh provides Web pages that have been indexed in the past thirty days).

RESEARCH RESULTS: ShiftCentral has developed dozens of detailed competitor profiles using this approach. In most cases it is much like a puzzle. If you can sift through the potentially millions of sources and extract just the relevant pieces, you can put together a robust and powerful tool for competitor information.

SUMMARY OF SOLUTION: By using the approach indicated above, competitor profiles can be developed quickly and cost-effectively. The majority of "competitive information" on publicly traded companies is available in the public domain, and by using a combination of specific sources and general Web searches, you can develop comprehensive and relevant competitor profiles.

CONTRIBUTOR NAME: David Campbell
AFFILIATION: ShiftCentral Inc.

USEFUL TIPS

- Specific sources of competitor information such as Hoover's, One-Source, Morningstar, and Yahoo! Finance provide good and timely data.
- Public company information sources such as the U.S. SEC and Canada's SEDAR are excellent sources of competitive information.
- General Web searches, date restricted, should be used to uncover valuable nuggets of competitor information.

PROBLEM NUMBER 9: WHAT ARE SOME ALTERNATIVE APPROACHES FOR IDENTIFYING COMPETITORS?

RESEARCH BACKGROUND: Who are a firm's true competitors? Are they obvious or are they lurking in the shadows? Are they niche players below the radar screen of the business press, or are they giants not yet openly associated with the industry, market, product, or service in question? The answers are not always obvious. Fortunately, there are online sources available that put some of the answers at the fingertips of an analyst. Our analyst is interested in learning more about the medical products industry, specifically the manufacturing of stethoscopes. She has been retained to develop a list of potential competitors for a company seeking to diversify its portfolio of manufactured products.

RESEARCH BUDGET: All of the information necessary for finding a solution to this problem is available for free on the Internet.

RESEARCH STRATEGY EMPLOYED: There are a number of Web sites useful for identifying competitors of this firm. A starting point is to do a keyword search by product type (offered by the firm) using Thomas Register (*http://www.thomasregister.com*). This will offer a list of companies with facilities in the United States that manufacture the product at hand. A second option involves the use of patent information. The patent database, found on the United States Patent and Trademark Office (USPTO) Web site (*http://www.uspto.gov*), can also be helpful in this regard. A search using the keyword *stethoscope* by patent title will list those patents including the term *stethoscope* in the title.

A third angle of attack is to undertake a second keyword search of a Web site such as Business.com (*http://www.business.com*). Once a group of firms is identified, other angles can be pursued. For those that are publicly traded, a researcher may want to do a search using the benchmarking function of EdgarScan (*http://www.edgarscan.pwcglobal.com*). This will list companies that fall under the same SIC classification. One need simply search by company name.

RESEARCH RESULTS: As noted above, we began our search by looking at Thomas Register. Thirty-eight companies were listed under the heading of Stethoscopes. A number of these were manufacturers, and names included Newman Tools, Davis Inotek Instruments, and APT Instruments. A search using the Business.com Web site revealed a large number of firms associated with stethoscopes. These included World Diagnostics, 3M, Supreme Enterprises, and Oakwood Laboratories. Using this initial listing, it was apparent that both 3M and World Diagnostics were publicly traded companies, with the latter's product being more focused toward stethoscopes and similar medical devices.

Using World Diagnostics as an example, the EdgarScan Benchmark tool was used to obtain a list of other companies operating under the same SIC code, 3841. Again, a large list of companies was revealed. In this instance, all were publicly traded. These included major players such as 3M, Becton Dickinson, Baxter International,

Neoprobe Corp., and Oxboro Medical. A search of the word *stethoscope* in the title of patents listed on the USPTO Web site revealed 263 patents since 1976 associated with the term, thus offering another indication of companies actively involved in the development of this type of product or accessories related to it.

SUMMARY OF SOLUTION: Use of free online information sources, including Thomas Register, Business.com, EdgarScan, and the USPTO Web site, reveals a crowded field in the area of stethoscope manufacturing. Worrisome to any new potential entrant to this field should be evidence of a large number of publicly traded companies active in this arena.

CONTRIBUTOR NAME: Conor Vibert

AFFILIATION: Acadia University

USEFUL TIPS

- When using Thomas Register, keep in mind that many of the listed companies may be small and privately owned. It is an excellent starting point when seeking to move out of the realm of publicly traded companies.

PROBLEM NUMBER 10: WHO ARE THE KEY DECISION MAKERS OF AN ACQUISITION TARGET?

RESEARCH BACKGROUND: Before it was acquired recently, Open Market.com was an increasingly influential player in the content management industry. Because of its size, however, it was apparent that it was a target for acquisition by a larger industry participant. Place yourself, at that time, in the role of an analyst with a competitor. If your company had Open Market in its sights, which individuals would your firm want to keep on board in the event of an acquisition? Who are its key decision makers? They are typically individuals who own significant numbers of shares of the company, are higher up in the hierarchy, bring much-needed resources or new business opportunities to an organization, make others dependent upon themselves, do things that put themselves in the limelight, and reduce uncertainty for the company.

RESEARCH BUDGET: The information needed to solve this problem was available online for free.

RESEARCH STRATEGY EMPLOYED: A number of online sources are useful for identifying and assessing key decision makers. Among the most important is, once again, the Web site of the Securities and Exchange Commission (*http://www.sec.gov*), which hosts corporate regulatory filings in its EDGAR database. In most instances, the company DEF 14A Form, along with information obtained from the company home page, should offer insight into hierarchy. Specifically, the former form will list and identify the corporate officers, their backgrounds, and their titles. Those who are in the spotlight can be identified by a number of means. A search of the company press releases by the names of senior executives should give an indication about whom the company is talking. A search for senior executive names using Google (*http://www.google.com*) and excluding hits originating from the company Web site should give an indication about whom outside observers are talking.

RESEARCH RESULTS: A search of the company Web site (*http://www.openmarket.com*) revealed a senior management team comprising a chairman and president (Harland Lavigne), a chief financial officer (Ed Durkin), a vice president and CTO (B. C. Krishna), a senior vice president of Worldwide Marketing (Joe Alwan), a vice president of Engineering (Eswar Priyadarshan), and a vice president and G.M. International (Alan Cornwell). A scan of Open Market's most recent (at the time) DEF 14A filing revealed that only three executives (Krishna, Lavigne, and Alwan) owned significant numbers of shares.

A search of the press releases on the Open Market Web site revealed a ranking in terms of exposure per executive in the following order, from top to bottom: Lavigne, Cornwell, Priyadarshan, Krishna, Alwan, and Durkin. A similar ranking of externally generated stories using Google revealed a slightly different ordering: Alwan, Krishna, Lavigne, Durkin, Cornwell, and Priyadarshan.

A brief examination of stories mentioning Open Market employees suggests an important role for B. C. Krishna, Harland Lavigne, and Joe Alwan to reduce uncertainty for the company. Finally, a glance at the profiles of each executive found that the most recent DEF 14A filing revealed a number of dependence patterns. Alwan, Priyadarshan, and Cornwell have the longest tenure as employees. Alwan and Priyadarshan used to work for Sun Microsystems, and Lavigne and Durkin used to work for Starburst Software. Lavigne and Durkin joined the firm within the last year. Krishna has been on board since a merger two years earlier.

SUMMARY OF SOLUTION: When the data was summarized in spreadsheet form and summarized, the key decision makers at the time turned out to be Harland Lavigne, B. C. Krishna, and Joe Alwan.

CONTRIBUTOR NAME: Conor Vibert
AFFILIATION: Acadia University

USEFUL TIPS

- When trying to assess dependencies, look for a common background such as the same previous employers, alma mater, places of birth, and so on.
- When doing counts of references in stories obtained through Google.com, be careful when searching for common names such as John Smith. It should come as no surprise that there often exists more than one individual with the same name who has a significant profile on the Internet.

PROBLEM NUMBER 11: HOW MIGHT A RESEARCHER OBTAIN BACKGROUND INFORMATION ON A PRIVATE COMPANY?

RESEARCH BACKGROUND: The marketing director of Boxes, Etc., a large packaging company, has just learned about a competitor called National Packaging. He is impressed by National's company Web site and believes its business model may offer the secret to improving his own company's profits. According to its Web site, National Packaging specializes in serving as an outsource for large companies with customized jobs, offering quick turnaround and direct shipping to the end customer and using the company's packaging and labels. The marketing director has heard through the grapevine that National Packaging is owned by a chemical company. He assumes the partnership plays a role in the success of the business, and he asks the staff researcher to learn all she can about the company, its ownership, and its way of doing business. This information will be used to determine whether adjustments should be made to Boxes, Etc.'s marketing strategy.

RESEARCH BUDGET: Although the information is of high interest, the marketing director would like to keep database costs at less than $100 until he believes there is reason to spend more.

RESEARCH STRATEGY EMPLOYED: The researcher begins by checking the National Packaging Web site. Given the marketing manager's desire to keep expenses down, she'll also check the Internet for information and then proceed to Factiva, where she can search for free, paying only for the articles she decides to purchase. She will also check Hoover's Online to see whether they have a free company profile or other facts on the company.

RESEARCH RESULTS: The researcher follows seven steps in an effort to gather information about the company:

Step One. She starts by visiting National Packaging's Web site. The marketing director was right—it presents a strong image. The site is well organized and provides detailed information about the company and its operations. It says that National Packaging has a 70,000-square-foot facility in Dubuque, Iowa, with five manufacturing lines—more than most companies in the industry. The Web site boasts an extensive range of manufacturing capabilities and customized products, highlighting the company's strength in dealing with quick turnaround orders. Its customer list includes specialty paper houses, auto manufacturers, electronics companies, and other industrial manufacturers.

Step Two. From here the researcher expands her search to the Internet. She goes to Google (*http://www.google.com*) and searches using *"National Packaging Corporation."* The quotation marks will limit the hits to documents that use this exact combination of words. The results are limited. There are seventeen hits; all are customer or supplier directory listings.

Step Three. The next stop is Factiva (*http://www.factiva.com*). The researcher again enters the company name as the search term, selecting All Dates and All Content for her search. The results are disappointing; there are only two very small articles. One announces the company's investment in new equipment, and the other mentions its new industry certification. For a seemingly large company, it certainly keeps a low profile.

Step Four. The researcher proceeds to Hoover's Online (*www.hoovers.com*) to see what she can uncover there. She starts on the home page with a Search by Company Name and again enters *National Packaging Corporation.* Hoover's lists several companies with similar names, but National Packaging Corporation in Dubuque, Iowa, is not among them. However, toward the bottom of the page, under the header Business Reports, Hoover's offers a search of Dun & Bradstreet (D&B) Business Background Reports.

The researcher again enters the name of the company. Voila! D&B has a Business Background Report available for National Packaging Corporation in Dubuque. It offers six tiers of reports, providing a variety of information, from very brief facts (address, annual sales, number of employees) to credit scoring and supplier evaluations. (Note, however, that not all information is available on all companies.) Pricing is graduated, starting as low as $5. She decides to purchase the report at $37. She knows some of the information provided in these reports is supplied by employees and may not be 100 percent accurate. Still, it will give her a place to start.

Although the company's annual sales are not provided, she learns that it has only thirty employees, and even this number is said to fluctuate with the work in progress. Now it's becoming clearer why there is so little information on this company in other sources. It's small! The company has been in business since 1950 and is fully owned by S&G Holdings, a holding and management company that also owns another subsidiary. The report also provides details of a past plant fire and the company's resulting investments in upgrades to the building and equipment.

Step Five. The researcher now decides to conduct a similar search for a D&B Business Background Report on S&G Holdings to learn more about the holding company and its subsidiary. A report is available, so she makes the purchase for $37. According to the report, the holding company was recently formed by two relatively recent Harvard graduates, whose last names begin with *S* and *G*. They are the only employees listed, operating from a small leased office space in Florida.

Step Six. The report mentions that S&G Holdings's second subsidiary is called Chemical Technology. A "Search by Company" search in Hoover's retrieves a free "At a Glance" company profile, which reveals that Chemical Technology is also a small business, with sales of $1–$2 million and fewer than twenty employees.

Step Seven. Now the pieces fit. It has become clear to the researcher that National Packaging is a small manufacturing business with several small manufacturing lines that provide it with the flexibility to offer customized products, quick product adjustments, and speedy turnaround. In contrast, Boxes, Etc. has very large manufacturing lines, making product switches much more difficult and time-consuming to make. Because this company is a very small player in the business, she's unlikely to find more published information, so she ends her search.

SUMMARY OF SOLUTION: The researcher's initial visit to the National Packaging Web site led her to believe the company was a large entity. A search of the Internet for company news proved fruitless, but this didn't prove anything. But when a search for company mentions in trade publications yielded only two very small entries, it became clear that this company was either a *very* low-profile company, or a smaller business than it appeared to be. The D&B Business Background Report confirmed that the company is quite small. The company's ownership by a holding company and its sister subsidiary also ended up being not quite what they first appeared to be. D&B reports revealed that both are also quite small, and in fact, National Packaging is the largest entity of the three.

   This information placed the success of the business model in perspective: National Packaging's small size and variety of smaller manufacturing lines gave it the flexibility to produce customized or infrequently ordered products at a profit. Given its greater size, Boxes, Etc. would find it much more difficult to execute this approach successfully.

CONTRIBUTOR NAME: Michelle Fennimore
AFFILIATION: Competitive Insights

USEFUL TIPS

- Don't be deceived by appearances when it comes to company Web sites. If the site is well done, even a one-person business can appear to be a large corporation.
- D&B reports can be a good source of basic facts about a company's operations. For a very nominal fee, a Company Profile provides estimated sales and the number of employees. More extensive reports are also available. The researcher should keep in mind, however, that the data is reported by the company itself and is only as accurate as the person reporting it.

PROBLEM NUMBER 12: WHERE IS COMPUTER DISPLAY MONITOR TECHNOLOGY HEADED?

RESEARCH BACKGROUND: MonitorQuest, an industry leader in the production of computer display monitors for desktop and laptop computers, has an extensive understanding of the display market, but its marketing manager wants to be sure he's not missing something. To maintain the company's competitiveness, he wants to know what new technological developments are affecting the computer display industry. He also wants to know what innovations are in the works that might result in alternatives to the cathode ray tube (CRT) or the liquid crystal display (LCD). He assigns the project to an in-house researcher in MonitorQuest's market research group.

RESEARCH BUDGET: The marketing manager does not approve any budget for expenses and allows only about an hour of professional research time. Raw data with a summary will be adequate.

RESEARCH STRATEGY EMPLOYED: The researcher concludes that more current and extensive information on computer products and technology will be found via the Internet than through the more commonly used aggregators. With this type of search, a number of directions can be pursued; he decides that the best place to start is Webopedia (*http://www.Webopedia.internet.com*) because it is important to first identify the terminology used in the industry, so he can use that terminology in the search language. The other benefit of Webopedia is that it provides access to a number of articles and links to relevant information.

The second direction would be to use a search engine to look up monitor display organizations. In the computer industry, standardization is critical to getting any product to the market. Monitor display organizations will provide information on technological advances and the feasibility of standardization.

The last place to check is market research reports, where information can be gleaned from the abstracts and table of contents of individual reports. Full-text market research reports are very expensive, but sometimes single pages from the report can be purchased. These sites might also provide other linkable material.

RESEARCH RESULTS: A search using *"display screen" OR monitor* at Webopedia brings up a short description and a sidebar with related categories and terms. Selecting Monitors under Related Categories brings up a broader series of categories and terms: Parent Categories, Subcategories, and Terms. Selecting the subcategory Flat-Panel Displays leads to more defined terminology, listed by Parent Categories and Terms, and clicking Flat-Panel Display again brings up a series of articles. One article, "Flat-Panel Display Technology Overview" (*http://www.pctechguide.com/07panels.htm*), provides a very good overview on the technology.

If the researcher needs more information later, he will perform a search-engine search using *computer display organizations* or *computer display monitor organizations,* which would probably provide some interesting results. Display Search Links directs him to a list of organizations and industry resources. One of them is United States Display Consortium (U.S.D.C.) (*http://www.usdc.org*). On the U.S.D.C. site is a tab marked Industry Resources. Clicking one of the subtitles under that tab, Business and Market Info., brings him to a page of market forecasts, overviews, and statistics (*http://www.usdc.org/resources/GDN_business_market.htm*). Here there are a number of excellent reports, but the first one mentioned, "Analyst's Outlook: Boston, Display Search (pdf) (7/01)," is quite informative. Another subtitle under the Industry Resources tab is Tutorials, which offers more reports on forecasts and display technologies.

The researcher then looks at market research report material. The U.S.D.C. has a link for such a report from its forecasts page to iSuppli/Stanford Resources, Inc. (*http://stanfordresources.isuppli.com/index.asp*). On the iSuppli/Stanford Resources site under Market Intelligence Products there is access to an excellent abstract and table of contents for "Emerging Displays Review." This information will complement and support previous research already accomplished. The researcher also uses a search engine to search for *display monitor reports.* This search retrieves the Display Reports Web site (*http://www.displayreports.com*), where free information can be found by selecting Press Room on the sidebar. Here there are a number of articles, including "Display Search's Annual *LCD Monitor Strategy Report* Projects LCD Monitors to Overtake CRT Monitors in 2004" (*http://www.displaysearch.com/press/2002/102302.htm*), which highlights trends and leading technological directions.

CONTRIBUTOR NAME: Kent A. Sutorius
AFFILIATION: Informed Solutions, Inc.

USEFUL TIPS

- Use a glossary or thesaurus to verify terminology, especially if it is unfamiliar.
- Look for market research report summaries and abstracts, which often provide useful information at no charge.

- Trade associations often have specialized information not available elsewhere.

PROBLEM NUMBER 13: HOW CAN AN HR DIRECTOR USE A PATENT SEARCH TO DISCOVER THE CREDENTIALS THAT WILL HELP HER COMPANY SUCCEED?

RESEARCH BACKGROUND: Alva Sweeney, human resources director at Ibirix Life Sciences, has a problem. The recently formed lab has won a significant grant from the National Institute of Health, but the company's scientists and researchers are busy fulfilling the obligations and requirements of another large government grant. They will have to hire additional human talent.

To improve recruiting efforts at Ibirix, Alva needs to identify the credentials and the areas of interest that may be involved in achieving stellar research results. After looking through the company records and identifying the qualifications of her top researchers, she is struck with the idea that perhaps she should investigate her competitor organizations, specifically Haydon BioLabs. Alva knows that in the field of science, especially biomedicine, researchers holding patents are particularly productive and are attractive to organizations such as hers. She decides to do some investigating.

RESEARCH BUDGET: Since she must keep track of the research being done in her own company and because she likes to keep an eye on who's doing what in the field, Alva has become familiar with the United States Patent and Trademark Office (USPTO) Web site. Knowing that the information she requires should be available for free, she decides to take advantage of the database.

RESEARCH STRATEGY EMPLOYED: Because identifying patent holders can indicate who are key players in terms of human resources, Alva launches her quick research at the USPTO Web site (*http://www.uspto.gov*).

RESEARCH RESULTS: The USPTO Web site displays several navigational buttons. Two categories, Patents and Trademarks, are on the left-hand side of the home page. Since Alva is interested in knowing who holds patents in her competitor organization, she looks at the choices listed below that heading. She selects Search.

Selecting the Search option retrieves a Web page titled Patent Full-Text and Full-Page Image Databases. Again, options for Alva's search are presented. The left-hand column, titled Issued Patents Full-Text Since 1976, provides options for searching the database for the patents *issued*, and the right-hand column provides options for searching patent applications. Alva selects the Issued Patents option.

She looks at her options under this category and decides on Quick Search. From there, she is presented with query boxes. In the query box on the left (Term 1), she enters her competitor's name and moves to the query box on the right to select Assignee Name from the pull-down menu (Field 1). Thinking that this choice will provide sufficient information for her preliminary purpose, she then clicks the Search button.

A page containing a list of patents assigned to Haydon BioLabs is presented. Alva clicks on each of the links to read the abstracts and to identify the "inventors" associated with each patent. Because the Haydon BioLabs holds eight patents, Alva is able to complete this preliminary investigation in less than ten minutes.

SUMMARY OF SOLUTION: Alva discovers that Haydon BioLabs holds eight patents, six of which are held by a team of three individuals. She decides that this result could indicate that members of this team are the key players in Haydon's human resources. Since it is unlikely that a small company such as Ibirix would be able to lure the team away from Haydon, Alva decides to list the credentials and areas of research that it holds in hopes of finding candidates with similar credentials and qualifications.

CONTRIBUTOR NAME: Kendra Carmichael

AFFILIATION: Acadia University

USEFUL TIPS

- Ms. Sweeney could conduct a follow-up search of citation patterns to see how important that team is in the field. She would simply return to the query boxes and input the company name in Term I and assignee name in Field I; then she should proceed to input the inventor's name in Term 2 and choose inventor name in Field 2. A click of the Search button should take her to a list of the patents held by that individual.

PROBLEM NUMBER 14: HOW MIGHT AN EMPLOYER FIND INVENTIONS DEVELOPED BY A PROSPECTIVE EMPLOYEE?

RESEARCH BACKGROUND: The owner of a small electronics firm receives a resume from engineer Charles A. Lemaire, who indicates that he works with producing LED (Light Emitting Diode) flashlights and illumination devices. Rather than contacting him immediately, the owner first wants to find patents for Lemaire's inventions. He believes that the patents will provide some useful information about the kinds of technologies the inventor has developed. Moreover, the owner wants to confirm Lemaire's employment, which he will do in part by reviewing the companies listed on the patents.

RESEARCH BUDGET: The owner has to watch what he spends. But since the research involves a prospective employee, he will spend as much as $100. He wants to perform the search himself. Then, he will consider whether or not to obtain full-text copies of the patents he finds.

RESEARCH STRATEGY EMPLOYED: In the real world, the owner would access a single source for locating, and obtaining copies of, patents. To provide a short comparison of patent resources, though, the strategy below illustrates several methods for obtaining the same information. Table 5-2, highlighting some of the differences between the research services used, follows.

RESEARCH RESULTS: The search process described below involved two free patent research services and one fee-based source. It targeted patents issued in the United States.

1. **Delphion Research Intellectual Property Network:** After registering for a free account, called Delphion Basic, the owner performed the following:
   - Using the Quick Text Search option, he checked the box next to Limit to an Inventor or Company.
   - Following the example provided for a name query—Smith John—he entered Lemaire Charles.
   - The query yielded eleven patent records. He followed the hyperlinked patent number to display information about an invention and to find an option for purchasing the full text.

2. **DialogWeb:** After signing on, the owner followed this path: Intellectual Property → Patents → Patent Sources → Patents (the option under the heading Targeted Search). This displayed a search form with various fielded search options.
   - He checked the box next to U.S. Patents Fulltext, and then reviewed the help documentation for entering searches. The online help does not specify a format for entering a query by inventor name. Rather, it illustrates how to use Boolean and proximity connectors. The owner entered *lemaire( )charles* in the field labeled Inventor. The syntax translates into Find the word *lemaire* next to the word *charles* in any order.
   - The initial search results consisted of eleven hyperlinked patent titles. To discover the inventor, the search must display the documents in another format.
   - To do this, the owner clicked the Show Rates button. (The price to the far right of each hyperlinked title indicates the price of a full display.) In this case, medium represents the cheapest format available that also includes inventors' names. From the format pull-down menu, he then chose Medium. This displays details such as the patent number, patent title, inventors, assignees (possibly the inventor's employer), and more.
3. **United States Patent and Trademark Office Web site:** After clicking the Patents button on the home page, the owner followed this path: Search Patents Quick Search.
   - Encountering two search boxes with no visual clues for how to query the database, the owner opted to display the help documentation. He discovered that searching by an inventor's name requires the use of the Field menu. Next, following a link labeled Field Search Help Page, he learned that the proper format for entering such a query is last name-first name-initial (hyphens included). It provides the example Doe-John-E.
   - Returning to the search page, the owner entered lemaire-charles$, in the first search box, and selected Inventor Name from the drop-down menu marked Field 1.
   - The query returned eleven documents, which searchers can display in full text.

SUMMARY OF SOLUTION: The research reveals that eleven United States patents list engineer Charles A. Lemaire as an inventor.

Note: United States patents are issued with sequential numbers, which now exceed six million. Many research services index patent numbers without the commas. But the front page of a granted patent displays the patent number as shown above. Moreover, a published patent reproduces the number in the header of each page.

When an inventor applies for a patent as an employee of a company, he or she usually assigns the patent to the company. Consequently, in this research scenario, the patents were assigned to PPT Vision, Inc. (Eden Prairie, Minnesota) and International Business Machines (IBM) (Armonk, New York). Patent dates indicate the day on which the U.S. Patent and Trademark Office issued and granted the patent. When you verify employment based on information from a patent record, note the patent application date, rather than the patent date. In this example, one patent assigned to IBM was issued after one filed for PPT Vision.

Table 5-2. Summary of Search Comparisons

	DELPHION	DIALOGWEB	U.S. PATENT & TRADEMARK OFFICE
Search Cost	No cost for searching U.S. patents for inventor names. Monthly fees of $75 or $200 available for additional search features.	Pricing depends on the database. Display formats are priced per record. Use the SHOW RATES command to discover database costs.	Searching is free, but the U.S.P.T.O. reserves the right to limit access to those who perform excessive searching and downloading.
Notes on Usage	Many search options are unavailable for free accounts.	Advises searchers to check the help documentation for coverage, or call 800-3-DIALOG for assistance.	Uses unfamiliar search syntax, which can be confusing. Check the online help documentation.
Ordering Patents	Patents can be ordered using a credit card.	An ORDER button appears on each search screen.	Patents can be ordered online, but users need to establish an account before purchase.

CONTRIBUTOR NAME: Roger V. Skalbeck

AFFILIATION: George Mason University School of Law

USEFUL TIPS

- For inventors with common surnames (e.g., Smith), construct the query to include a first name and middle initial.
- Many United States patents reveal the city and state where the inventor works or resides. Sometimes you can add this information to narrow the scope of a query.
- Inventors do not have to be consistent about the formatting of their names in patent records. In the above scenario, the inventor appears as either Charles A. Lemaire or Charles Arthur Lemaire.

PROBLEM NUMBER 15: HOW CAN AN ANALYST IDENTIFY TOXIC CHEMICAL RELEASES AFFECTING THE ENVIRONMENT?

RESEARCH BACKGROUND: A grassroots environmental group has hired you to report to them the total volume of releases of the chemical cadmium by the petrochemical and coal mining industries in the United States for the years 2000 and 2001. Your client is particularly interested in which facility made the emission and where it was located.

RESEARCH BUDGET: The budget for this project will cover less than one hour of your research time.

RESEARCH STRATEGY EMPLOYED: The U.S. Environmental Protection Agency (EPA) keeps track of all on- and off-site toxic chemical releases. This is called the Toxic Release Inventory. This is a free site and fairly easy to use once you get the hang of it. This should be the only site you will have to visit.

RESEARCH RESULTS: First, go to the EPA Web site (*http://www.epa. gov*). On the sidebar you should find an option for Information Sources. Click on this, then click on Databases and Software. Click Alphabetical List of Databases and Software, then scroll down to find Toxic Release Inventory. As you scroll through this list, you will find a wealth of information that the EPA has stored (you can come back to explore this later). Find Search TRI data, The TRI Explorer.

Since the client would like to know not only how much of a particular chemical was released but from which facility, you must select the Facility option under Reports. Once Facility Reports is highlighted, leave the geographic location as it is, because we want a report for the entire United States. Select Chemical Released, and select the specific chemical(s). Scroll down the list provided in the pop-up box and select Cadmium and Cadmium Compounds, then Done. Next, select the box under Industry and choose Select from the list of SIC codes. Scroll down the list to find SIC 12—Coal Mining, and SIC 29—Petroleum. Then, press Done. As for the Year of Data, it is possible to select only one year at a time. First, make sure you have the Year 2001 selected, then press Generate Report. Once the report has been generated, you will be able to either print or download the file. Next, change the Year of Data to 2000 and generate a second report. Now your research is complete.

SUMMARY OF SOLUTION: Your reports will tell you that for the year 2000, a total of 255 pounds of cadmium and cadmium compounds were released by only one petroleum facility. Other facilities are listed, but no amount of chemical release is indicated. This means that the facility left that cell on the EPA forms blank. For the year 2001, your report should list two companies reporting a total of 67 pounds of total on-site releases and ten pounds of off-site releases. Three other companies are listed for the year 2001, but again they have listed their releases for these chemicals as not applicable.

Although this is the most reliable source for this type of data, it is still limited. The EPA requires companies over a certain size to report all of their on- and off-site releases of a specific list of chemicals. However, these are self-reports, and unless there is some compelling reason, the EPA rarely conducts on-site checks to validate the information reported. Thus, we must presume that all the information that is applicable is reported and is reported accurately.

CONTRIBUTOR NAME: Edith Callaghan
AFFILIATION: Acadia University

USEFUL TIPS

- An alternative site for accessing information about toxic chemicals is the Right to Know Network available at *http://www.rtknet.org*.
- Occasionally, the EPA Web site is slow to respond to queries. Be patient; the information is worth the wait.

PROBLEM NUMBER 16: HOW MIGHT A BUSINESS OPERATOR ASSESS THE EFFECT OF A PUBLIC HEALTH CRISIS ON ITS COMPETITORS?

RESEARCH BACKGROUND: The owner of a downtown Toronto hotel property has been hit by a serious downturn in business in 2003. A number of factors could have contributed to the large number of cancellations his hotel has experienced over the last year. Factors that have been mentioned include the following:

- Severe Acute Respiratory Syndrome (more commonly known as SARS),
- Continuing fallout from the terrorist attacks of 9/11,
- The economic crisis in the United States caused by the war in Iraq with a resultant downturn in the economy, and
- Several smaller factors.

Other operators in the city think the vast majority of the downturn in business can be attributed to the SARS crisis. The owner of the hotel would like to confirm that this is the case, because he has to allocate his marketing budget for the upcoming year and wishes to target specific factors over which he has direct control, rather than ones outside his control. He wishes to undertake some research to determine the degree to which SARS has been the cause of the downturn in his business.

RESEARCH BUDGET: The owner would like to undertake some research on his own. To truly understand the exact nature of the effect of SARS on his cancellations he would have to conduct a primary research study whereby he would survey individuals who had actually canceled their reservations. This option isn't really appropriate, because it would be a costly and time-consuming process. There is also a sampling problem, whereas it is impossible to identify individuals who might have come but changed their minds before actually making a reservation. He would like to spend a maximum of $300 to conduct this research.

RESEARCH STRATEGY EMPLOYED: The owner has proposed that a tourism program co-op student, who is working in the hotel for a semester, conduct the research project doing online research. When she joined the hotel staff, she indicated on her resume that she was familiar with doing Internet research. Her school transcript also showed that she had completed a course in research methods. In discussing the situation with her, she said that she was aware of several sources where statistics were available with respect to Canada, as a whole, and that the Canadian Tourism Commission also provided tourism-related statistics. She also thought the government would have some specific information about SARS.

RESEARCH RESULTS: As usual, the student began her search by accessing Google.ca for a general search on the topic area. Unfortunately, such a broad search returned SARS information from sources worldwide. SARS, with a limiting factor of "search only Canadian Web sites" and "I'm feeling lucky," brought up *http://www.SARS.gc.ca*, which takes one to Health Canada's Web site on the topic. This site looks only at the health aspects of SARS but is quite exhaustive in that area. The business aspects of SARS are more difficult to track down.

The next area of search involved searching tourism-related sites. A search of the Canadian Tourism Commission Web site, using the term *SARS*, provided three PDF (Adobe Acrobat) documents related specifically to the decline in markets in Ontario and Canada, in general, which seemed to indicate that the SARS outbreak was independent of the war in Iraq and that it was totally responsible for an 18 percent downturn in business in the metropolitan Toronto area. In studying the projected tourism arrivals information in these documents, it is apparent that even with the advent of a "benign SARS scenario," the next few years will be bleak, and that if the "expanded SARS scenario" comes to pass, the outlook will be disastrous.

The owner was somewhat satisfied that the information gleaned thus far provided a good insight into the actual effect of SARS on his business. However, the student thought the search could be further refined to differentiate between the effect of SARS and other possible causes of the decline in business. Numerous other government departments, both provincial and federal, conduct research on the tourism industry, and a further search turned up Web sites for the Ontario Ministry of Tourism and Recreation (OTMR) and the Canadian Tourism Research Institute.

A report generated for the OTMR mentions travel intentions of individuals from outside and within Canada. The summary of these statistics shows that SARS was not seen as a big impediment to travel. Citizens of Ontario who indicated that they would not travel this year rated SARS at only 2.9 on a scale of 10 as a reason why they wouldn't travel. Other reasons were fear of flying at 8.7, West Nile Virus at 8.2, and the poor economic outlook at 8.0. On the other hand, seventeen percent of Americans polled as to why they would not travel to Canada said that SARS was the main reason. A whopping 66 percent gave the war in Iraq as their number one reason, and fear of terrorism, in general, was cited as number one by 18 percent of those surveyed.

In addition, a major 202-page report done by PKF for the OTMR titled "Monitoring Canada's Accommodation Industry 2003" (*http://www.tourism.gov.on.ca/english/tourdiv/research/studies/pkf_report1_june2003.pdf, http://www.canadatourism.com*) provided the following information:

An Ipsos-Reid poll conducted on behalf of the Canadian Tourism Commission shows that the vast majority of Americans (89 percent) are aware of SARS, although only 50 percent were aware that there was an outbreak in Canada. Approximately 60 percent of Americans indicated that SARS would have no effect on the likelihood of their traveling to Canada. About one-third said they would be less likely to visit Canada because of SARS. Among those respondents less likely to visit Canada now versus six months ago, Canada's position on the war (10 percent) and economic uncertainty (6 percent) were of more concern than SARS (4 percent). The poll measured the U.S. public's reaction to the SARS situation in Canada, and in general. The questions were asked as part of an Ipsos-Reid U.S. Omnibus conducted between April 11 and April 13, 2003.

Most of the information provided by hotels and restaurants was anecdotal evidence, and although it represented a grassroots evaluation of individual situations, it did not provide adequate empirical evidence to support any conclusions. Generally speaking, though, operators were convinced that the SARS outbreak was most responsible for their lack of business.

In terms of the actual figure respecting the Toronto region, one source (*http://www.hotel-online.com*) reports that as of the end of March 2003:

> The immediate effect has been that over one-third of the 95,000 workers in the tourism industry in Toronto have been laid off, with many more working only part-time. Smith *Travel* Research has reported RevPAR results for downtown Toronto, compared to last year: for the week ending May 3, a decline of 71.5%; for the week ending April 26, a decline of 56.3%; for the week ending April 19 (including Easter), a decline of 54.2%; for the week ending April 12, a decline of 40.0%; and for the week ending April 5, a decline of 15.4%. This translates into hotel occupancy rates in Toronto in the 30% to 40% range, instead of the seasonal 70% range.

SUMMARY OF SOLUTION: After spending a day visiting numerous tourism-related research sites, it became apparent that general opinion held that the effect of SARS on the metropolitan Toronto tourism market was severe and that forecasts were for tourism to recover slowly over the coming year. Positive factors include (a) economic projections for the United States appeared to be upward as the 2003 holiday season approached, despite the lingering war in Iraq, (b) SARS no longer appears to be a major deciding factor with respect to intent to travel to Toronto, and (c) occupancy rates and RevPAR (revenue per available room) are on the increase. On the downside, (a) the potential for SARS to return creates a high level of uncertainty, and (b) the location of this hotel near Toronto-Pearson International Airport, combined with the high emphasis put on the fear of flying and terrorism, in general, may mean a continuation of low occupancy rates.

The owner concluded that despite the vast amount of information available at no charge on the Internet regarding the tourism industry, the conclusions that could be drawn with respect to his property were based on anecdotal evidence from other operators, government research, and industry association research. If he wants hard and fast information that is property specific, he will have to undertake primary research. Given the information at hand, however, he believes he has sufficient information available to make decisions about his marketing budget for next year. He was also delighted that the retrieval of this information took less time than forecasted and was therefore under the budget that he had proposed.

CONTRIBUTOR NAME: Jim Macaulay
AFFILIATION: Acadia University

USEFUL TIPS

- Insights into public-health-related crises such as the 2003 global SARS scare and the mad cow calamity that hit the U.K. beef industry are increasingly well documented and easy to access online.

PROBLEM NUMBER 17: HOW MIGHT A RESEARCHER EXPLORE PRODUCT QUALITY ISSUES AMONG CONSUMER GOODS MANUFACTURERS?

RESEARCH BACKGROUND: The search for a reputable, dependable supplier is a common occurrence for many companies. The costs associated with putting defective products on a store shelf can be devastating. Not surprisingly, taking the time to check the track record of a supplier can pay future dividends by ensuring a surprise-free business relationship. One company that is both a significant importer and manufacturer of consumer goods intended for its clients is Avon Inc. To understand some of the supplier concerns that it may have in the consumer goods arena, a researcher was assigned to gather information.

RESEARCH BUDGET: Aside from the research time of the analyst, this research is free.

RESEARCH STRATEGY EMPLOYED: In a simple sense, the approach for addressing this problem is to examine what a company is saying about its particular products and what outsiders are saying about the products. Outsiders refer to regulators, consumers, and members of the media. Assuming that most companies will be full of praise for their own products, their Web sites and their SEC regulatory filings should be scanned using keywords such as *product recalls* or *product defects*. In particular, special attention should be paid to their 10-K annual report filed with the SEC. In terms of outsiders, a place to begin searching is the Web site of the U.S. Consumer Product Safety Commission (*http://www.cpsc.gov*). One can search the CPSC site by Date, Company, Product Type, Product Description, and Product Category. A second location is the home page of the U.S. Food and Drug Administration (*http://www.fda. gov*). Interested observers can scan through recall notices and warning letters in search of any concerns. Finally, a growing number of Web sites offer consumer feedback on products. One site to search is PlanetFeedback by Intelliseek (*http://www.planetfeedback. com*).

RESEARCH RESULTS: Our research began the task by examining the Web site of Avon (*http://www.avon.com*) looking for evidence of product recall notices. Using the terms *recall, defect,* or *mislabel,* no evidence was found on the Web site or in its press releases to suggest any issues. Indeed, the terms were not found at all, nor was there any mention of any defective products or packaging.

The next Web site to be searched was that of the U.S. Consumer Product Safety Commission (*http://www.cpsc.gov*). Under the heading Recalls and Product Safety News, a search was then conducted by Company. Using the scroll-down bar, the term *Avon Products* was noted. Clicking on it led to the discovery of one recall notice for a Recall to Repair Jack in the Box Toys, dated December 29, 2003. The toy had been imported from overseas.

Our researcher then moved on to explore quality issues associated with Avon's main product line, cosmetics. From the FDA home page (*http://www.fda.gov*), a link was offered to a listing of Recalls, Market Withdrawals and Safety Alerts Archive, for 2003. A search by the keyword *Avon* found no reference to the company. A search of the Enforcement Reports on the Web site, again using the term *Avon,* revealed only two references to the company in the last four years. Both involved the recall of the same product, Little Soothers cold packs, within a span of sixty days in May and July of 2002. In this instance, two separate overseas manufacturers were involved.

Finally, the researcher moved on to the consumer feedback online service, PlanetFeedback of Intelliseek (*http://www.planetfeedback.com*). Upon entering the site, our analyst chose the Customer Feedback option. Once in the site, the Shared Letters tab was clicked on. In the next window, Avon is typed in the Company Name slot and Complaint is chosen from the Feedback Types options. Hitting the Enter button reveals 68 letters of complaint submitted to this consumer feedback service. Although many of these are related to customer service, others specifically mention product quality concerns.

SUMMARY OF SOLUTION: Are there major product quality issues at consumer goods manufacturer Avon Inc.? The evidence suggests no. Although two products have been recalled in recent years, this figure appears to be within reason for a large cosmetics player such as Avon. Although consumer complaints are evident on the PlanetFeedback Web site, the number of issues directed specifically toward products are few, relative to the overall size of the company.

CONTRIBUTOR NAME: Conor Vibert

AFFILIATION: Acadia University

USEFUL TIPS

- When searching in the 10-K documents or other regulatory filings, consider using the Ctrl F key on your keyboard to open the keyword search option.
- Transparency is hot these days with corporations. Although they may not be put right on the home page, product recall notices are now becoming easier to find on company Web sites. Do take an extra minute when searching on these sites.

PROBLEM NUMBER 18: HOW MIGHT AN ONLINE RESEARCHER LEARN HOW ENVIRONMENTAL PLANS ARE BEING IMPLEMENTED IN THE HOTEL INDUSTRY?

RESEARCH BACKGROUND: A large hotel, with approximately 400 rooms, wished to become environmentally responsible by implementing a Green Team initiative. They began by delegating the task to a project manager who had no written guidelines to work from. Thus, the first hurdle to overcome was to discover what other hotels were doing. In other words, what were some of the best practices being used in the industry that could be adopted and/or customized for this property? Once these could be identified, then guidelines could be established and presented to the department managers and general manager for approval and adoption.

RESEARCH BUDGET: The project manager had a budget of $1,000 for this initiative.

RESEARCH STRATEGY EMPLOYED: The manager used a research team from a local university that required a project for a third-year course on facility management in the tourism and hospitality degree program. The team had three months to undertake the research and present its findings.

RESEARCH RESULTS: The research team found the following information on the Internet and presented an implementation plan to the management team that consisted of four steps, as outlined below.

A search of the Web sites of the major hotel chains led to the following three environmental plans:

- Fairmont Resorts and Hotels (*http://www.fairmont.com*): Under About Fairmont, their environmental plan called The Fairmont Resorts and Hotels Green Partnership Plan is outlined. Also noted is their unique Department of Environmental Affairs, which was contacted.
- Intercontinental Hotels Group (*http://www.ihgplc.com*) has a section titled "*Environment and Community*," which contains a newsletter called *Our Planet* and a copy of their Environment and Social Report. Other information includes Corporate Governance, Our Environmental Responsibilities, and Guidelines for Business Conduct.
- The International Hotel Environmental Initiative (*http://www. ihei.org*) promotes responsible business practices for hotels. Practical guides, benchmarking tools, and case studies are available.

The Department of Environmental Affairs at Fairmont was contacted, and a guidebook published by them was purchased at a cost of $30. It outlines, in detail, how to create a Green Team, and the policies and procedures of environmental responsibility for hotels are explained fully.

Through this research, the team discovered that the Hotel Association of Canada had embarked on an initiative called the Green Leaf Rating Program, which assists hotels in acquiring a Green Leaf rating from one to five leaves, depending on their level of environmentally responsible practices. This Green Leaf program includes a guide that is helpful in setting practices and goals. It covers all areas of energy and water conservation, waste management, handling toxic materials, and procurement procedures.

Information garnered from these resources enabled the development of a four-step implementation program, as follows:

- **Identify Areas of Focus:** includes waste management, water conservation, energy conservation, and procurement policies.
- **Form a Green Team:** Choose natural leaders and give training on areas of focus. Brainstorm ideas.
- **Identify and Implement Objectives:** Measure current consumption rates to use as a baseline and set benchmarks. Use of a Web tool (*www.benchmarkhotel.com*) is very useful for tracking a hotel's consumption rates and comparing it with other similar hotels for evaluation.

- **Measurement and Evaluation:** Measure on a monthly basis and compare with the previous year to track progress. This can also be used to give incentives to best-performing teams.

SUMMARY OF SOLUTION: The research team's findings were crucial for the successful implementation of the Green Team initiative. The discovery of the best practices set a baseline for the hotel to use in creating its own procedures and policies. The Fairmont Green Partnership Guide was an excellent purchase value because it contained a step-by-step approach to implementing an environmental program.

CONTRIBUTOR NAME: Candace Blayney
AFFILIATION: Mount Saint Vincent University

USEFUL TIPS

- Finding the Fairmont Hotel and Resorts and the Intercontinental Hotels Web pages with their environmental policies was very encouraging. However, out of a list of approximately ten large hotel companies, these were the only two with their environmental policy embedded on their home page.
- There is also some information on the Environment Canada Web sites, but it is very general and does not relate specifically to the hotel industry.

PROBLEM NUMBER 19: HOW CAN NONTEXT COMPETITIVE INTELLIGENCE BE FOUND AND CAPTURED?

RESEARCH BACKGROUND: With the emergence of broadband, more and more Web content is in image, audio, or video formats. Searching for this type of information can be very challenging because many search engines index text only for keywords and phrases. Banner advertisements, video presentations, and other Web-based marketing is not indexed by the major search engines. This vignette summarizes strategies for finding this content and capturing it.

RESEARCH BUDGET: Many of the search tools summarized below are fee-based because they focus on specific target markets. However, a comprehensive program to search and analyze image, audio, and video files for relevant competitive intelligence can be achieved on a modest budget by employing a mix of general (free) search engines and specific search engines (fee-based), depending on the type of content required.

RESEARCH STRATEGY EMPLOYED: The amount of image, audio, and video files available through the Internet and peer-to-peer file-sharing software is estimated to be in the hundreds of millions of files. There is no single search tool that allows users to comprehensively search this content, but there are a number of different sources that can be used to complete a more robust search. Image, audio, and video content searching is a vital part of any Web-based competitive intelligence program because it allows users to find competitor advertisements, product demonstrations, and third-party product reviews, as well as charts/graphs not indexed through traditional text-based search engines.

Three types of tools are available to help search for images, audio, and video content: general multimedia search engines, specific search engines focusing on a specific technology or segment of the market, and peer-to-peer file sharing, as follows:

(1) General multimedia searching. A number of the major Internet search engines have integrated image and/or multimedia search tools. Google's Image Search (*http://images.google.com*) is the most comprehensive image search on the Web, with more than 425 million images indexed and available for viewing. Google analyzes the text on the page adjacent to the image, the image caption, and dozens of other factors to determine the image content. For example, a search on Toyota finds more than 162,000 images, including product images, advertisements, cars for sale, product specifications, pictures of key Toyota management, and so on. The search can be further refined for more precision.

AlltheWeb.com (*http://www.alltheWeb.com*), a service of Overture Services, Inc., claims to have indexed hundreds of millions of multimedia files. For example, a search on Toyota finds 437 video files, including advertisements, case studies, product reviews, and product demonstrations.

Lycos Multimedia (*http://multimedia.lycos.com*) is one of the most comprehensive image, audio, and video search tools available. A search of Toyota finds 459 video files, including product demonstrations, "bloopers," advertisements, and technical support videos.

Ditto.com (*http://www.ditto.com*), published by TLS Technologies, claims to be a general Internet search engine organized by images. Users search for terms and "see the Web" with the results of their search. A search on Toyota finds thousands of images.

(2) Specific technology or category searching. Imagio Technology (*http://www.imagiotech.com*) has developed a tool that specifically indexes Flash video files. Flashseek extracts and indexes all text that appears on stage within a movie. This includes dynamic text, static text, or input text that has an initial value assigned. This search tool is unique because its indexing is based on text images within the Flash movie and not in the text on the page surrounding the movie or in the meta-tags. Users must buy the software to search for Flash files.

Quebec-based Eloda Inc. (*http://www.eloda.com*) offers an interesting service that acts as a bridge between traditional TV advertising and Web-based search tools. The Eloda software indexes product advertisements shown on Canadian television. Users can search through their database and download recent advertisements by product line and geographic market. This is a fee-based service.

NewspaperDirect Inc. (*http://www.pressdisplay.com*) provides digital reproductions of 160 newspapers from 40 countries available minutes after they are published at home. This allows the user to search through content manually for images and also text content in the newspapers not usually picked up by other search tools. This is a fee-based service.

(3) Peer-to-peer searching. Although peer-to-peer search tools have come under fire for rampant downloading of copyright-protected audio and movie files, they can still be potentially valuable tools for finding competitive intelligence. A search on Kazaa (*http://www.kazaa.com*) finds thousands of multimedia files referring to Toyota, including advertisements, personal videos, product comparisons, and so on. At any given time, millions of users are connected to the Kazaa system, sharing hundreds of millions of audio and video files. Limewire (*http://www.limewire.com*) is another popular peer-to-peer file-sharing tool.

RESEARCH RESULTS: By employing a mix of general and specific image-, audio-, and video-searching techniques, as well as peer-to-peer file searching, users can complete a comprehensive search of multimedia content available through Web-based sources.

SUMMARY OF SOLUTION: Using a mix of general multimedia search engines such as Lycos, AlltheWeb, and Google to access widely available content; specific (fee-based) services such as Flash-Seek and Eloda to find content not indexed by the general search engines; and peer-to-peer file-sharing software should provide a comprehensive image, audio, and video search program.

CONTRIBUTOR NAME: David Campbell

AFFILIATION: ShiftCentral Inc.

USEFUL TIPS

- Use the free multimedia search engines such as Lycos Multimedia and AlltheWeb first before advancing into the specialized, fee-based services. In many cases the content is available through the free sources.
- Be careful of violating copyright laws when downloading content from the Web and peer-to-peer sources.
- Check each specific search engine that you use to determine how they are indexing multimedia content. Understanding how they index images, audio, and video files will help you craft successful search strings.

PROBLEM NUMBER 20: HOW MIGHT AN ANALYST RESEARCH THE FEASIBILITY OF OPENING A BOOKSTORE?

RESEARCH BACKGROUND: A retired couple is considering opening up a small bookstore in Halifax, Nova Scotia. Because they have no previous entrepreneurial experience, they have to identify a starting point for the project, identify competitors and their strategies, look for any niches that may exist in the local market, and determine a rough estimate of potential sales.

RESEARCH BUDGET: The couple would like to find free information via the Internet but would be willing to pay $500 to access the necessary material.

RESEARCH STRATEGY EMPLOYED: The couple contacted a local university and proposed that the project would fit the requirements of a small-business consultancy course. After discussing the assignment with the professor, it was determined that two students would have one month to research the problem and present the findings in a written report. After reviewing the request, the students identified a number of research objectives. They included the following: gather educational information on starting and running a small business; identifying competitors and their strategies; identifying any niche in the marketplace; and estimating sales.

RESEARCH RESULTS: The students started with a broad search using both Google (*http://www.google.ca*), and Dogpile (*http://www.dogpile.com*), and the search headings *Opening a Business in Canada* and *Starting a Business in Canada.* After reviewing numerous Web pages, the students determined that the following four Web sites contained the most detailed information on starting and managing a small business:

- the Royal Bank of Canada Web site (*http://www.royalbank.com*);
- the federal government–sponsored Web site (*http://www.rc.gc.ca*);
- the Atlantic Canada Opportunities Agency Web site (*http://www.acoa.ca*); and,
- the Business Development Centre Web site (*http://www.bdc.ca*).

During the initial research phase, the students concluded that a proper business plan would be essential for the couple's success. After reviewing the Web sites, the students discovered a free interactive business plan on the Business Development Centre Web site, (*www.bdc.ca*). The students concluded that the site's business plan best suits the inexperienced couple because it lists a series of questions for the potential entrepreneur(s) to answer, which, upon completion, results in a printable business plan. The Web site also stores information allowing for updating and revisions, and provides a section for frequently asked questions.

The next phase in the research project was to identify the number of local competitors and their strategies. The students completed a search using 411.ca (*http://www.411.ca*) and Yellow Pages.ca (*http://www.yellowpages.ca*) and determined there were 41 competitors. After listing the competitors, the students visited the stores in the local region, several times taking detailed notes and trying to determine whether competitors were basing their strategy on service, location, and/or price. The students also determined that online retailers Chapters (*http://www.chapters.ca*) and Amazon.ca (*http://www.amazon.ca*) were competitors and visited the Web sites to determine strategies and future plans.

The final phase in the research was the calculation of a simple feasibility study. The Atlantic Canada Opportunities Agency Web site (*http://www.acoa.ca*) provided an easy quantitative formula where entrepreneurs determine the market potential, market share, and potential income for their business.

To complete the calculations, the students visited the Statistics Canada Web site (*http://www.statcan.ca*) and determined that there are 132,000 households in Halifax with annual expenditures of $299 on books. By following the formula on the ACOA Web site, the students multiplied the number of households by their expenditures on books to determine a market potential of $39,527,000. To determine a rough estimate of market share, the students divided their store by the number of competitors, including the potential store (1/42), to estimate a market share of 2.3 percent and multiplied this figure by the market potential, resulting in estimated annual sales of $941,138.

SUMMARY OF SOLUTION: The students were successful in accessing a vast amount of free information on starting and running a small business in Canada, including developing a business plan, identifying the number of competitors, and calculating market potential and market share. However, the research team concluded that a primary research campaign would have to be conducted to clearly identify competitors' strategies and to determine if any niche exists in the marketplace. Based on the findings of the research, the couple has decided to continue exploring the idea and plans to complete a business plan for the venture in the coming months.

CONTRIBUTOR NAME: Peter Mombourquette
AFFILIATION: Mount Saint Vincent University

USEFUL TIPS

- ACOA is a federal ministry that supports economic development in Atlantic Canada.
- The Stats Canada Web site is very user-friendly.

6

Competitive Intelligence Research Data Source Evaluations and Reviews

The World Wide Web is growing at an amazing pace and now offers business professionals countless opportunities to gain competitive intelligence. However, the size and nature of the Web's organization can make it difficult to find results. Business researchers can no longer afford to rely on serendipity by "surfing" the Web. As the online information industry continues to shape the cost and quality of Internet offerings, effective Web-based research demands that one keep current with the search environment and have the strategy and skills to efficiently use the available tools and data sources.

According to a survey conducted by FIND/SVP in March 2003, 73 percent of businesses responded that they use the Internet as a source of information. 95 percent of these businesses also question whether that information is reliable. The survey reported that of those companies buying or subscribing to online sources, nintey-five percent expanded on the variety of information tools they used a year ago, and a third of these companies are looking for new sources to tap for competitive intelligence. Strategic use of the Web requires following an important principle: the best and most complete information on any topic is found by using more than one source. An analysis of the survey results shows a strong need for high-quality online data sources for competitive intelligence. Good searchers know that it pays to have a variety of trusted tools in their search belt.

The world of online business information has seen the inevitable transition from free information to a fee-based market. The Web has exploded with companies offering professional, content-enhanced services and value-added features to give organizations a competitive edge. Dot-com sites that made money primarily through their advertising contracts went belly up, and companies that charged for everything did not appeal to those prospective clients on limited budgets. There is still a middle ground to using the Internet to your advantage. Direct access to subscription-based databases, such as LexisNexis, is one option. However, as the cost of computer technology falls, more companies are able to provide affordable access directly from their own Web site rather than marketing their information through an aggregate service provider. A growing breed of information providers, such as Hoover's, combine free and fee-based sources with different pricing structures to suit their clients' needs. These products continue to draw customers to customizable, convenient, and relatively inexpensive "one-stop" research shops. Primary research tools have not been replaced, but the Web has made secondary research simpler, cheaper, and faster.

There is a reason why online fee-based sources of information stay in business. Information on the Web can be invaluable; it can also be inaccessible, irrelevant, and inaccurate. Analysts need to be critical about the data they gather, because anyone can publish and charge for anything via the Web. This should caution researchers to assess the sources of information that they are paying to access. Proficient users of the Web follow simple principles to evaluate online information: investigate the authority of the source, check for data accuracy and currency, assess objectivity, inspect the scope of information, and make decisions about the usability of the Web site resource. Reviews and evaluations written by professionals can also help the business researcher.

OVERVIEW OF MAJOR SEARCH ENGINES

Before there were search engines, there was absolute disorder on the Web. If you needed to find a site, you had to know the exact address. Knowing the URL of a specific site is still the easiest way to find anything on the Web. However, with the daily proliferation of Web sites, it has become virtually impossible to meet information needs by simply collecting useful Web addresses. In this environment, search engines become essential.

Anyone who has used more than one search engine knows that they are not all created equal. There is one cardinal rule when searching the Web: If you want to find the best and most complete information on any topic, use more than one engine. Always. Your experiences, good or bad, will be what ultimately form your own judgment about which to use. Because opinions continually shift, depending on new features and the task at hand, outlining the options available in numerous search engines or trying to size them up is not the answer. However, it will be useful to highlight the features of a few favorite general and specialized search tools as well as some notable meta-search newcomers.

The Little Search Engine That Can

As far as general search engines go, Google has consistently kept pace with the competition. Don't let its clean interface fool you. Google has powerful indexing capabilities and performs sophisticated relevancy ranking. It takes into account the number of times your search terms appear in a Web page and measures link importance. The more links pointing to a particular site, the higher this site will be weighted in your results.

Searchers can take advantage of more advanced options such as date range, domain, field searching, language, and all aspects of Boolean logic, including exact phrase searching. Google's reverse link search allows researchers to seek out affiliations and relationships to a specific Web site. For example, to establish relations to a company home page, simply key *link:http://www.thecompanyinquestion.com* and all URLs pointing to this site will appear in the results list.

Documents surface, are altered dramatically, or even completely disappear on the Web. Can't find a page you found just yesterday? Google's spider program takes a snapshot of every page and archives it in a cache, providing a unique way to redisplay this information. A recent Google innovation has been its Image Search feature. It is now the only major search engine that lists not only PDF files but also files in Microsoft Word, the Microsoft PowerPoint presentation graphics program, Microsoft Excel, Adobe PostScript, and Rich Text Format (Sherman, "Google," 2001). Researchers can view the file in its original format or as an HTML file. For those who wish to keep Google close by their side, the Google toolbar is available as an add-on to the Internet Explorer browser.

So far, everything about Google remains free. It is a staple search tool, with a no-nonsense interface and indexing power that brings back results with both speed and accuracy.

An Enterprising Solution

One of the biggest industry innovations is enterprise information portals. These are single-port entry sites to specialized topical information. The market has exploded with vendors offering professional content-enhanced services. Catering to the corporate community, the Northern Light business portal harbors one of the best business search services in the industry. Using a variety of specialized search options, Northern Light sorts retrieved information into customized subject folders to ease the burden of sifting through results. All retrieved information is given a percentage rank corresponding to its relevance to the query.

Portals are a different breed from general search engines in the information they provide. For a long time, the content of Northern Light was either gathered from the Web and viewed for free or pulled from a Special Collection database, including the full text of popular business journals and investment reports written by industry analysts. As one of the first models of half application service provider, half outsourced service provider, Northern Light has recently switched over to a completely fee-based business model. Another service is RivalEye. This service gathers data on the Web specifically for tracking competitors. Portals such as Northern Light are designed for instances when a simple Web search won't do because a researcher's information needs include subject analysis and dependable sources. Advanced features and value-added services are going to cost a company money, but Northern Light knows its clients will pay for timely on-demand service and especially for reliable content.

The Power of Diversity

Because any good search depends on using a variety of search tools, meta-search engines were a natural development. Actually, meta-search engines are not, in fact, search engines at all. They are sites designed to search numerous engines at one time. Why use only one search engine when you can use several simultaneously? There is no better way to experience firsthand the vast differences in the way search engines work than by using a meta-search tool for retrieving information from the Web.

Since its arrival in the search world, the meta-search engine Vivísimo has improved. It now has a clean, simply designed interface and provides comprehensive Web coverage using some of the more popular search engines and sources in the industry. What is different about Vivísimo is its document-clustering capability. A search will display collapsible detailed categories of information conveniently placed on one side of the screen, emulating Northern Light's topical results folders. Clicking Details will display a chart showing how each search engine performed in the query.

Vivísimo's system plays to the ideal of "no more tedious lists," addressing the overwhelming task for the user of dealing with reams of information spewing out of popular search engines. Easily navigated while at the same time offering a sophisticated advanced search syntax, this new-generation search tool is a fast and organized alternative to many of its competitors.

A fairly recent addition to the meta-search scene is SurfWax. Clean and reminiscent of Google, it has customized search settings and anywhere from 250 to more than 1,200 sources to choose from. SurfWax provides access not only to most search engines and directories but also to other Web resources not available or searchable by other meta-search engines.

With SurfWax's My SearchSets, a user can set a relative weight for sources within each set according to selected search criteria. ContextZooming allows the searcher to zoom directly into portions of a Web page document and then use SiteSnap to save a snippet of information. Once we were limited to bookmarking site addresses for the valuable information they contained. Now the actual information can be extracted and saved instead. It can then be sent to an InfoCubby, a personal repository of the information gathered. Web search industry guru Chris Sherman describes InfoCubby as "a collection of bookmarks on steroids" (Sherman, "Power Searching," 2001). Multiple InfoCubby SearchSets may be created for different topics and queries and then either e-mailed to other researchers or placed in a public folder for others to search.

Following the trend of the new-generation search engines, SurfWax offers many of its advanced features with a price tag attached. Free, silver, and gold subscriptions allow for the creation of varying numbers of search sets, and the availability of sources depends on the money the researcher is willing to spend. SurfWax is more than a meta-search engine. It is a search management tool. Far from the simplicity of Google and much more ambitious than Vivísimo, SurfWax's current feature-rich, yet fairly complicated mechanism is not for everyone. Yet its extensive set of tools and variety of sources make SurfWax an interesting new breed of search system that any organizational analyst should consider for ongoing Web research.

DATA SOURCE RATINGS

All of the data source reviewers were asked to rate each source on the basis of the following eight categories, using "10" as the highest rating and "1" as the lowest ("80" being a perfect score):

1. Relative cost-to-value (a "10" would be very cost-effective)
2. Relative timeliness of data
3. Relative comprehensiveness of data
4. Ease of use
5. Search options available
6. Level of support services
7. Level of training offered
8. Amount/kinds of special services offered

The editors also provided the following general rating instructions to the reviewers: "Under this section we would like you to be critical but fair, bearing in mind that no source is perfect, complete, and free. It would be most useful if you always compare this source to similar sources when answering the following questions:

- How would you rate/describe the cost in terms of other sources? Do you feel the source is cost-effective for the applications/questions/data you are using it for?
- Describe the various cost schedules and/or options as you know and use them.
- How timely is the data? How often is it updated? Is the updating partial or complete?
- How comprehensive is the data? Consider such factors as breadth, depth, and completeness of coverage.
- How easy is the source to search? What do you like best about the user interface?
- What is the level and value of technical support offered? What is the cost for this?
- What type of training is offered, and how effective is it? What is the cost for this?
- Summarize and comment on a total rating you would apply to this data source using the guidelines from the rating scale above."

Many of the initial source review ratings were double-checked by editors and other contributors, but in the end, these opinions are expressed by individuals whose professional experience with the source under review was honestly given. A different set of reviewers might very well arrive at different conclusions, and the reader is advised to use these ratings with some caution. A broad-based survey of one thousand users of the same source would be necessary to ensure reliable quantitative results, but that more elaborate process was not feasible for this series.

The rating results for the source reviews in this chapter are shown in Tables 6-1–6-10 below, with one table for each rating category and sources ranked from high to low. A summary table showing the comparative ranking of all sources is also provided (see Table 6-2). Ratings tables for *all* sources reviewed in *all* volumes of this series are provided in Appendix C, both alphabetically by publisher and as a total ranking for all eight rating categories, from high to low.

Table 6-1. Data Source Ratings: Alphabetical by Data Source

DATA SOURCE	1. RELATIVE COST-TO-VALUE	2. RELATIVE TIMELINESS OF DATA	3. RELATIVE COMPREHENSIVENESS OF DATA	4. EASE OF USE	5. SEARCH OPTIONS AVAILABLE	6. LEVEL OF SUPPORT SERVICES	7. LEVEL OF TRAINING OFFERED	8. AMOUNT/KINDS OF SPECIAL SERVICES OFFERED	TOTAL
ABI/Inform	6	10	8	10	10	9	9	10	72
Bureau of Labor Statistics	10	10	10	7	8	8	7	8	68
CEOExpress	9	9	8	9	8	9	9	8	69
CI Resource Index	10	8	8	9	8	5	5	7	60
Competia	8	7	6	7	5	8	9	9	59
CorporateInformation	9	9	7	8	8	6	6	7	60
Epinions	10	10	10	9	8	6	6	7	66
Factiva	9	10	10	8	7	6	6	9	65
FreeEDGAR/ EDGAR Online/ EDGARpro	6	9	7	6	7	8	8	6	57
Global Financial Data	8	9	10	10	8	10	8	7	70
Hoover's Online	9	8	8	8	8	9	8	9	67
LexisNexis	9	10	9	7	9	8	8	10	70
LexisNexis Statistical	7	8	8	7	9	7	9	8	63
LIVEDGAR	9	9	9	8	9	8	9	9	70

Table 6-1. Data Source Ratings: Alphabetical by Data Source (cont.)

DATA SOURCE	1. RELATIVE COST-TO-VALUE	2. RELATIVE TIMELINESS OF DATA	3. RELATIVE COMPRE-HENSIVE-NESS OF DATA	4. EASE OF USE	5. SEARCH OPTIONS AVAILABLE	6. LEVEL OF SUPPORT SERVICES	7. LEVEL OF TRAINING OFFERED	8. AMOUNT/ KINDS OF SPECIAL SERVICES OFFERED	TOTAL
PlanetFeedback	10	8	7	9	8	8	7	8	65
SEDAR	10	9	9	9	8	8	7	7	67
TableBase	8	8	8	9	9	7	7	7	63
U.S. Consumer Product Safety Commission	10	10	10	8	8	8	8	7	69
U.S. Securities and Exchange Commission	10	10	8	9	5	6	2	2	52
Vault	9	8	7	9	9	8	8	9	67

Note: Reviewers were asked to rate each research data source on the basis of a "10" being the highest, most complimentary, rating and "1" being the lowest or least complimentary. A perfect score would be "80."

Table 6-2. Data Source Ratings: Ranked by Overall Rating

DATA SOURCE	1. RELATIVE COST-TO-VALUE	2. RELATIVE TIMELINESS OF DATA	3. RELATIVE COMPREHENSIVENESS OF DATA	4. EASE OF USE	5. SEARCH OPTIONS AVAILABLE	6. LEVEL OF SUPPORT SERVICES	7. LEVEL OF TRAINING OFFERED	8. AMOUNT/KINDS OF SPECIAL SERVICES OFFERED	TOTAL
ABI/Inform	6	10	8	10	10	9	9	10	72
Global Financial Data	8	9	10	10	8	10	8	7	70
LexisNexis	9	10	9	7	9	8	8	10	70
LIVEDGAR	9	9	9	8	9	8	9	9	70
CEOExpress	9	9	8	9	8	9	9	8	69
U.S. Consumer Product Safety Commission	10	10	10	8	8	8	8	7	69
Bureau of Labor Statistics	10	10	10	7	8	8	7	8	68
Hoover's Online	9	8	8	8	8	9	8	9	67
SEDAR	10	9	9	9	8	8	7	7	67
Vault	9	8	7	9	9	8	8	9	67
Epinions	10	10	10	9	8	6	6	7	66
Factiva	9	10	10	8	7	6	6	9	65
PlanetFeedback	10	8	7	9	8	8	7	8	65
LexisNexis Statistical	7	8	8	7	9	7	9	8	63
TableBase	8	8	8	9	9	7	7	7	63
CI Resource Index	10	8	8	9	8	5	5	7	60

Table 6-2. Data Source Ratings: Ranked by Overall Rating (cont.)

DATA SOURCE	1. RELATIVE COST-TO-VALUE	2. RELATIVE TIMELINESS OF DATA	3. RELATIVE COMPRE-HENSIVE-NESS OF DATA	4. EASE OF USE	5. SEARCH OPTIONS AVAILABLE	6. LEVEL OF SUPPORT SERVICES	7. LEVEL OF TRAINING OFFERED	8. AMOUNT/ KINDS OF SPECIAL SERVICES OFFERED	TOTAL
CorporateInforma-tion	9	9	7	8	8	6	6	7	60
Competia	8	7	6	7	5	8	9	9	59
FreeEDGAR/ EDGAR Online/ EDGARpro	6	9	7	6	7	8	8	6	57
U.S. Securities and Exchange Commission	10	10	8	9	5	6	2	2	52

Note: Reviewers were asked to rate each research data source on the basis of a "10" being the highest, most complimentary, rating and "1" being the lowest or least complimentary. A perfect score would be "80."

DATA SOURCE RATINGS: RANKED BY INDIVIDUAL CRITERIA

Table 6-3. Ranked by Relative Cost-to-Value

DATA SOURCE	1. RELATIVE COST-TO-VALUE	TOTAL
U.S. Consumer Product Safety Commission	10	69
Bureau of Labor Statistics	10	68
SEDAR	10	67
Epinions	10	66
PlanetFeedback	10	65
CI Resource Index	10	60
U.S. Securities and Exchange Commission	10	52
LexisNexis	9	70
LIVEDGAR	9	70
CEOExpress	9	69
Hoover's Online	9	67
Vault	9	67
Factiva	9	65
CorporateInformation	9	60
Global Financial Data	8	70
TableBase	8	63
Competia	8	59
LexisNexis Statistical	7	63
ABI/Inform	6	72
FreeEDGAR/EDGAR Online/EDGARpro	6	57

Note: Reviewers were asked to rate each research data source on the basis of a "10" being the highest, most complimentary, rating and "1" being the lowest or least complimentary. A perfect score would be "80."

Table 6-4. Ranked by Relative Timeliness of Data

DATA SOURCE	2. RELATIVE TIMELINESS OF DATA	TOTAL
ABI/Inform	10	72
LexisNexis	10	70
U.S. Consumer Product Safety Commission	10	69
Bureau of Labor Statistics	10	68
Epinions	10	66
Factiva	10	65
U.S. Securities and Exchange Commission	10	52

Table 6-4. Ranked by Relative Timeliness of Data (*cont.*)

DATA SOURCE	2. RELATIVE TIMELI-NESS OF DATA	TOTAL
Global Financial Data	9	70
LIVEDGAR	9	70
CEOExpress	9	69
SEDAR	9	67
CorporateInformation	9	60
FreeEDGAR/EDGAR Online/EDGARpro	9	57
Hoover's Online	8	67
Vault	8	67
PlanetFeedback	8	65
LexisNexis Statistical	8	63
TableBase	8	63
CI Resource Index	8	60
Competia	7	59

Note: Reviewers were asked to rate each research data source on the basis of a "10" being the highest, most complimentary, rating and "1" being the lowest or least complimentary. A perfect score would be "80."

Table 6-5. Ranked by Relative Comprehensiveness of Data

DATA SOURCE	3. RELATIVE COMPREHENSIVE-NESS OF DATA	TOTAL
Global Financial Data	10	70
U.S. Consumer Product Safety Commission	10	69
Bureau of Labor Statistics	10	68
Epinions	10	66
Factiva	10	65
LexisNexis	9	70
LIVEDGAR	9	70
SEDAR	9	67
ABI/Inform	8	72
CEOExpress	8	69
Hoover's Online	8	67
LexisNexis Statistical	8	63
TableBase	8	63
CI Resource Index	8	60
U.S. Securities and Exchange Commission	8	52
Vault	7	67
PlanetFeedback	7	65

Table 6-5. Ranked by Relative Comprehensiveness of Data (*cont.*)

DATA SOURCE	3. RELATIVE COMPREHENSIVE- NESS OF DATA	TOTAL
CorporateInformation	7	60
FreeEDGAR/EDGAR Online/EDGARpro	7	57
Competia	6	59

Note: Reviewers were asked to rate each research data source on the basis of a "10" being the highest, most complimentary, rating and "1" being the lowest or least complimentary. A perfect score would be "80."

Table 6-6. Ranked by Ease of Use

DATA SOURCE	4. EASE OF USE	TOTAL
ABI/Inform	10	72
Global Financial Data	10	70
CEOExpress	9	69
SEDAR	9	67
Vault	9	67
Epinions	9	66
PlanetFeedback	9	65
TableBase	9	63
CI Resource Index	9	60
U.S. Securities and Exchange Commission	9	52
LIVEDGAR	8	70
U.S. Consumer Product Safety Commission	8	69
Hoover's Online	8	67
Factiva	8	65
CorporateInformation	8	60
LexisNexis	7	70
Bureau of Labor Statistics	7	68
LexisNexis Statistical	7	63
Competia	7	59
FreeEDGAR/EDGAR Online/EDGARpro	6	57

Note: Reviewers were asked to rate each research data source on the basis of a "10" being the highest, most complimentary, rating and "1" being the lowest or least complimentary. A perfect score would be "80."

Table 6-7. Ranked by Search Options Available

DATA SOURCE	5. SEARCH OPTIONS AVAILABLE	TOTAL
ABI/Inform	10	72
LexisNexis	9	70
LIVEDGAR	9	70
Vault	9	67
LexisNexis Statistical	9	63
TableBase	9	63
Global Financial Data	8	70
CEOExpress	8	69
U.S. Consumer Product Safety Commission	8	69
Bureau of Labor Statistics	8	68
Hoover's Online	8	67
SEDAR	8	67
Epinions	8	66
PlanetFeedback	8	65
CI Resource Index	8	60
CorporateInformation	8	60
Factiva	7	65
FreeEDGAR/EDGAR Online/EDGARpro	7	57
Competia	5	59
U.S. Securities and Exchange Commission	5	52

Note: Reviewers were asked to rate each research data source on the basis of a "10" being the highest, most complimentary, rating and "1" being the lowest or least complimentary. A perfect score would be "80."

Table 6-8. Ranked by Level of Support Services

DATA SOURCE	6. LEVEL OF SUP-PORT SERVICES	TOTAL
Global Financial Data	10	70
ABI/Inform	9	72
CEOExpress	9	69
Hoover's Online	9	67
LexisNexis	8	70
LIVEDGAR	8	70
U.S. Consumer Product Safety Commission	8	69
Bureau of Labor Statistics	8	68
SEDAR	8	67
Vault	8	67
PlanetFeedback	8	65

Table 6-8. Ranked by Level of Support Services (*cont.*)

DATA SOURCE	6. LEVEL OF SUPPORT SERVICES	TOTAL
Competia	8	59
FreeEDGAR/EDGAR Online/EDGARpro	8	57
LexisNexis Statistical	7	63
TableBase	7	63
Epinions	6	66
Factiva	6	65
CorporateInformation	6	60
U.S. Securities and Exchange Commission	6	52
CI Resource Index	5	60

Note: Reviewers were asked to rate each research data source on the basis of a "10" being the highest, most complimentary, rating and "1" being the lowest or least complimentary. A perfect score would be "80."

Table 6-9. Ranked by Level of Training Offered

DATA SOURCE	7. LEVEL OF TRAINING OFFERED	TOTAL
ABI/Inform	9	72
LIVEDGAR	9	70
CEOExpress	9	69
LexisNexis Statistical	9	63
Competia	9	59
Global Financial Data	8	70
LexisNexis	8	70
U.S. Consumer Product Safety Commission	8	69
Hoover's Online	8	67
Vault	8	67
FreeEDGAR/EDGAR Online/EDGARpro	8	57
Bureau of Labor Statistics	7	68
SEDAR	7	67
PlanetFeedback	7	65
TableBase	7	63
Epinions	6	66
Factiva	6	65
CorporateInformation	6	60
CI Resource Index	5	60
U.S. Securities and Exchange Commission	2	52

Note: Reviewers were asked to rate each research data source on the basis of a "10" being the highest, most complimentary, rating and "1" being the lowest or least complimentary. A perfect score would be "80."

Table 6-10. Ranked by Amount/Kinds of Special Services Offered

DATA SOURCE	8. AMOUNT/ KINDS OF SPECIAL SER- VICES OFFERED	TOTAL
ABI/Inform	10	72
LexisNexis	10	70
LIVEDGAR	9	70
Hoover's Online	9	67
Vault	9	67
Factiva	9	65
Competia	9	59
CEOExpress	8	69
Bureau of Labor Statistics	8	68
PlanetFeedback	8	65
LexisNexis Statistical	8	63
Global Financial Data	7	70
U.S. Consumer Product Safety Commission	7	69
SEDAR	7	67
Epinions	7	66
TableBase	7	63
CI Resource Index	7	60
CorporateInformation	7	60
FreeEDGAR/EDGAR Online/EDGARpro	6	57
U.S. Securities and Exchange Commission	2	52

Note: Reviewers were asked to rate each research data source on the basis of a "10" being the highest, most complimentary, rating and "1" being the lowest or least complimentary. A perfect score would be "80."

DEVELOPMENT OF THE REVIEWS

This chapter offers detailed evaluations of selective, yet important, online sources and services. These source reviews are subjective and reflect the opinions of the authors and those of other professional researchers. The chapter includes two types of data sources, loosely defined as "general" and "special." General data sources are those that are used widely and contain information that ranges over a spectrum of business research. Special sources are narrower in scope and usually cover data that is of immediate application to this volume on Competitive Intelligence Research. The chapter also distinguishes between sources that are free and those that are available for a fee. Each review is organized into eight sections: Alternate/Previous Data Source Name, Service/Portal Name,

Source Description, Pricing, Source Content, Source Evaluation, Source Value Ratings, and Source Reviews. Reviews also include useful tips for practicing researchers.

ORGANIZATION OF THE REVIEWS

The business data source reviews within this chapter are organized under six distinct headings. Under the heading of *Competitive Intelligence Business Portals,* four sources are reviewed: Competia, CorporateInformation, CEOExpress, and CI Resource Index. Grouped together under the title of *Industry Analysis/Company Information* are reviews of Hoover's Online, LIVEDGAR, FreeEDGAR, the Web site of the U.S. Securities and Exchange Commission, and SEDAR. Reviews are also offered of Factiva, ABI/Inform, and LexisNexis, which are put together within the *News/Alerts/Literature* category. Under the heading of *Consumer Information,* readers will find reviews of the Web site of the U.S. Consumer Product Safety Commission, as well as Epinions and PlanetFeedback. Researchers interested in information sources rich in *Data and Statistics* will be interested in learning more about the Web site of the U.S. Bureau of Labor Statistics, TableBase, LexisNexis Statistical, and Global Financial Data. Finally, for readers interested in *Employer Insights,* a review of Vault is offered.

COMPETIA

ALTERNATE/PREVIOUS DATA SOURCE NAMES: Facts-on-Tap

SERVICE/PORTAL NAME: *http://www.competia.com*

SOURCE DESCRIPTION: Competia is a company based in Montreal. Their target market includes analysts and senior executives in all areas of strategic planning and competitive intelligence. The company's business portal is Competia.com, offering professionals an information gateway that provides current news sources and articles along with techniques for industry analysis and networking possibilities. Competia provides additional services that can supplement or replace a regular subscription, including specialized and customizable industry-intelligence reporting.

PRICING: Two primary pricing options, *individual* and *student,* are available for the portal subscription. *Individual* is based on an annual subscription of $109 per year (plus tax). Students who attend universities registered with Competia receive a reduced rate of $49 per year. Multi-user subscriptions are also available and vary for institutions; organizations are asked to e-mail *subscriptions@competia.com* for pricing structures.

Competia has a myriad of prices for specialized training and customized research services. Facts-on-Tap provides customers with secondary data and information sources customized to a company's needs. The price is $500 plus $150 per hour to organize and synthesize this information. The Competitive Landscape Profile service is priced at $18,000. A Bookmarking service is available at $1,500. Company or industry screening and other customizable searches are priced according to the request.

The Competia Academy division provides competitive intelligence training both online and on-site, with varying prices. In conjunction with the Media Institute, Competia organizes annual symposiums offering in-depth client training. The 2004 symposium ranges from individual to group rates of $1,950 to $2,150.

The searchable Competia Library, with access to more than a thousand full-text articles, is available for a reasonable price of $99 in addition to a regular subscription. A complete listing in the CI Directory will cost a company $300 per year.

SOURCE CONTENT: The Competia.com portal is divided into ten sub-linked sections that provide subscribers access to immediate information resources, all of which are described below:

1. **Magazine.** Membership to Competia offers a subscription to the online monthly magazine. The table of contents has monthly sections and other articles on areas relevant to the current environment. Content and coverage can include briefings on the industry, online CI search tips and source reviews, highlighted issues in the field, book reviews, and sections such as the Competia "Member of the Month" and "Friendly Sites," which are Web sites that have linked to Competia.com. The magazine is an excellent information source aggregator for various areas of interest. The back file of all published issues, sorted by topic, is also available.

2. **Academy.** The Competia.com portal is building its information sources for member subscribers, but also uses the site to market the company's main business focus, consultancy and training. The Competia Academy section offers a wide selection of professional development ideas and opportunities for enhancing strategy education, including public seminars and in-house training. The academy is available for service in North America and Europe.

Figure 6-1. Example of Competia Magazine Table of Contents

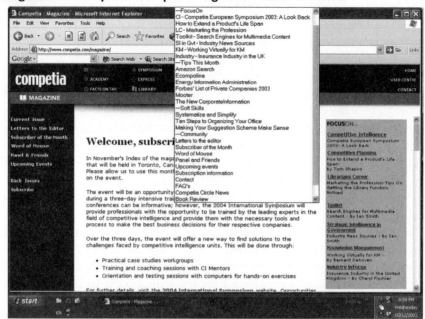

Reprinted with permission of Competia, Inc.

3. **Facts-on-Tap.** This section is dedicated to Competia's information and research services. Facts-on-Tap is a service that customizes data and information for companies with a guaranteed response time of less than twenty-four hours. The Competitive Landscape provides a company with a detailed synopsis of up to five key competitors. Also included is a bookmarking service to compile, organize, update, and circulate bookmarks. Industry and company screening, as well as other defined customizable searches, are available upon request. (See Pricing section above for cost details.)

4. **Symposium.** In 2001, Competia hosted its first symposium. The event offered presentations from national and international industry experts. Competia has expanded to include three separate annual events: the Competia International Symposium, Competia European Symposium, and Competia Public Service Symposium. Proceedings of each can be purchased from the Symposium section of the Competia.com site.

5. **Express.** Competia Express offers members a selective, well-organized page of important Web site links alphabetized by industry. Each industry section contains annotated links to help the user easily select choices. Although not comprehensive, Competia advertises this as a "superb head start" to online industry research.

6.   **Library.** The Competia Library (now in Version 1.1), although not included in a regular membership subscription, can be accessed annually for an additional $99. The library is a database of links, arranged by topic, to full-text articles. The content is updated every six months and currently includes more than a thousand selected articles. The company anticipates a new version of the library with a search interface to be available by May 2004. Categories include defining competitive intelligence processes, online searching, gathering intelligence, analyzing competitive intelligence information, communicating findings and insights, industry specific articles, and strategic planning.

Figure 6-2. Preview of the Competia Library, Version 1.0

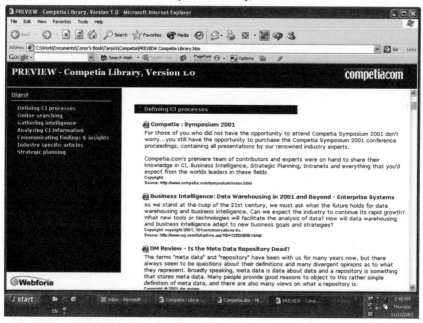

Reprinted with permission of Competia, Inc.

7.   **News & Articles.** A variety of free monthly e-newsletters is available, including *CompetiaNews* for news briefs on the CI industry, *CompetiaTools* for the latest in information tool technology, and *Competia Government News* for resources in the areas of knowledge management and economic development. The CI Industry News is a compilation of news accessible from the Web site but available in a convenient monthly digest delivered directly to a user's inbox. The value of this section is the recent selection of full-text online articles published from various

publications in the competitive intelligence and strategic planning fields. Titles link to the content directly from the published online source. Sources include *KM World Magazine, Searcher, Course and Direction, ONLINE, DM Review, CIO,* and *Strategy + Business.*

This section of the site also has a selection under the heading Competia Libraries, which houses two archives: a list of selective books in the field, where titles link conveniently to the Amazon "record for purchase," and a presentations library, where subscribers can scan a variety of sessions and request the template of information for their own use.

8. **Circles.** An attractive feature of Competia is a forum to bring like-minded, and geographically located, professionals closer together. Competia Circle membership is available at no cost and provides the opportunity to create and join "communities." Each has its own "home" on the Competia pages, including a coordinator and the ability to contact members of your circle. Although circle members have the ability to engage in discussions online, they are encouraged to be non-virtual in nature and offer people an opportunity to network face –to face in organized or individual meetings. They are as active as their members want them to be. Current circles include those in London, Montreal, Northern California, Pune (India), Quebec City, Saskatchewan, and Washington, D.C.

9. **Awards.** Competia presents annual awards to honor exceptional professionals in the fields of competitive intelligence and strategic planning. Applications are free and encouraged for young professionals to gain visibility and recognition through Competia-sponsored award ceremonies and press releases.

10. **CI Directory.** Competia publishes an online directory of its members, 30 percent of which are European, 40 percent American, and 30 percent from other parts of the world, according to its Web site. A short listing of a company and contact information can be included in the CI directory at no cost. For a more detailed entry, including the company description and logo, the cost is $300 per year. This price also includes a one-year, one-user licensed subscription to the online magazine. Competia's Web site claims the directory provides high visibility for organizations, with more than 750,000 hits per month.

SOURCE EVALUATION: A fairly new company on the competitive intelligence business portal landscape, Competia.com has come a long way. Following the trend in the post-"dot-com meltdown," the

Figure 6-3. Example of a Competia Circle

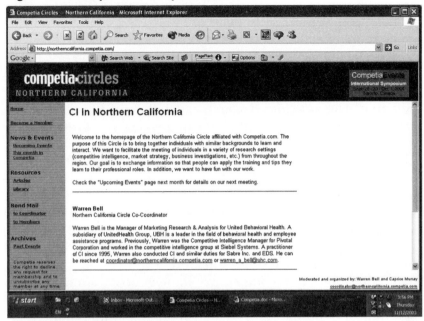

Reprinted with permission of Competia, Inc.

company no longer offers a lot of free information. Although the information and services are now fee based, subscriptions are relatively inexpensive if you do not purchase other add-ons offered by the Facts-on-Tap services. A majority of the information is available freely on the Internet, and although students attending academic institutions have library access to much more comprehensive business information sources, the "packaging" of the content is the selling point. Corporate librarians and other information management professionals will appreciate Competia's recognition of the importance of their profession in the business of competitive intelligence. The magazine features a Librarians'Corner, and some of the subscription articles are chosen from sources such as the Informed Librarian. Competia.com offers convenience and information reliability for the entire member audience, saving time for today's strategy professional.

The only glaring problem with the site is that it is not searchable and does not have a site index. The Competia Library, referred to as a "database," is in fact a rudimentary hypertext linking system. The magazine is also not searchable and is sorted only by topic. Competia would be wise to recognize that subject is just as important as currency. Allowing several different ways to limit a search (especially by date) or to organize content would be much more effective.

Despite the lack of search capability, the site has an organized, clean interface design that makes content relatively easy to navigate and access. Its current Web site size is small but has greater potential. The anticipated search capabilities of the site and the library in the near future will allow Competia.com to grow, manage their content more easily, and increase the value for its customers. The current subscription price is reasonable, and it will be interesting to watch whether pricing structures change with the sophistication of the site.

Competia.com is an inexpensive alternative for high-priced information resources such as LexisNexis, Factiva, or ABI/Inform, although certainly not a replacement. Competia.com is a useful aggregator of mostly free information, a source for considering staff education and competitive intelligence training, and a resource for customized intelligence services to increase the competitiveness of businesses. For industry players who require accurate, professionally compiled information, the Competia portal offers an effective access point to enhance their work.

SOURCE VALUE RATING: All of the data source reviewers were asked to rate each source on the basis of the following eight categories, using "10" as the highest rating and "1" as the lowest ("80" being a perfect score):

1. Relative cost-to-value:	8
2. Relative timeliness of data:	7
3. Relative comprehensiveness of data:	6
4. Ease of use:	7
5. Search options available:	5
6. Level of support services:	8
7. Level of training offered:	9
8. Amount/kinds of special services offered:	9
Total Rating:	59

SOURCE REVIEWS:

Duberman, Josh. 2001. Competia Symposium 2001: A Strategically Competitive and Intelligent Choice. *Searcher*

(September): 26–32. Competia prides itself on professional development in addition to its information services. Highlights the first Competia Symposium held in Quebec City, 2001. Most notable is the fifth track of the symposium that focuses on resource tools and tips of particular sessions.

CONTRIBUTOR NAME: Tanja Harrison
AFFILIATION: Acadia University

USEFUL TIPS

- Sign up for Competia's variety of free monthly electronic newsletters, including *CompetiaTools,* the source to "stay informed on the latest tools to search, collect and disseminate information."
- The Competia Express page jump-starts a search for key industry Web sites.
- Check News & Articles frequently for current industry press releases and access to articles covering competitive intelligence and strategic planning issues.
- Members should take advantage of the free company listing in the CI Directory, offered at *http://www.competia.com/yellowpages.*

CORPORATEINFORMATION

ALTERNATE/PREVIOUS DATA SOURCE NAMES: CI, Wright Investors' Service

SERVICE/PORTAL NAME: *http://www.corporateinformation.com*

SOURCE DESCRIPTION: CorporateInformation.com (CI) is a business information Web portal and search tool that provides industry professionals an effective starting point for a variety of research needs. The CI site emphasizes international industry research, giving quick and easy access to exchange rates, company and industry reports, country profiles, a useful definition and company "extension" directory, and a newly added U.S. state company search. Other features include a browseable alphabetical listing of companies that have been analyzed by CI, as well as a weekly market commentary written by Wright Investors' Service employees.

Figure 6-4. CorporateInformation Registered Member Home

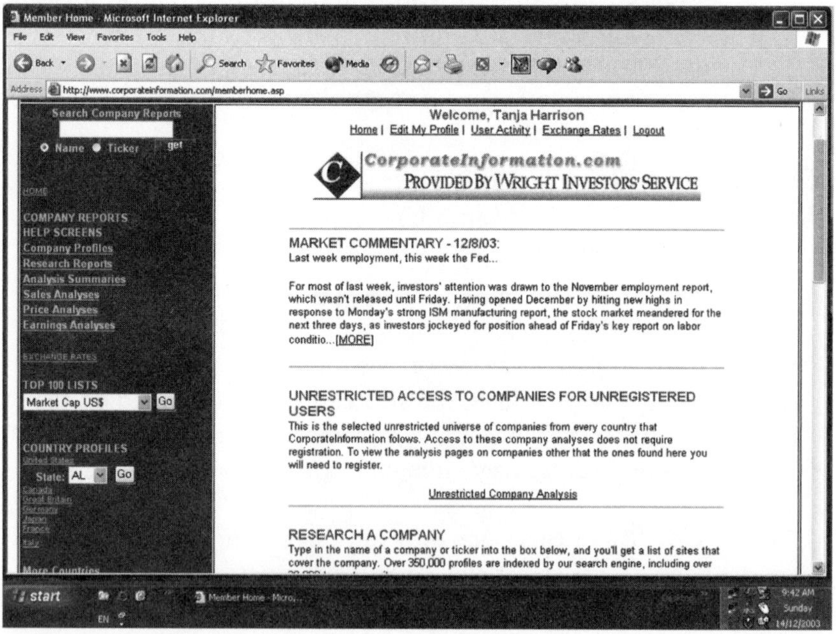

©2003 The Winthrop Corporation. All Rights Reserved. Information is believed reliable, but accuracy, completeness and opinions are not guaranteed. Reprinted with the permission of the publisher.

PRICING: The CI site houses a combination of free and fee-based information. Selected company reports from North America and around the globe are available without registration, but registering is necessary to gain access to the majority of information and search engine capabilities. Registering requires a valid e-mail address and a password that will generate a confirmation message.

The site invites users to take a "test run" and to contact Wright Investors' Service to "discuss pricing on accessing more companies per your need," indicating that some enhanced services are fee based. The Wright Investors' Service Profiles and other features are not available for long. A common message that greets trial users without a paid subscription is: "We're sorry. You have exceeded the maximum number of viewable pages for your Account." However, the company and industry search results, which show Wright Investors' Service profiles, also include lists of resources from freely available sources, such as Hoover's, FreeEDGAR, and Yahoo! Finance.

SOURCE CONTENT: The CorporateInformation portal is divided into several sections, including the following:

1. **Research a Company.** Using a search engine, users can search for company information by name or ticker symbol. If available, the Wright Investors' Service company profile is provided along with other links to information from freely available sources. According to the CI site, more than 350,000 records are indexed, including 20,000 from the internal site.

Figure 6-5. Company Report Search Results by Ticker

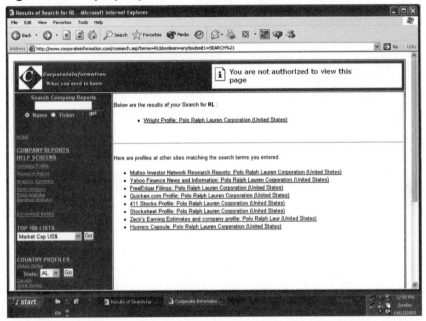

2. **Research a Country**. From an easy-to-use drop-down menu, users can select from a long list of countries and link from the results to a variety of different company information resources for that country.

3. **Research a Country's Industry**. This search combines the first two options by using two drop-down menus, allowing the user to indicate the industry and country of origin to research. Similar to the results in other searches, hits include those provided through the service and outside the site. Some of the links to external information are annotated, describing other national and international services that provide the user with the opportunity to purchase profiles.

Figure 6-6. Industry by Country Company Profile Example

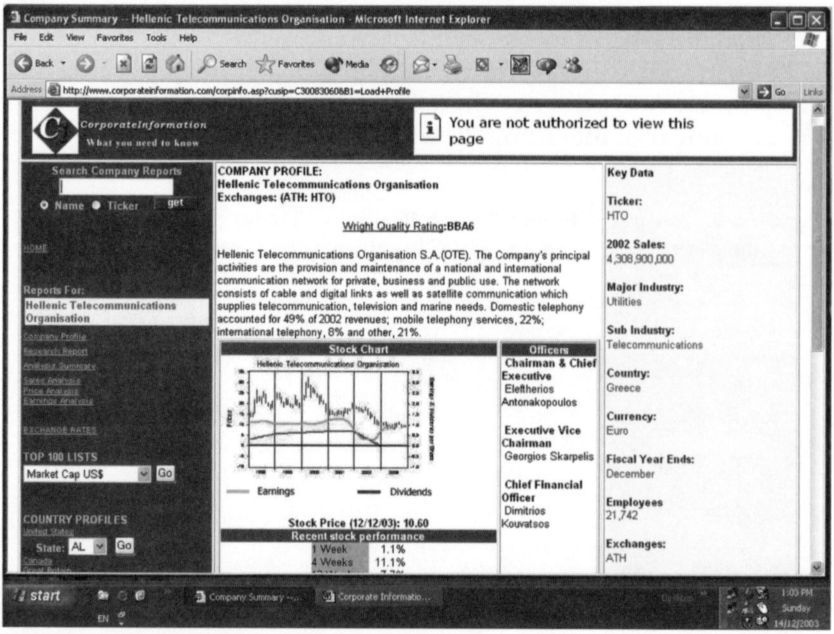

©2003 The Winthrop Corporation. All rights reserved. Information is believed reliable, but accuracy, completeness and opinions are not guaranteed. Reprinted with the permission of the publisher.

4. **Research a U.S. State**. A new addition to the CI site, this option is similar to the country research search. A drop-down menu of U.S. states is provided, and selections will retrieve a list of companies within those states, providing links to internal profiles and general external links.

5. **Research the Top 100**. Users may select this option to retrieve and view information on the top 100 companies around the world. Companies may be sorted by market capitalization, sales, operating margin, fifty-two-week price change, and three-year sales growth.

6. **Definitions and Company Extensions**. This section provides the user with definitions of "security identifiers," such as CUSIP and identifies company "extensions," such as GmbH. The user must scroll through an alphabetical list; note that the "security identifiers" are in the lower portion of the page.

SOURCE EVALUATION: The CorporateInformation site has recently been updated with a whole new look, claiming that it has been "redesigned to improve functionality and navigation." The site is clear and offers a good color scheme with a user-friendly

Figure 6-7. Top 100 Companies Worldwide

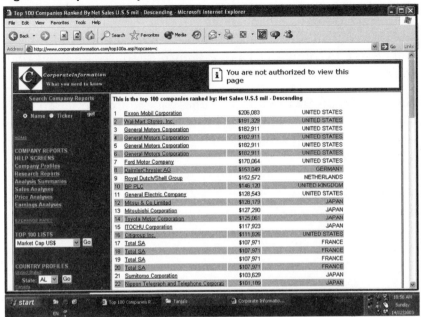

design. The content is relatively current, and exchange rates appear for the last business day.

Assuming we know the company name when searching, *all* should be the default search to retrieve targeted results. There are minor typos on the site, and occasionally broken links appear in a results search. The box that appears at the top of every screen, "You are not authorized to view this page" could be avoided. It is not entirely clear what the User Activity option is from the main home page, as the function does not appear to be working. Users must e-mail the service to gather information about the pricing structure. Although there doesn't appear to be online help for using the actual site, there are areas that welcome and encourage feedback by sending a message to *ci@wisi.com*. It would be wise to add an FAQ or Help area for users, especially to indicate the extent of the "free views" of the Wright Profiles available before charging a fee. Usability problems have been reported to the Wright Investors' Service, and it is hoped that some will be resolved in the near future.

Despite these areas, CorporateInformation is an excellent starting point for international company and industry information. The content is current and useful for business intelligence research. The information industry has transformed itself over the last few years, and many similar sites once offering business research services have disappeared. Wright Investors' Services CI portal has remained one of the information gateways that offers free, or comparatively inexpensive, analyzed information. Users will be able to count on CI as an all-purpose source for many years to come.

SOURCE VALUE RATING: All of the data source reviewers were asked to rate each source on the basis of the following eight categories, using "10" as the highest rating and "1" as the lowest ("80" being a perfect score):

1. Relative cost-to-value:	9
2. Relative timeliness of data:	9
3. Relative comprehensiveness of data:	7
4. Ease of use:	8
5. Search options available:	8
6. Level of support services:	6
7. Level of training offered:	6
8. Amount/kinds of special services offered:	7
Total Rating:	60

SOURCE REVIEWS:

The New CorporateInformation. 2003. *Competia* magazine] (December). Discusses the new look, services, and added content of CorporateInformation, the meta-search tool and portal for company information.

CONTRIBUTOR NAME: Tanja Harrison
AFFILIATION: Acadia University

USEFUL TIPS

- When using the Research a Company engine, change the default word search option menu from *any* to *all* if you know the exact name of the organization.
- Choose to view company or industry profiles wisely when first trying out the site. Viewing privileges of the detailed information expires quickly.

CEOEXPRESS

ALTERNATE/PREVIOUS DATA SOURCE NAMES: CEOExpress Select

SERVICE/PORTAL NAME: *http://www.ceoexpress.com*

SOURCE DESCRIPTION: CEOExpress is a Web portal that provides an organized gateway to relevant and timely business-related sites. Aimed at an executive audience, the company's CEO and editor Patricia Pomerleau says the site receives up to seventy-five thousand visits daily. The content is not original, but the value of this one-stop shop is the convenience of selection, organization, customization, and navigation.

Figure 6-8. CEOExpress Select Desktop Interface

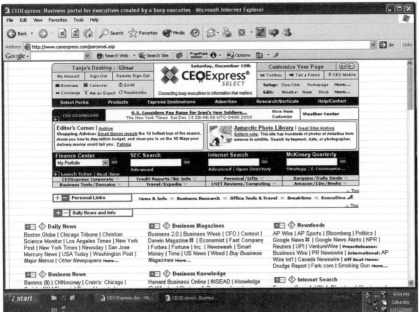

Reprinted with the permission of CEOExpress Company.

PRICING: CEOExpress Select is available for an annual subscription of $59 or on a month-by-month basis of $6.95. Premium features marketed by other companies are available through the Web site and offer discounts to CEOExpress subscribers. Individuals can sign up for a fourteen-day trial from the home page.

SOURCE CONTENT: The main page "desktop" immediately greets the user with a myriad of information sources. The main screen is divided into separate sections with two highlighted boxes of options.

The first is dedicated to customizable options. It offers several fee-based services such as links from Briefcase, MyDocsOnline, and Ask an Expert, which is a service providing online research assistance. A free online calendar is also available to keep track of business contacts and appointments with an import and export feature compatible with MS Outlook. Framing the bottom of the first box is a toolbar of options with more links, including Select Perks (highlights some of the site information and services); Products (outlines CEOExpress Corporate, a customizable portal for "companies of all sizes"); Express Destinations (including CEO@home, books, and reviews, as well as other "express" links to information); an Advertise link; Research/Verticals; Help/Contact, which has an extensive user manual; a quick tour; and numerous contact and feedback options.

The second box allows users to customize the look of the desktop. Users can show or hide features such as the CEO Dashboard, which runs news captions across with clickable links to the full story. The Ticker scans current stock and indices and is also collapsible. The Editor's Corner contains Pomerleau's selected news item of the day, and the Great Sites feature displays the editor's current pick and the archive of recently featured Web sites.

Four search boxes are displayed for quick and easy access to various types of information:

1. **Finance Center.** This has a drop-down menu for information such as stock quotes, indices, market overviews, what's hot, what's not, top stocks, mutual funds, futures, and sectors.
2. **SEC.** There is an advanced search engine for sifting through the Securities and Exchange Commission.
3. **Internet Search.** This is a meta-search tool for seven difference search services that clusters information into broad subjects with the results next to each subject. The search also offers an advanced function with an open directory option for browsing by topic.
4. **McKinsey Quarterly.** This option searches a subset of full-text articles from the online accompaniment to the *McKinsey Quarterly*. There is also an option to browse by topics such as strategy, e-commerce, marketing, operations, finance, and technologies. The Quarterly publishes articles in the areas of business strategy, management, finance, and technology. The archive goes back to 1993.

The remainder of this information box includes categories of links to various other information services, including Business Tools/Domains, Credit Reports/Biz Info, Travel/Expedia, Personal/Gifts, CNET Reviews/Computing, Bargains/Daily Deals, and Amazon/CDs/Books.

The lower portion of the desktop is devoted to a variety of links, many of which are clickable directly from the desktop. All categories can be customized to display or stay hidden by selecting the symbol, and links can be added or deleted by selecting the ✧ icon, depending on the user's preference. The remaining ⊞⊟ categories are the following:

1. **Personal Links.** This section subdivides to produce links pertaining to personal life and leisure, ready reference links, and CEOExpress features for customization. There are three separate categories that users can name and add links to.

2. **Daily News & Info.** Takes the user to sources for information with subcategories titled Daily News, Business News, International News, Online Television News, Cell Phone Messaging, Track Packages, Business Magazines, Business Knowledge, Tech Magazine & News, Lifestyle Magazines, Time & Weather, News Feeds, Internet Search, Website Locator/Registration, and Health.

3. **Business Research.** This category also provides extensive information in subcategories such as Financial Markets, SEC, Government Agencies, Statistics, Internet Research & Surveys, Quotes and Market News, Online Investor Services, Banking and Finance, Small Business, Online Marketing, Company Research, International Business, Investing and IPO Research, and Bankruptcy.

4. **Office Tools & Travel**. Subcategories with links to various resources include Office Tools, Speech and Writing, Reference, Directory Search, Essential Downloads, Tech Tools, Airlines, and Travel.

5. **Breaktime.** This section is presumably what users will be looking for on their "break," such as Sports, Real Estate, Leisure, Unwind, Autos, and Shopping.

6. **ExecuDiva.** This link takes the user to a Web page of resources compiled specifically for the female executive. Beginning with Diva on the Go, the collection of links includes the work portfolio, travel, nutrition, and child care. The page continues to highlight sources for News & Information, Research & Resources, Beyond the Office, and Career & Associations, all geared specifically with the businesswoman in mind.

Source Evaluation: CEOExpress is an excellent, inexpensive resource for anyone working in the business world. The site features a variety of different links, and although the majority are related to the office, the other part of a user's life is not forgotten, with desktop features such Breaktime and CEO@home. It's refreshing to see the special feature ExecuDiva for female executives. The Editor's Choice, distinguishable by small CEOExpress logos next to each link, helps the user choose recommended links. There is some duplication of links in different categories, but users may look for information differently, and it certainly is better to have links twice than not at all. Despite not finding update dates on the pages, all links were found to be active and current. The site is well organized, and it's amazing how much information is linked in such a small space. For competitive intelligence professionals, this site offers many resources at their fingertips. It even includes a remote sign-out to remove cookies from computers other than their own. The online support is exceptional, and when contacted, friendly and personable company employees are quick to follow up. CEOExpress is highly recommended as a business portal for industry professionals.

Source Value Rating: All of the data source reviewers were asked to rate each source on the basis of the following eight categories, using "10" as the highest rating and "1" as the lowest ("80" being a perfect score):

1. Relative cost-to-value:	9
2. Relative timeliness of data:	9
3. Relative comprehensiveness of data:	8
4. Ease of use:	9
5. Search options available:	8
6. Level of support services:	9
7. Level of training offered:	9
8. Amount/kinds of special services offered:	8
Total Rating:	69

Source Reviews:

Marien, S. 2002. CEOExpress: Business Portal for Executives. *Choice* (August): 132. The Web site *www.ceoexpress.com,* which offers information on relevant business sites, is reviewed.

CONTRIBUTOR NAME: Tanja Harrison
AFFILIATION: Acadia University

USEFUL TIPS

- Take advantage of numerous customization features to suit your needs.
- Open the lower categories only when necessary, to produce a clean user interface.
- Out of the office on business? Select CEO Mobile to subscribe for your PDA or cell phone.
- Female executives should look for the "red shoe" to discover the ExecuDiva resources.

CI RESOURCE INDEX

ALTERNATE/PREVIOUS DATA SOURCE NAMES: CISeek, Competitive Intelligence Resource Index

SERVICE/PORTAL NAME: *http://ciseek.com, http://www.bidigital. com/ci*

SOURCE DESCRIPTION: The CI Resource Index site targets an audience of executives and managers working in competitive intelligence. The site offers a variety of industry resources complete with annotated links organized by category, including associations, books, companies, documentation (consisting of industry magazine articles and tutorials), education, jobs, and software. Many of these groups are further divided into subcategories for easy access to specific areas of interest. The CI Resource Index is available free of charge.

SOURCE CONTENT: The CI Resource Index is browseable and searchable, with an advanced search option engine to efficiently retrieve lists of relevant Web site links. Links to information include the date added to the index, the number of hits received by users, and a "vote" option to read what people are saying about the particular resource. Another option for users is to choose and rate particular sites.

Many of the link annotations include several eye-catching icons, including one to four blue stars indicating the rating of the site, a turquoise box with the abbreviation "pop" indicating the popularity of the site, and a bright red "new" icon signifying whether the site is a recent addition. Search results are organized chronologically.

The Companies category contains the highest number of sites, followed by Software, Books, Associations, Documentation, Publications, and Education. Only five links are currently in the job category, which is oddly missing some big industry employment sites such as Vault, WetFeet, and Monster.

There are features and services other than the clearly labeled categories. Notable mentions are those available to the right of the screen under the section titled Services and the links along the navigation bar on the lower portion of the screen.

Under Services to the right:

1. **Free Newsletter**. After entering your name and e-mail address, you can subscribe to a free electronic newsletter delivered directly to your inbox.
2. **Recommended.** Selecting this link sends the user to a form that allows them to e-mail resources of interest to themselves and/or up to five colleagues.
3. **Popular Links.** This link takes the user to a section titled Cool Links, which is a collection of heavy traffic sites based on the large amount of accumulated hits accessed directly from the index.
4. **CI Bookstand.** This feature somewhat duplicates the main Books category, but provides a shorter, more directed list of books, including publisher information and jacket images. Listings are linked to Amazon.com for price and availability.
5. **Advertising.** The index offers advertising and sponsorship packages, and links interested companies to pricing structures.
6. **Alexa Toolbar.** A free, handy, downloadable browser toolbar is provided by CI Resource Index's main sponsor, Amazon.com. Users should take note of the terms of use before downloading. The first caution listed is that the data searched with the toolbar will be collected and stored. Although the information is aggregated, some may be identifiable.

On the lower navigation bar:

1. **Add a Site.** Users are invited to add sites to the index in the area of competitive intelligence. To perform this task they are prompted to write a description of the site, select a category, and submit a contact name and e-mail address. The site says it

adds all submitted resources to the index within two to three days. If your site is selected and added to the index, a "premier resource" CI Resource Index logo is available for downloading and posting to your Web site for added exposure.

2. **Modify a Site.** Users can also choose to modify a site, either to change the URL in question or add a deeper link to direct users to a different Web page from a site already included in the index. This feature also asks users to select a category, write a description, and leave a contact name and e-mail address.

3. **What's New.** Choosing this feature provides the user a list of dates within the last couple of months, where after each date is a number in brackets indicating the number of sites added to the index on that particular day.

4. **What's Cool.** Selecting this link sends users to the same What's Cool site mentioned above under the heading Popular Links.

5. **Top Rated Sites.** This link provides a list of top ten sites separated into two different tables; the first ranked by user rating and the other by number of votes received.

6. **Random Link.** This is a unique feature that displays a new Web site each time you click on the link. It is assumed the sites chosen for viewing have been paid for through advertising services. All Web sites that are open pertain to the competitive and market intelligence information and service industry.

7. **Search.** A useful addition to the index is the Advanced Search option that allows for more sophisticated information-seeking techniques. Options include the ability to limit by number of results, search by keyword or phrase, apply the Boolean operator AND to combine terms, or choose the operator OR for using synonyms.

SOURCE EVALUATION: The CI Resource Index is an excellent place to begin competitive intelligence research. The information links in the database, "rated" data, indication of number of hits, alerts to "new" additions, and the "popularity" symbol all combine to assist users in making better decisions about the resources they find, even before they decide to pursue them further. The site is updated weekly, which is acceptable. There are not the numerous ads that usually plague many sites, and considering that the index is freely available for use, ads are predictable but not obtrusive.

Some older indexed sites tend to include dated annotations that may not reflect current pricing or services. The CI Bookstand is somewhat dated, and unless one is interested specifically in gathering the index user's ratings, it is recommended to go to Amazon.com directly for more a precise retrieval, including the ability to search for books by subject.

Overall, the CI Resource Index is one of the best, most economical sources on the Web for compiling useful Web sources for business intelligence. It is a unique combination of directory and database, full of valuable information leads and sources. The index will assist industry professionals in finding the information they need to do their jobs better.

SOURCE VALUE RATING: All of the data source reviewers were asked to rate each source on the basis of the following eight categories, using "10" as the highest rating and "1" as the lowest ("80" being a perfect score):

1. Relative cost-to-value:	10
2. Relative timeliness of data:	8
3. Relative comprehensiveness of data:	8
4. Ease of use:	9
5. Search options available:	8
6. Level of support services:	5
7. Level of training offered:	5
8. Amount/kinds of special services offered:	7
Total Rating:	60

CONTRIBUTOR NAME: Tanja Harrison

AFFILIATION: Acadia University

USEFUL TIPS

- Use the Advanced Search options to better target your search strategies.
- Periodically check Cool Links and Top Rated Sites for new, popular resources.
- Remind yourself, or tell a colleague, about great sites discovered by e-mailing them with the Recommend link on the right side of the screen.

HOOVER'S ONLINE

ALTERNATE/PREVIOUS DATA SOURCE NAMES: Hoover's

SERVICE/PORTAL NAME: *http://www.hoovers.com*

SOURCE DESCRIPTION: Hoover's Online delivers company information through short company fact sheets and more in-depth company records. It also contains industry snapshots, market intelligence, and sales prospecting tools. Although significant portions of Hoover's database were available freely in the past, much of the no-cost content has been eliminated and is now offered only on a subscription basis. Hoover's targets business professionals who need to retrieve a standard amount of competitive information on a regular basis. It also works well for interviewees, small businesses, and personal investors.

PRICING: Hoover's continues to offer limited free information accessible from their free site at *http://www.hoovers.com/free*. The page presents "padlock" icons indicating what is available only to subscribers.

Hoover's subscriptions are reasonably priced. With three cost structures in place, Hoover's Lite, Pro, and ProPlus (in addition to Hoover's Corporate), a user can choose the level of access. For individual subscriptions to Hoover's Lite, options begin at $50 per month or $400 per year. This gives a user access to what the company refers to as a single business intelligence database, along with basic search functions. An upgrade to Hoover's Pro starts at $1,995/year for a one–five seat license. This increases access to tools and databases by adding more international company data and executivequeries as well as increasing the sophistication of the search tools. Hoover's Pro Plus is the ultimate standard subscription next to the customized corporate options. The pricing begins at $4,995/year for a one–five seat subscription and includes all Lite and Pro features, plus search functions for more international information and report-building options. Data can be customized to fit user needs.

SOURCE CONTENT: Hoover's Online contains three main parts: The Hoover's Online home page for company and industry information, IPO Central, and Hoover's Books (see Figure 6-10).

1. **Hoover's Company and Industry Coverage.** Hoover's covers more than 35,000 public and private companies worldwide, 600 industries, and 190,000 corporate executives. It also covers

Figure 6-9. Hoover's Free Site Home Page

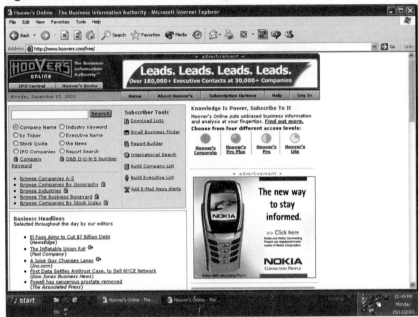

Reprinted with the permission of Hoover's, Inc. (*http://www.hoovers.com*).

Figure 6-10. Hoover's Subscriber Home Page

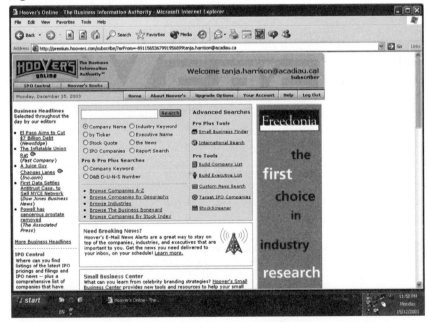

Reprinted with the permission of Hoover's, Inc. (*http://www.hoovers.com*).

more than 12 million companies from Dun & Bradstreet and nine thousand non-U.S. firms from Mergent. All information can be accessed from the main home page, either by using the main search box offering fields such as company name, ticker, and industry keyword, or alphabetically by company name, geographic location, stock index, or by industry. There is also the Business Boneyard, a unique feature offering an alphabetical listing of companies that no longer exist.

From a company record, one can access the History of the company, Industry Information, Top Competitors, related News items, SEC filings, Key Financials, and Key People. Users can also discover how a company has changed over time with the new archived Products and Operations Charts. Many of the records contain in-depth company descriptions, financial comparisons for each competitor, and industry benchmarks. News items are primarily press releases and articles from a variety of online sources. The News page also links to company press releases. A "reverse" search capability called Find Similar Companies locates companies with similar attributes.

Industry Records contain a descriptive snapshot of the trade, links to Most Viewed Companies, where the user's choice lies in the linkable Industry Family Tree, current news, a glossary of industry terms, lists of related associations, selected Web sites, print sources, and associated SIC and NAICScoding. These industry snapshots are an excellent source for an overview of an industry and its key players.

At the bottom of every record is a yellow box titled Related Products from Our Trusted Partners. In this area, users can access more than forty-five thousand reports from more than ninety publishers, including Dun & Bradstreet, Datamonitor, Freedonia, Harris, Jupiter, and Reuters. These reports are available for fees ranging from $5 for a D&B Credit Report, to approximately $500 for an industry report. A detailed description for each report assists in making a purchasing decision.

The ProPlus with Downloads subscription features additional fields for searching, including Net Income Range, Net Income Growth, Industry Keyword, and SIC or NAICS Codes. The Small Business Finder features additional fields to further filter and refine your search, such as SIC, NAICS, Metro Area, Asset Range, Company Type, and/or Fiscal Year-End.

2. **IPO Central.** Here users can search for initial public offerings (IPOs) by either the company name or ticker symbol. Subscribers can also click on Target IPO Companies to search for IPOs by location, underwriter, industry, filing, or trading date ranges, offering amount, price range, or annual sales. Proposed or recently trading companies are featured in the weekly

Figure 6-11. Hoover's Online Company Record Example

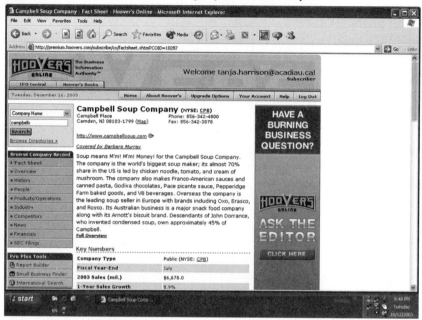

Reprinted with the permission of Hoover's, Inc. (*http://www.hoovers.com*).

Figure 6-12. Hoover's Online Industry Record Example

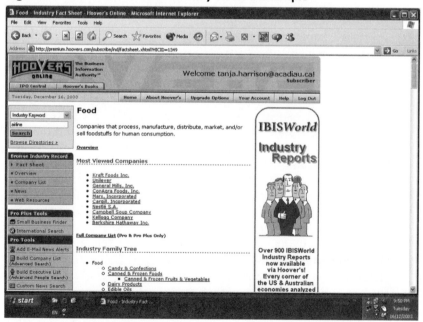

Reprinted with the permission of Hoover's, Inc. (*http://www.hoovers.com*).

IPOs On Deck list with links to the company record for more information. Once IPOs are identified, Hoover's links to the appropriate company record.

3. **Hoover's Books**. A large part of the Web site is now devoted to Hoover's Business Press publications, including the Hoover's Handbook and MasterList series. They also publish a variety of other titles and make available those from third parties, such as international guides and business resources. The career guides and industry reports are published by Plunkett Research, who also supply information for industry overviews of the database. Prices vary and can range anywhere from $20 to $300 for each book. A free catalog of products is available by filling out an online form.

SOURCE EVALUATION: Dun & Bradstreet acquired Hoover's in March 2003, forming part of Dun & Bradstreet's E-Business Solutions Group. Since then, Hoover's has revamped its interface by making it easier to search for business information. The site design has significantly improved, and although much of the information is now licensed content, it is presented in an easy-to-understand format. The URL takes the user to a clear log-in page for free versus subscription-based access, differentiating the content access levels and user experience.

The new search box on the streamlined home page is a nice addition. Company and industry records now share consistent, clear organization, including new record navigation in blue highlighting. A new green toolbox on the left side of every company or industry record showcases all relevant tools for finding, manipulating, and downloading information. Common features have been intuitively renamed to better reflect the content or the function performed; for example, Advanced Company Search is now Build Company List. Company financials (including listing auditor, stock price, and other popular elements) save time for the user, as they now appear all on one page. Users can easily track companies and industries with the news alerts tool for more than six hundred industries, and can set up multiple ticker symbol alerts through this same interface. Links to external content are clearly identified and open in a new browser window. Fewer ads appear on the subscriber site, which is a welcome change.

Since the acquisition by Dun & Bradstreet, the move hasn't significantly changed the basic content of the old offering. The site has added more companies to their roster and industry coverage has expanded from three hundred to more than six hundred Hoover's defined industries. Although much of the licensed content is available from other sources, Hoover's is known for their company and industry narratives, which have always formed one of the strongest parts of the resource. The content is interesting and well written without using jargon. Hoover's continues to be an industry leader for providing easily accessible, inexpensive, and valuable information for the business professional to research competition.

SOURCE VALUE RATING: All of the data source reviewers were asked to rate each source on the basis of the following eight categories, using "10" as the highest rating and "1" as the lowest ("80" being a perfect score):

1. Relative cost-to-value:	9
2. Relative timeliness of data:	8
3. Relative comprehensiveness of data:	8
4. Ease of use:	8
5. Search options available:	8
6. Level of support services:	9
7. Level of training offered:	8
8. Amount/kinds of special services offered:	9
Total Rating:	67

SOURCE REVIEWS:

Dodd, D. 2003. Hoover's and Northern Light End Free Services. *Information World Review* (February): Discusses the decision to pull free services in reaction to a continuing downturn in ad revenues and the inability to make "pay-per-view" services profitable.

Fulton, Marsha L., Denise G. Rabogliatti, and Jan M. Rivers. 2002. Company Directories: Past, Present, and Future. *Searcher* (September): 39+. Compares three resources: Directory of Corporate Affiliations through Dialog and LexisNexis, Hoover's through LexisNexis, and Standard & Poor's via Dialog and LexisNexis.

O'Leary, Mick. 2002. Business Site Seeing: The New Hoover's: Complete Company Content. *Link-Up* (May/June). Analysis of *http://www.hoovers.com site.*

"What Does Hoover's Pro Offer Information Pros?" 2002. *Information Advisor* (September): 6–8. Discusses the Companies and Industries section of Hoover's, along with the sales prospecting tools offered to Hoover's Pro subscribers.

CONTRIBUTOR NAME: Meryl Brodsky / Patricia A. Watkins / Tanja Harrison

AFFILIATION: Consultant / Thunderbird School of International Management / Acadia University

USEFUL TIPS

- Before beginning, explore Hoover's Help Center and FAQ section (under Help).
- Target a search quickly from the home page by using the variety of fields available to search within, such as Company Name, Executive Name, Ticker and Industry Keyword.
- Make use of the Find Similar Companies link from within a company record to explore companies with similar characteristics.
- Can't find a company? Check Hoover's Business Boneyard for companies that no longer exist (available to Pro and Pro Plus Subscribers only).

LIVEDGAR

ALTERNATE/PREVIOUS DATA SOURCE NAMES: GSIonline, Global Securities Information

SERVICE/PORTAL NAME: *http://www.gsionline.com*

SOURCE DESCRIPTION: Global   Securities   Information's LIVEDGAR contains corporate Securities and Exchange Commission filing information for U.S. public companies as well as for non-U.S. companies whose stock is traded on U.S. exchanges. The database also contains Securities and Exchange Commission compliance information in the form of releases, rules and rulings, corporate finance and mergers and acquisitions data, and news and alerts. In early 2004 LIVEDGAR revamped the look of its product. It also added a couple of new features: SEC Staff Reviews Database and the SEDAR (database of Canadian filings).

LIVEDGAR is useful for obtaining a company's 10-K filing, for example, but is really aimed at people doing in-depth corporate securities research or who are looking for comparative data on companies. The product provides a variety of options for locating targeted information, as well as preformatted searches contained in its Topical Research Library.

Figure 6-13. Main Menu Screen for LIVEDGAR

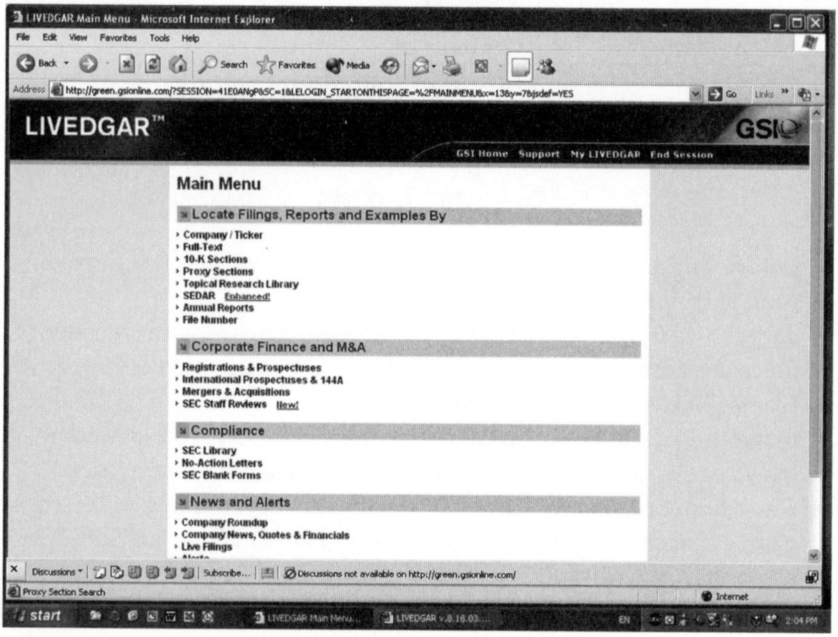

Reprinted with the permission of Global Securities Information, Inc.

PRICING: A monthly fee based on number of users per institution. There is also a "pay-as-you-go" feature: each time a user logs on, the account is charged $10. The account is also charged $1.75 for each minute the user stays on LIVEDGAR. (Source: *http://www.gsionline. com* Web site.)

SOURCE CONTENT: This review summarizes the following seven content areas within LIVEDGAR:

- **Corporate Filings**: Users are able to search company filings via a variety of options, including company ticker symbol, full-text keyword searching, 10-K section search limiting a search to specific areas of the 10-K filing, Topical Research Library, Annual Reports to Shareholders, and filing number. The Topical Research Library consists of hundreds of preconstructed searches, listed alphabetically by topic. Users select and run these preconstructed searches. If necessary, the searches are also editable if there are additional criteria needed to be added, such as date restrictions. The Topical Research Library can also be accessed by subject category, such as Tax/Accounting or Intellectual Property, as well as browsed alphabetically. Filings can be e-mailed or downloaded in .pdf, .rtf, write, or text format. Annual reports to shareholders are in .pdf format.

- **Corporate Finance and M&A**: Registration Filings and Prospectuses can be searched in this section via customized search templates. International prospectuses and 144A filings are also included. This area also includes lists of the most recent original and final initial public offerings (IPOs). The lists are in reverse chronological order and can be used to generate Transaction Data Reports to be exported into Excel format. These reports contain data elements the user selects from a large checklist of options and contain comparative information for the IPO deals listed in this section. This same functionality can be found in the International Prospectuses and 144A section of this LIVEDGAR category. Rankings League Tables are also available in the Corporate Finance and M&A section; however, they are not available in the International Prospectuses and 144A area.

- **The League Tables** rank the top twenty-five Registrations and Prospectuses for specific time periods by Issuer Counsel, Target Counsel, or Lead Underwriters or the top twenty-five Mergers & Acquisitions for specific time periods by Target Counsel, Target Financial Advisor, Acquiror Counsel, or Acquiror Financial Advisor. Tables include Rank, Law Firm, or Underwriter Firm or Financial Advisor name, number of deals, and total transaction values for the time period selected (that is, last ninety days, year to date, and so on). The Mergers and Acquisitions database is also searchable via custom templates with a wide variety of available search criteria. Users can search for comparable deals or comparable events, as well as obtain a list of most recent additions.

- **Compliance:** You can search the following via the SEC Library contained in this section: regulatory actions, staff interpretations, news and public statements, litigation information from the Securities and Exchange Commission (including proposed and final rules), administrative proceedings and litigation releases, speeches and testimony, exemptive orders, and staff accounting bulletins. All are searchable via a custom template. A No-Action Letter Database is also contained in the Compliance section and is keyword searchable. Blank SEC forms are contained within Compliance as well.

- **SEC Staff Review Database:** contains more than 600 completed SEC staff reviews, incorporating more than 20-500 letters and 15,000 pages of valuable SEC insight. The basis of this collection is the publicly released staff comment letters issued as part of the SEC's 2002 Fortune 500 Review. This database provides important regulatory information that is necessary in a compliance-based environment.

Figure 6-14. M&A Screen from LIVEDGAR

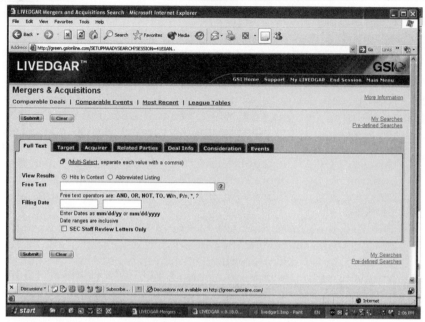

Reprinted with the permission of Global Securities Information, Inc.

Figure 6-15. SEC Library Search Screen from LIVEDGAR

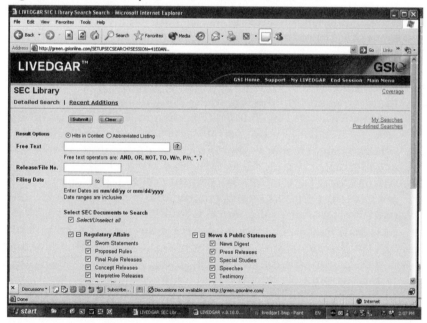

Reprinted with the permission of Global Securities Information, Inc.

Figure 6-16. SEC Staff Review Database Search Screen

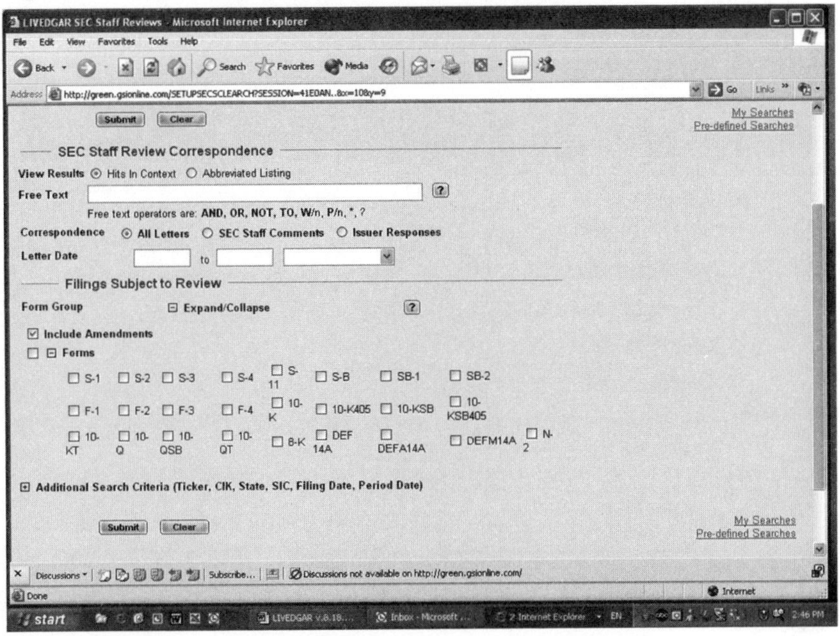

Reprinted with the permission of Global Securities Information, Inc.

- **SEDAR:** System for Electronic Document Analysis and Retrieval is the Canadian equivalent of the EDGAR system in the United States. This database provides access to more than one million filings from public companies and mutual funds in Canada. Filings go back to 1997. Searching SEDAR is simple and is integrated into the full-text search screen as an option.
- **News and Alerts**: The Live Filings area lists SEC filings in reverse chronological order as soon as they are filed with the SEC. You can also set up alerts in this area by company name, ticker symbol, or full text. Full-text alerts run across all Edgar documents, No-Action Letters, and foreign SEC filings in the LIVEDGAR database. Alerts run daily and results are sent via e-mail to you.

SOURCE EVALUATION: LIVEDGAR is a cost-effective source for corporate filings or SEC-related research. It is easy to use and offers a broad range of search alternatives, broad categories, and other means of targeting information. It is a richer resource than the SEC's Web site, Securities Mosaic, or other EDGAR resources. The log-in fee plus per-minute charge is cheaper than obtaining the same information via LexisNexis, Westlaw, or Dialog. Multiple documents can be downloaded simultaneously in PDF format.

Figure 6-17. LIVEDGAR's SEDAR Search Screen

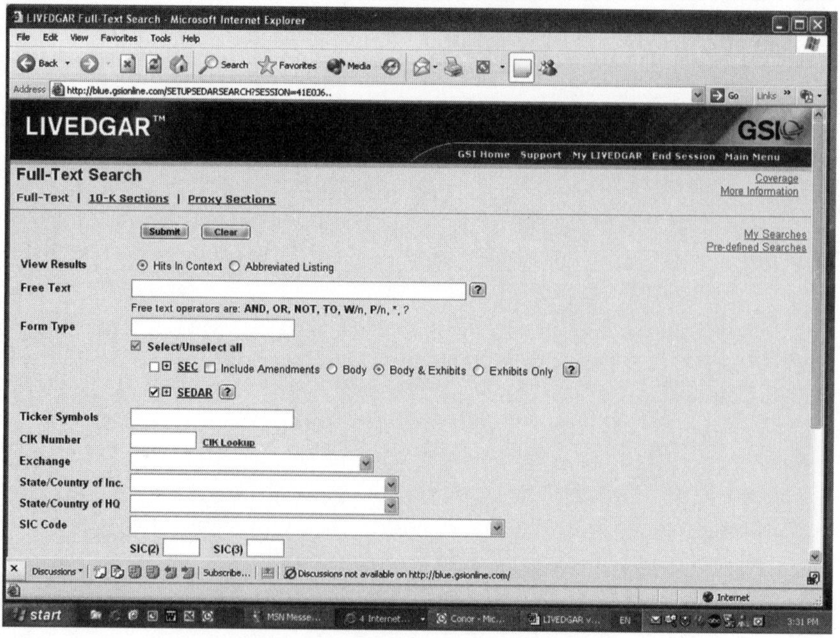

Reprinted with the permission of Global Securities Information, Inc.

Searchers using keywords can elect to see their keywords in context. Users can also elect to obtain portions of the SEC filing, another option not always available in free EDGAR resources. Frequently run searches can be saved under My Searches. Additionally, both online help and toll-free telephone help options are available, and customers have the option of receiving updates via e-mail. LIVEDGAR continues to improve and add value to its product. The new look is clean and user-friendly, and the customer service is exceptional.

SOURCE VALUE RATING: All of the data source reviewers were asked to rate each source on the basis of the following eight categories, using "10" as the highest rating and "1" as the lowest ("80" being a perfect score):

1. Relative cost-to-value:	9
2. Relative timeliness of data:	9
3. Relative comprehensiveness of data:	9
4. Ease of use:	8
5. Search options available:	9
6. Level of support services:	8
7. Level of training offered:	9
8. Amount/kinds of special services offered:	9
Total Rating:	70

SOURCE REVIEWS:

Kassel, Amelia. 1999. Disclosure, the SEC, and LiveEdgar: Some Musings and Elucidations. New Jersey: Information Today Inc., *Searcher (1999)*. (*http://www.infotoday.com/searcher/jul99/kassel.htm*). Accessed February 3, 2003.

Story, Laura. *New Research Tools from LiveEdgar: Customized Research and Web Pages.* Law Library Resource Exchange. (*http://www.llrx.com/features/livedgar.htm*). Accessed February 3, 2003.

CONTRIBUTOR NAME: Jan Rivers / Patricia A. Watkins / Jennifer Richard

AFFILIATION: Dorsey & Whitney LLP / Thunderbird School of International Management / Acadia University

USEFUL TIPS

• The results from the preformatted searches may be too general in some instances. You may have to edit or further customize the preformatted searches from the Topical Research Library to retrieve more relevant information.

- Remember LIVEDGAR covers only U.S. public companies and for-eign companies that file with the Securities and Exchange Commission. Private companies are not included and will not be represented in any "top company" lists or tables. This is especially important to remember when using the Ranking League Tables tool.
- You may have to click on View multiple times before you are able to view the entire filing.
- Rather than printing individual documents, you may select docu-ments to be saved to your work list for downloading and printing later.

FREEEDGAR/EDGAR ONLINE/EDGARPRO

SERVICE/PORTAL NAME: FreeEDGAR (*http://www.freeedgar.com*), EDGAR Online (*http://www.edgar-online.com/start.asp*), and EDGARpro (*http://www.edgarpro.com*) are related Web sites from the same parent company. All contain public company filing infor-mation from the U.S. Securities and Exchange Commission (SEC).

SOURCE DESCRIPTION: Public companies in the United States and foreign companies trading on U.S. stock exchanges are required to file various types of disclosure documents with the SEC. Begin-ning in 1996, these filings were required to be made electronically. EDGAR is an acronym for Electronic Data Gathering and Retrieval, the term the SEC uses for the electronic gathering and storing of these company filings. The term has also enjoyed wide-spread use as a generic term for an electronic archive or repository of company filings made with the SEC.

EDGAR Online, Inc. produces three resources to give users access to SEC filings. These resources vary in content and functionality. The free resource, FreeEDGAR, requires users to register before they can access information on the site. EDGAR Online is a fee subscription site that builds on FreeEDGAR's functionality, resulting in more advanced searching and other capabilities. EDGARpro is a fee subscription site aimed at professionals. It contains the same functionality as EDGAR Online, only with some additional features. These three services are exam-ined in the following section.

SOURCE CONTENT: This summary provides information on the three EDGAR resources: FreeEDGAR, EDGAR Online, and EDGARpro.

FreeEDGAR. This resource provides access to thousands of SEC filings, updated as the filings are received. You can search for filings for a specific date or by form type (for example, 10-K) or you can perform a quick search by company name or ticker symbol. A Watchlist feature allows users to track the filings for companies they select.

Figure 6-18. FreeEDGAR Home Page

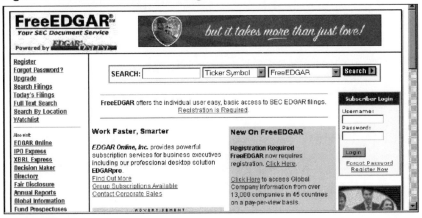

Reprinted with the permission of EDGAR Online, Inc.

You can search for companies by name, ticker symbol, or SIC (Standard Industrial Classification) code by clicking on the Search Filings link. Enter up to ten ticker symbols per search.

A search by ticker symbol brings up a Search Results page, which offers two options: View Filings or Add to Your Watchlist. The page also includes a More Info box with links to EDGAR Online and other options; some of these options and the Watchlist require a subscription to EDGAR Online to use.

Filings appear in a frames format, which can be changed to no-frames if desired. The filings can be navigated via a table of contents.

Although you will note a link to a filing when using the frames version of FreeEDGAR (see Figure 6-21), you cannot download filings in Rich Text Format (RTF) from the link. You can print the

Figure 6-19. FreeEDGAR Company Search

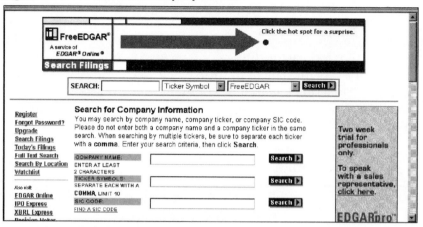

Reprinted with the permission of EDGAR Online, Inc.

Figure 6-20. FreeEDGAR Ticker Symbol Search Results Page

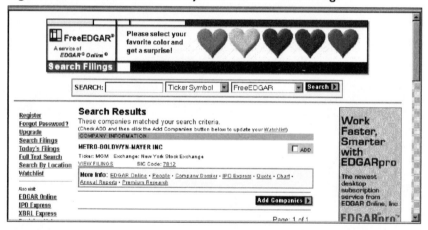

Reprinted with the permission of EDGAR Online, Inc.

filing from your browser screen and you can also change the font size, but any downloading requires a subscription to EDGAR Online. This is an example of the minimum functionality that exists within FreeEDGAR.

EDGAR Online. This resource functions almost identically to FreeEDGAR. A quick search feature allows searches by either company name or ticker symbol, and you can also view today's filings. The added value that comes with the subscription is that you can now download your filings in RTF format, create a Watchlist, and search the full text of filings. In EDGAR Online, you can search full-text filings by company name, ticker symbol, CIK

Figure 6-21. Sample View of Company Filings in FreeEDGAR

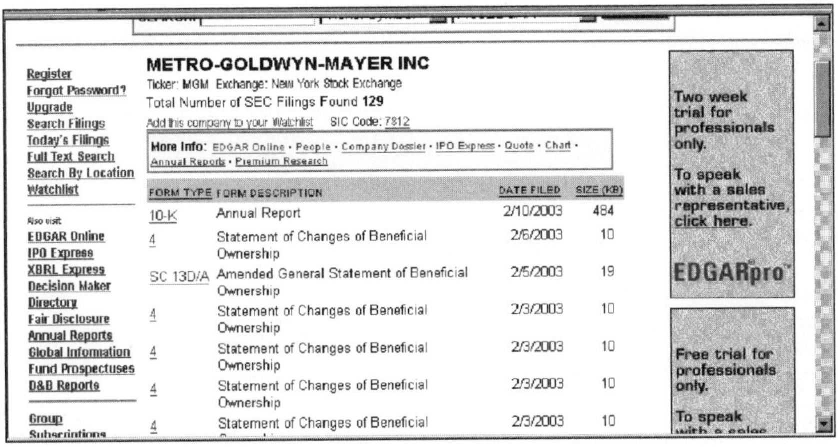

Reprinted with the permission of EDGAR Online, Inc.

(the Central Index Key is a unique identifier assigned by the SEC to each filing company), industry, sector, city, state, and form type, and you can limit by date range or target by a specific date. Full-text searches will go back to 1994.

Figure 6-22. Sample EDGAR Online Search by Ticker Symbol

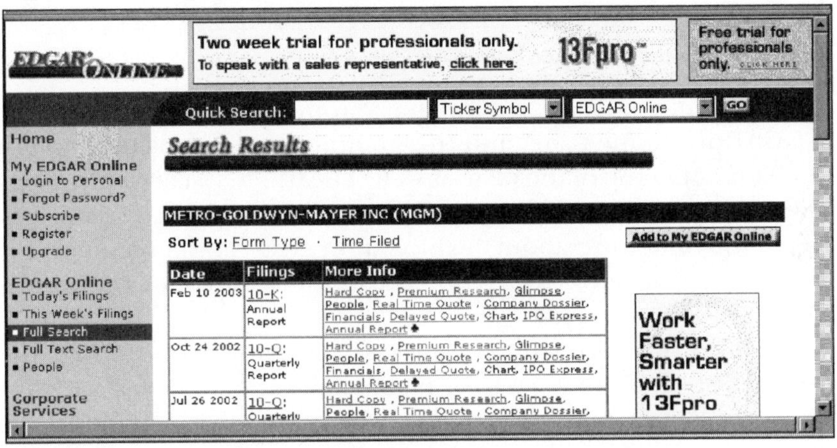

Reprinted with the permission of EDGAR Online, Inc.

Users can order hard copies of a company's annual report or obtain further information, such as a company dossier, financial information, stock quotes and charts, free analyst research, initial public offering (IPO) information, or a list of executives and directors. With the Premium Research tool, users can link to other, fee resources, such as Dun & Bradstreet and Multex. EDGAR

Online also provides a link to Global Information, a section that covers some non-U.S. companies. These can be browsed by company name, country, index, or exchange or accessed via a quick or advanced search.

EDGARpro. This resource is a subscription site with EDGAR Online's functionality, as well as additional features. It allows users to enter "tracker" numbers that appear in usage reports, allowing for the charging back of research costs to clients.

Figure 6-23. EDGARpro Home Page after Login

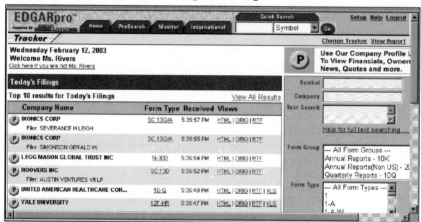

Reprinted with the permission of EDGAR Online, Inc.

The full-text search template automatically appears on the EDGARpro home page, and the ubiquitous Quick Search option appears at the top of the page as well. The full-text search functions identically to that in EDGAR Online. For example, a search of 10-Ks for disclosure about "exploitation costs," which include the marketing and advertising of feature films, retrieves the results shown in Figure 6-24.

EDGARpro allows users to access company profiles from the results list (see the *P* icon in Figure 6-24), as well as download filings in RTF or Excel format. You can also track which filings you have viewed via the check mark in the Viewed column. Searches can be saved using the Save or Save As links. You can administrate your saved searches by clicking on the Monitor tab. Filings in EDGARpro are more professional in appearance than those in FreeEDGAR, and the results also print well without any need for formatting by the user. EDGAR Online filings also print well.

Figure 6-24. Sample EDGARpro Search Results List

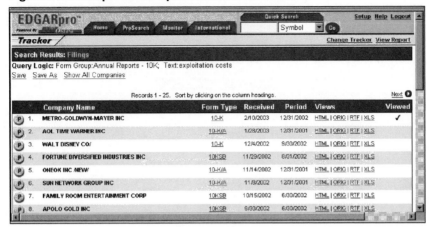

Reprinted with the permission of EDGAR Online, Inc.

Figure 6-25. Sample 10-K Filing in EDGARpro

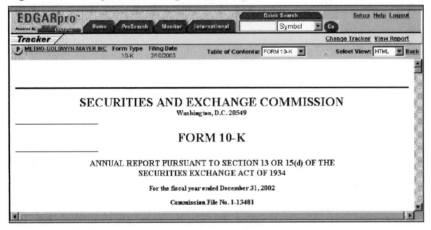

Reprinted with the permission of EDGAR Online, Inc.

EDGARpro's ProSearch feature allows for full-text searching of filings, with the option to include or exclude paper filings.

As previously noted, EDGARpro enables users to charge back their usage or to track it through its Tracker feature. Information entered into the Tracker appears on usage reports you can download from the EDGARpro site.

SOURCE EVALUATION: FreeEDGAR is aimed at the layperson and has limited functionality. Even though links to such features as full-text search appear on the FreeEDGAR home page, those features require a subscription to EDGAR Online. FreeEDGAR is

Figure 6-26. EDGARpro's ProSearch Screen

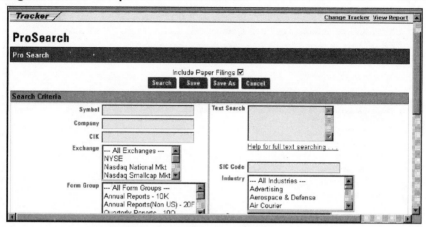

Reprinted with the permission of EDGAR Online, Inc.

Figure 6-27. EDGARpro Usage Reports Generator

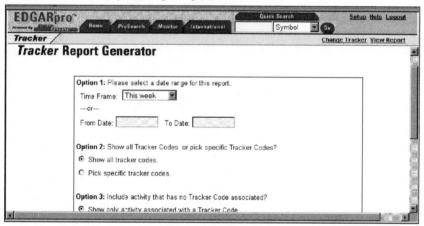

Reprinted with the permission of EDGAR Online, Inc.

very basic in its offerings and can be a quick, free resource to use when simply trying to locate company filings by SIC code and when it does not matter whether the filings "look pretty." It can also be a quick resource for locating company filings in general, but the EDGAR database at the U.S. Securities and Exchange Commission Web site is just as quick and easy to use, with about the same functionality. In fact, the filings from the SEC Web site look better when printed. FreeEDGAR also contains *lots* of advertising, including pop-up ads, which distract from its usability and can make it difficult to locate information. Finally, every time you log into FreeEDGAR, you receive an "offer" page; you must scroll down the page and then accept the offer or decline the offer before you can proceed to using FreeEDGAR itself. This is very annoying and keeps appearing no matter how often you decline.

EDGAR Online is designed for the savvy layperson. Its increased functionality over FreeEDGAR, especially the full-text search and download capabilities, makes it worth the subscription price. In the subscription format there is also a sharp decrease in the number of ads on the site, which reduces clutter and confusion and increases usability. The search results are difficult to browse, however, because of the way they appear on the screen. With much of the emphasis on promoting EDGARpro and other areas of the site, the remaining screen area is "stuffed" with too much information for the limited space. Similar data sources, such as 10k Wizard, are easier to use and browse. (In EDGARpro, however, you are able to view your search terms in context within the filings by clicking on the HTML link next to the filing name in the search results list, and then using the First Hit/ Next Hit/ Last Hit buttons.)

EDGARpro is aimed at professional researchers and would be the best option for librarians and information professionals to use. Its search functionality and results lists are the best of the three related products. Ads are minimal, and download capability is extended to Excel format, which is important for the financial information in SEC filings. In late 2003, Microsoft announced a partnership with Edgar Online to incorporate Accelerator for XBRL (Extensible Business Reporting Language) to allow Edgar Online customers to extract and review financial information in Edgar's repository directly from within Microsoft Excel 2003. The Tracker feature allows for usage tracking and reporting—another vital feature of any subscription service used in a business research setting. The company summaries and profiles include financial ratio information, institutional ownership, newswire stories, and other information missing from both FreeEDGAR and EDGAR Online. One drawback is that you cannot see your search terms in context when viewing filings. Also, international content is accessed via Global Reports or Perfect Information, and not in the general search features.

SOURCE VALUE RATING: All of the data source reviewers were asked to rate each source on the basis of the following eight categories, using "10" as the highest rating and "1" as the lowest ("80" being a perfect score):

1. Relative cost-to-value:	6
2. Relative timeliness of data:	9
3. Relative comprehensiveness of data:	7
4. Ease of use:	6
5. Search options available:	7
6. Level of support services:	8
7. Level of training offered:	8
8. Amount/kinds of special services offered:	6
Total Rating:	57

SOURCE REVIEWS:

Ferguson, Renee Boucher. 2003. Microsoft, Edgar Online to collaborate on software. *Eweek,* (November 5).

O'Leary, Mick. 2003. Free sites for EDGAR data. *Information Today* (June).

CONTRIBUTOR NAME: Jan Rivers / Patricia A. Watkins / Jennifer Richard

AFFILIATION: Dorsey & Whitney LLP / Thunderbird School of International Management / Acadia University

USEFUL TIPS

- It is best to use FreeEDGAR solely for locating known entities, such as a specific company's 10-K filing.
- Full-text searching of any kind with these three products can be done only in EDGAR Online or EDGARpro.
- For obtaining copies of filings, use EDGAR Online or EDGARpro. If you wish to print free copies of filings without using a subscription resource, use the SEC's Web site (*http://www.sec.gov*).
- EDGARpro has the most functionality and value-add of the three resources.
- Two other free versions of EDGAR are available on the Web. Both are a few weeks behind in updates; however, EDGARSCAN (*http://edgarscan.tc.pw.com*), provided by PricewaterhouseCoopers, allows full-text searching within individual documents and EdgarIQ (*http://www.edgariq.com*), by Inverito, offers company-name, ticker, and full-text searching of the whole EDGAR database.

U.S. SECURITIES AND EXCHANGE COMMISSION

ALTERNATE/PREVIOUS DATA SOURCE NAMES: SEC

SERVICE/PORTAL NAME: *http://www.sec.gov*

SOURCE DESCRIPTION: The role of the Securities and Exchange Commission (SEC) is to protect investors and to maintain the integrity of the securities markets. It acts like a watchdog over public companies as well as accounting and investment banking professionals to ensure that appropriate disclosure regarding public corporate financial information is achieved. For the competitive intelligence researcher, the SEC site is most useful for its links to legislation, rules and interpretations, and "pressure points" relating to accounting governance, monitoring, and litigation. It is the SEC that provides the raw data to the EDGAR system. EDGAR is searchable through this Web site, though with fewer features than some other free and fee-based versions of this database. This review focuses on the non-EDGAR content found on the SEC Web site.

Figure 6-28. SEC Main Page

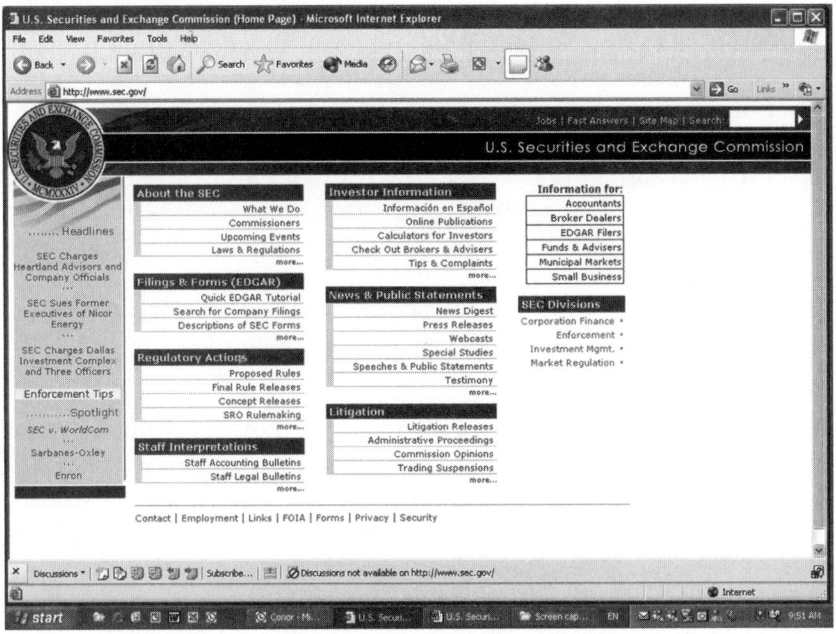

Reprinted with permission of U.S. Securities and Exchange Commission.

SOURCE CONTENT: The SEC home page is neatly divided into nine broad categories that clearly guide you to relevant content:

1. **About the SEC:** provides the mission statement and basic information about the department, including the commissioners, upcoming events, rules of practice, annual reports, laws and regulations, and guidelines.

2. **SEC Filings and Forms:** it is here that you can access the EDGAR database. Also included in the section is a quick EDGAR tutorial, SIC codes, and information for filers. Since most filings are now done electronically, the SEC's version of EDGAR includes same-day filings now.

3. **Regulatory Actions:** contains links to proposed and final rules, concept and interpretive releases, PCAOB and SRO rule making, Exchange Act Exemptive Applications, Exemptive Orders, and other commission orders and notices.

4. **Staff Interpretations:** provides access to written and verbal statements by the SEC staff. Note: these are only interpretations, are therefore not legally binding, and are for guidance on legal and accounting matters.

5. **Investor Information:** provides tools, such as calculators, links to brokers and advisers, tips, alerts, information about complaints, and education for investors. Some of the information in this section is also provided in Spanish.

6. **News & Public Statements:** links you to recent press releases, news digests, public statements, and more.

7. **Litigation:** provides links to federal court actions, notices and settlements, reports of investigations, and trading suspensions.

8. **Information For:** this section provides information broken down by area of interest. They include accountants, broker-dealers, EDGAR filers, funds and advisers, municipal markets, and small businesses.

9. **Divisions:** links to the Web sites of the four major divisions of the commission. They are Corporate Finance, Enforcement, Investment Management, and Market Regulation.

SOURCE EVALUATION: Virtually all of the content found on this Web site is critical to the competitive intelligence researcher and anyone concerned with conducting research in the area or staying abreast of current events and hot issues. The Web site is relatively well designed and organized into logical sections. In most cases the full text of recently released documents is available on the site; historical documents are much less consistently available, and, in fact, it is difficult to predict what older documents might be found here. From the research perspective, it would be nice if the SEC would consistently make more of the historical documents available via the Web site or at a minimum include comprehensive citations or abstracts. As it stands, the researcher still needs to subscribe to subscription-based electronic databases such as Lexis-Nexis or print loose-leaf services such as CCH's SEC Reporter to be ensured of complete historical and current content.

SOURCE VALUE RATING: All of the data source reviewers were asked to rate each source on the basis of the following eight categories, using "10" as the highest rating and "1" as the lowest ("80" being a perfect score):

1. Relative cost-to-value:	10
2. Relative timeliness of data:	10
3. Relative comprehensiveness of data:	8
4. Ease of use:	9
5. Search options available:	5
6. Level of support services:	6
7. Level of training offered:	2
8. Amount/kinds of special services offered:	2
Total Rating:	52

CONTRIBUTOR NAME: Brenda Reeb / Jennifer Richard
AFFILIATION: University of Rochester / Acadia University

USEFUL TIPS

- Web site that pertain to specific areas of interest.
- Headlines on the left sidebar provide information about enforcement issues and current activities of the commission.

SEDAR

ALTERNATE/PREVIOUS DATA SOURCE NAMES: System for Electronic Document Analysis and Retrieval

SERVICE/PORTAL NAME: *http://www.sedar.com*

Source Description: SEDAR (the System for Electronic Document Analysis and Retrieval) is the system used for electronically filing most securities-related information with the Canadian securities regulatory authorities. The database is operated by the Canadian Securities Administrators (CSA) and the Canadian Depository for Securities (CDS). Filing with SEDAR started January 1, 1997, and is now mandatory for most reporting issuers in Canada. For companies it allows filing of securities documents and the remittance of filing fees electronically. For researchers and other users the system facilitates immediate and intelligent access to public company and mutual fund information in the public domain. Information is provided in both of Canada's official languages, English and French. The target audiences for this Web site are investors, analysts, investment advisers, and regulators. It is also very useful to educators and students in business programs.

Figure 6-29. SEDAR Home Page

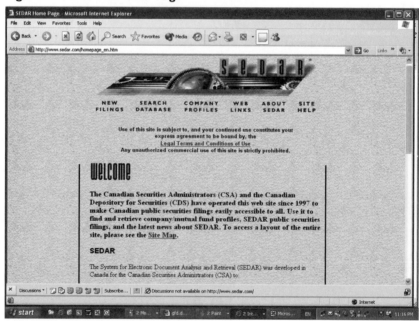

Reprinted with the permission of CDS, Inc.

Source Content: The SEDAR page is quite simple, with six options at the top of the page:

1. **New Filings**: all new filings, up to the close of the last business day, are available in the database. It is often the case that users want to track the most current filings, and for that purpose,

they are featured in this separate location. Included in this section of the Web site are the most current public companies filings, annual reports, financial statements, press releases, prospectuses, takeover and bid materials, as well as all new mutual fund filings. Documents are made available only after the security commission approves them for release, which, under normal circumstances, occurs one to two days after filing.

2. **Search Database:** The database is divided into two sections. One search screen is provided for public companies, as shown below, and a second search screen, with different options, is available for mutual funds.

Figure 6-30. Search for Public Companies on SEDAR

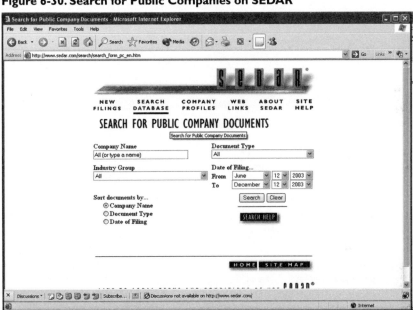

Reprinted with the permission of CDS, Inc.

Search results are clear, providing pertinent information about the file, including the name of the company, a brief description of the document, the date of filing, the format, and the size of the file.

3. **Company Profiles:** these are divided into two alphabetical lists, one for public companies and one for mutual fund groups. Profiles give relevant information about Canadian companies. Data includes, but is not restricted to, address and contact information, various industry codes and symbols, partners,

Figure 6-31. SEDAR Company Search Results

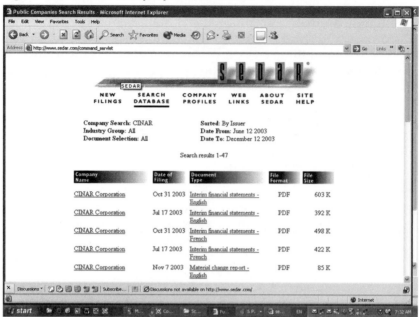

Reprinted with the permission of CDS, Inc.

auditors, jurisdictions, and size of issues.

4. **Web Links:** this page simply lists the provincial securities commissions. For U.S. content, links to EDGAR and SEC are provided as well as a few Canadian and U.S. links to stock market information. It is a relevant if not exhaustive or detailed list of additional resources.

5. **About SEDAR:** includes background and contact information, lists of fees, information for filers and subscribers, FAQs, and information for data resellers.

6. **Site Help:** includes a useful glossary of terms for novice and detailed searching assistance for the browser, database, and company profiles.

SOURCE EVALUATION: Overall, the Web site is easy to navigate and user-friendly. The Site Help section provides useful documentation to assist the user in searching both the Web site and the database. The information is current and relevant; however, the database is periodically unavailable for various reasons. One common reason is site maintenance. A minor flaw in the searching protocol was noted by Daphne Flanagan in her review. This was that the database searches for literal strings of letters, such that a search for the company name Inco retrieves words such as *incorpo-*

Figure 6-32. SEDAR Company Profile

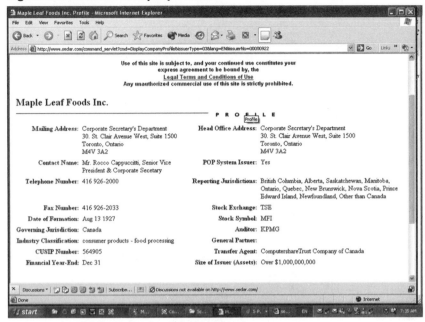

rated and *income*, resulting in a cumbersome, inaccurate results page. A way around this problem is to search INCO through the Company Profile section of the Web site. It is very important to point out the value of having a free resource that provides high-quality data about Canadian companies. Unfortunately, the formats are not yet consistent. This makes it easier for filers, but oftentimes more difficult for end users, though the majority of documents are now in PDF and the downloading time is quick.

SOURCE VALUE RATING: All of the data source reviewers were asked to rate each source on the basis of the following eight categories, using "10" as the highest rating and "1" as the lowest ("80" being a perfect score):

1. Relative cost-to-value:	10
2. Relative timeliness of data:	9
3. Relative comprehensiveness of data:	9
4. Ease of use:	9
5. Search options available:	8
6. Level of support services:	8

7. Level of training offered:	7
8. Amount/kinds of special services offered:	7
Total Rating:	67

Source Reviews:

Flanagan, Daphne. 1999. SEDAR. *Journal of Business and Finance Librarianship* 4 (4): 37–40.

Contributor Name: Jennifer Richard
Affiliation: Acadia University

USEFUL TIPS

- If you know the specific public company or mutual fund, go straight to the company profiles section of the Web site, rather than sorting through search results.

FACTIVA

Alternate/Previous Data Source Names: Dow Jones Interactive, Reuters Business Briefing, Dow Jones News/Retrieval

Service/Portal Name: *http://www.factiva.com*

Source Description: Factiva is a joint venture, formed in 1999 by Dow Jones & Co. and The Reuters Group. Its flagship product, Factiva.com, is the successor online service to Dow Jones Interactive (formerly Dow Jones News/Retrieval) and Reuters Business Briefing, both of which were known for their focus on international information sources. Factiva.com now includes almost all of the content of both of its predecessors, along with capabilities and services not previously available.

The heart of Factiva is its collection of nearly eight thousand publications in twenty-two languages from 118 countries, and its emphasis on acquiring content directly from publishers whenever possible. This enables the company to ensure that the updates are added as soon as they are available, and that the coverage of individual publications is as comprehensive as is feasible. Factiva data includes current news and selected photos, archived articles, company data, country and regional profiles, investment analyst reports, market data, historical stock price performance, and company financials.

PRICING: Factiva offers several basic pricing structures, including flat-fee access and individual, transaction-based pricing. Since flat-fee subscriptions start at $1,000 a month, low-volume searchers will probably want to use the Individual Subscription option, which offers articles at $2.95 each with an annual fee of $69. Note that individual subscribers do not have access to the News Pages or Companies/Markets areas of Factiva.

SOURCE CONTENT: Factiva offers four basic navigational tabs: Search, Track, News Pages, and Companies/Markets. (Note that News Page and Companies/Markets tabs are not available to Individual Subscription users.) Below is a detailed commentary on the content of each tab:

1. **Search.** Factiva provides access to eight thousand publications and content from ten thousand business-related Web sites in twenty-two languages, all judged to be of particular interest to business searchers. Areas within these sites are scanned daily, if appropriate, to retrieve and index content that is not otherwise available on Factiva. The Search function also includes pictures from Reuters and Knight Ridder, with more than four thousand images added weekly. Selected content is available in PDF format, and articles can be displayed and saved in rich text format (RTF) as well as in HTML and plain text. Factiva supports both free-text searching and searches with the Factiva Intelligent Indexing codes.

   Although most researchers will use the free-text search box to construct their search, Factiva does support full Boolean logic. A relatively small number of words cannot be routinely searched in Factiva, including *and, or, not, same, near* and *date*. However, even these words can be searched if enclosed in quotation marks. The search phrase *"to be or not to be"*—consisting entirely of words and quotation marks that are not searchable in most online services—is a valid search in Factiva.

   Researchers can also limit the search by field; these include Headline, Lead Paragraph, Author, Word Count, Date, Publication Title, Language, and Intelligent Indexing term. Most of the field restrictions can be indicated through pull-down boxes, with an option to add a custom list of fields from a collection of thirty specialized indexing fields. The Factiva

Figure 6-33. Factiva's Search Interface

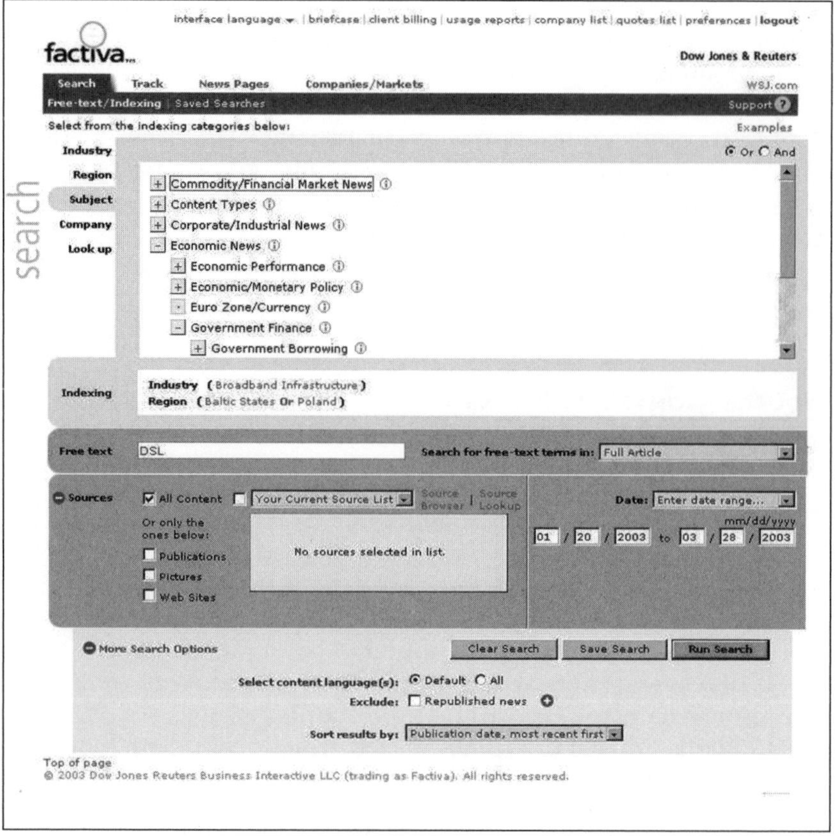

Intelligent Indexing terms are searchable through the links at the top of the Advanced Search page. Clicking on Company, Industry, Region, or Subject opens a new window to display the options available, as illustrated in Figure 6-34.

Each of the hierarchical categories that appear can be expanded by clicking the Plus icon. The default selection of sources to search is All Content, but sources can be specified by clicking the Source Browser link on the main search page, which allows the user to build a custom source list by selecting publications organized by title, industry, region, type, or language. Source lists can be saved for later use or selected for one-time searching. See Figure 6-35 for an example of the Publication Type Source Browser.

After a search has been executed, the default search results screen displays the complete citation, word count, and lead

Figure 6-34. Factiva Search Option, Intelligent Indexing Search by Industry

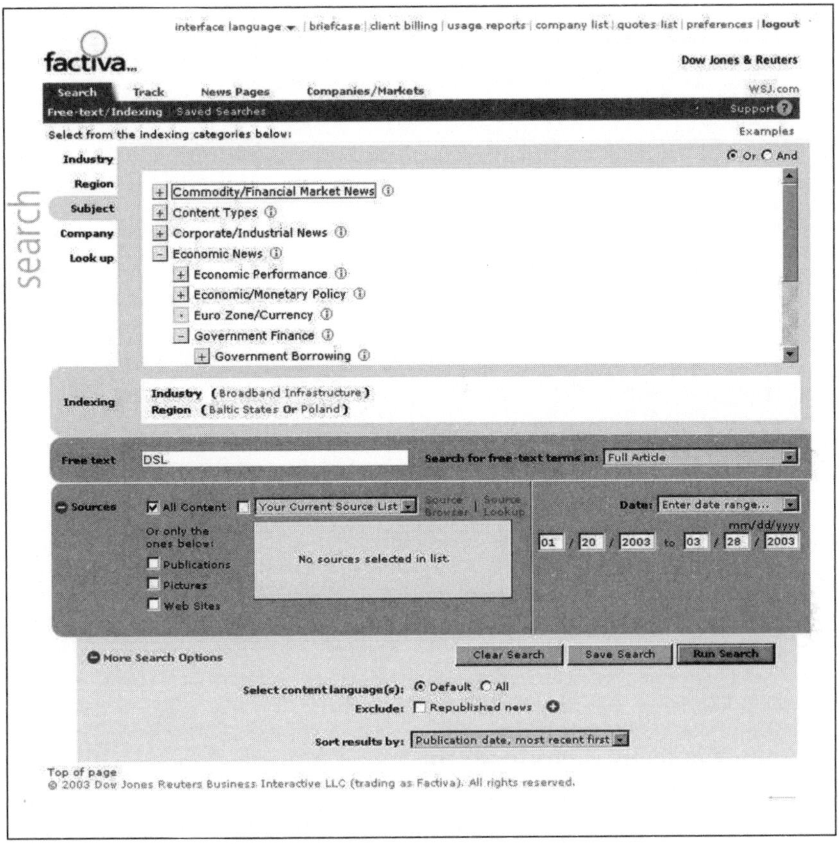

sentence. Articles can then be displayed in full or in one of several other formats, and the researcher can create customized display formats. The results can be viewed and saved in rich text format as well as plain text; they can be e-mailed to the researcher or a third party; or they can be placed in the "Briefcase," which stores up to one hundred documents for thirty days.

Factiva has recently developed an indexing process called Factiva Intelligent Indexing, which assigns company, industry, regional, and subject codes consistently across all content in its Search and Track areas. These codes are based on international indexing standards, such as NAICS (North American Industry Classification System) and ISO (International Standards Organization), and include up to five levels of hierarchy. For example, a search on the industry term *Computers* would

Figure 6-35. Publication Type Source Browser in Factiva

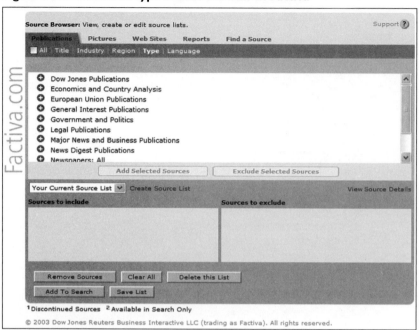

automatically include all the more granular terms within the computer industry hierarchy.

The advantages of Intelligent Indexing are that you can search non-English content by using the Intelligent Indexing terms in the language you wish to use. Indexing terms are consistently applied across all content providers. You can limit your search to a specific geographic region, to articles about a particular company, or even to a type of document (editorial, interview, or an overview of industry trends).

2. **Track.** There is the ability to use an alerting tool that monitors news from close to 6,000 publications and 750 Web sites. Track works continuously; the results can be viewed in the Track Folders, or they can be sent to an e-mail address, either throughout the day as articles are added or aggregated into a single e-mail once or twice a day. The search logic is similar to that of Search; both free-text searching and queries using Intelligent Indexing are supported. An interesting feature of the Track option is the ability to set the relevance level of the retrieved items to high, medium, or any degree of relevance. The relevance-level score is based on the number of search terms that appear in a document. Searchers can use the

relevance-level setting to restrict the Track Folder to articles that are directly about a particular topic or expand the folder to any articles that mention a topic or company.

Figure 6-36. Factiva's Track Folder Option

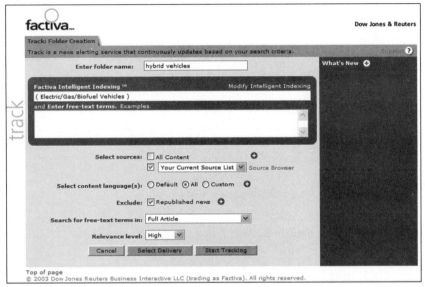

3. **News Page.** This provides access to several content areas of Factiva from a single screen. The default Factiva Pages include the top news from up to ten major news sources, based on the subscriber's region; key stock market indices; and Editor's Links to Web sites of topical interest (see Figure 6-37). Note that with the pull-down menu at the upper left of the screen, the Factiva Pages can be customized by geographic region and by industry category.

    Other types of News Pages include Group News, set up by an organization's administrator to provide customized current news for selected groups of users with the organization, and Personal News, which subscribers can set up individually to display the sources and sections from publications they want to monitor.

4. **Companies/Markets.** Access to detailed information on companies in seventy-two countries is provided in this section. Companies/Markets consists of five categories of content: financial data for 42,500 companies worldwide, 36.5 million Dun & Bradstreet records (with links to full Dun & Bradstreet reports), 30,000 investment analyst reports (in PDF format),

Figure 6-37. Factiva's News Page Option

stock quotes (often going back twenty-five years on publicly traded securities), and company profiles, snapshots, and news.

Subscribers can use the Companies/Markets area to build a list of companies that meet specific criteria, create charts of stocks, funds, and market indices, view investment reports on companies or industries of interest, and build customized company profiles. The Company Quick Search feature, shown below for Johnson & Johnson, is particularly useful when one needs to pull together content from a number of sources and areas within Factiva.

SOURCE EVALUATION: Factiva's strength lies in its focus on business and industry information sources and in its global content. It offers a powerful and flexible search interface, advanced search features, deep archives of content, and intuitive tools for pulling information together from a variety of sources. Keep in mind that because of its focus on business information, Factiva is *not* a one-stop source for researchers who also need access to scientific-technical, medical, or legal information.

Factiva has recently made some significant improvements to its service. One such improvement is the box on the Search screen that allows users to exclude republished news (common in newswire data sources) and other types of articles. Intelligent Indexing

Figure 6-38. Factiva's Company Quick Search Feature

is also an improvement, but it can be frustrating for professional researchers. Another limitation is that when one is using the More Like This function, it is not clear which indexing terms the system is keying on. The Help functionality could also be enhanced. Clicking on the question mark in the upper right-hand corner brings up a generalized Help menu that is difficult to navigate. Often the more detailed written guides on the Factiva site are more helpful.

Through its partnership with Reuters and SunGard (Tradeline), Factiva has taken the integration of market data and business news to a new level. It allows users to see the direct effect of company news and announcements on stock price. Factiva subscribers can view headlines to stories describing the cause of the rise or fall in stock price by dragging a mouse over the performance line or bar in a company's historical stock chart.

Factiva's user interfaces are both feature rich and intuitive. Many of the default settings can be customized through the Preferences screen, which further enhances the usability of the interfaces. The user interfaces are available in nine languages. Factiva offers several technical support and customer service options, available through Factiva's Membership Circle by clicking the Support icon. Flat-fee subscribers can also call a toll-free number for live customer service and technical support. User documentation, case studies, reports, and white papers are also available online (*http://www.factiva.com/collateral*). Some of these documents are available in multiple languages, including French, German, Italian, Spanish, and Japanese. In addition, Factiva offers free self-directed lessons and product tours, and online and face-to-face training sessions throughout the world. The schedules for these sessions are listed online (*http://www.factiva.com/learning*).

SOURCE VALUE RATING: All of the data source reviewers were asked to rate each source on the basis of the following eight categories, using "10" as the highest rating and "1" as the lowest ("80" being a perfect score):

1. Relative cost-to-value:	9
2. Relative timeliness of data:	10
3. Relative comprehensiveness of data:	10
4. Ease of use:	8
5. Search options available:	7
6. Level of support services:	6
7. Level of training offered:	6
8. Amount/kinds of special services offered:	9
Total Rating:	65

SOURCE REVIEWS:

Factiva is one of *KM World* magazine's "Top 100 Companies in Knowledge Management" and part of *EContent* magazine's "Top 100 Content Companies to Watch." Factiva is also recognized as a winner of the 2002 Software & Information Industry Association's Codie Awards in the Best Online Business, Corporate or Professional Information category. Other reviews include the following:

Hane, Paula. 2003. Serious About Customer Service. *Information Today* 20, no. 3 (March 1). Interview with Clare Hart, CEO of Factiva.com, in which she discusses the company's products and plans, as well as trends in the information industry.

O'Leary, Mick. 2001. Factiva.com: The New Dow Jones/ Reuters Synthesis. *EContent* 24, no. 5 (July). This in-depth article discusses the formation of Factiva.com and introduces the major Factiva.com modules.

Wood, Anthony. 2002. Factiva: The Way We Search Now. *Business Information Searcher* 11, no. 3/4 (February). Extensive review of Factiva's search module, its standard and advanced user interfaces, and output options.

CONTRIBUTOR NAME: Mary Ellen Bates / Meryl Brodsky / Tanja Harrison

AFFILIATION: Bates Information Services, Inc. / Consultant / Acadia University

USEFUL TIPS

- Save frequently run searches by clicking the Save Search icon at the bottom of the Search screen.
- How-to-use guides are available from the Factiva Web site (*http://www.factiva.com/collateral/download_brchr.asp?node=learning2*). You must have Acrobat Reader software to access them.
- The Search area provides a pull-down menu that allows sorting results by date (either chronological or reverse chronological) or by relevance. Another pull-down menu allows you to select the format of the results. Using these display functions can save time.
- Factiva.com offers a number of preferences that can be set by the user, including the default search interface, date, and language restrictions as well as the format of search results. The Preferences link is in the top right corner of the main screen.

ABI/INFORM

SERVICE/PORTAL NAME: *http://www.proquest.com; http://www.il.proquest.com*

SOURCE DESCRIPTION: ABI/Inform began in 1971 when three Portland State University, OR graduate students were responsible for designing a system that would improve corporate access to business literature. After being inspired by an information service developed by a local power company, and with contributions from a University of Wisconsin database project called Inform, the students succeeded in developing the system. After graduation they founded a small company that merged their new brand, ABI (Abstracted Business Information), with the Wisconsin database name Inform, and ABI/Inform was born. The product generated minimal interest and profits until a Kentucky newspaper owner purchased it in 1973 and made the file available in Dialog. In 1991, documents went from abstracts to full-text records, making the product a forerunner among document-delivery services. The Kentucky media giants sold ABI/Inform to UMI (University Microfilms) in 1986.

The ABI/Inform index supplies journal articles and abstracts that contain a broad range of North American and international business, advertising, marketing, human resources, finance, taxation, technology, and management content. The database includes information on more than sixty thousand companies and covers 1,116 periodicals, 65 percent of which provide their articles in full text. ABI is known for providing more extensive archival information than its competitors; some retrospective articles date back to 1971. The average date span covers the past ten years.

ABI/Inform targets all environments that depend on business information: academic, corporate, and public. Because the service provides prolific amounts of business literature, it can be expensive (depending on the institution size, number of users, and subscription details). Most subscribers are larger, research-oriented organizations. Broad topical coverage includes business conditions and trends, management techniques, corporate strategies, and industry information on both a domestic and global scale.

Aside from the ProQuest portal, ABI/Inform content may be accessed through any of the following products: Dialog (*http://www.dialog.com*), Ovid/Silverplatter (*http://www.ovid.com*), OCLC/FirstSearch (*http://www.oclc.org*), and the corporate version of LexisNexis (*http://www.lexis-nexis.com*).

ABI/Inform's collection of articles is available on Dialog. If you need to regularly search back more than five years for accounting issues, you may want to explore Dialog's pay-as-you go pricing options. For more recent articles, many of the journals have been added to the other business aggregators, such as Factiva and LexisNexis. Subscribing to the ABI/Inform database through the ProQuest portal offers the advantage of displaying most of the articles in PDF format, but because it is expensive, this may not be an option for many organizations.

PRICING: An annual subscription to ABI/Inform ranges from $6,000 to approximately $75,000.

SOURCE CONTENT: This section describes the content and related features of ABI/Inform under the following five categories:

1. **Origin of Information**. ABI/Inform does not create its content; rather, it gathers content created by others and provides the search engine and indexing that allows the information to be searchable. Journal aggregators such as ABI/Inform are evaluated on both volume and quality of the incorporated publications, and the effectiveness of their search engine.

2. **Navigation.** Six features are presented on the top horizontal navigation bar: Basic Search, Advanced Search, Topic Guide, Publication Search, and Marked List. The key to searching ABI/Inform lies in understanding how to successfully use the search tools. The Tools area contains the options for Search Tips and Browse Topics. Search Tips is the researcher's primary instrument. From here, users can discover effective search methods to use the index effectively and how to better target and refine their searches. It includes a browsable list of linked topics to more information as well as a searchable index and glossary of terms. The Help link in the top right-hand corner will also bring the researcher to the Search Tips section.

3. **Search Methods**. The Basic Search contains a drop box and two check-box options for fine-tuning a search. The search box allows for keyword searching of an article. The user is asked to fill in the box with a word, words, or specific phrase. The user then specifies the date range by choosing All dates, Last seven days, Last 30 days, Last three months, Last six months, Last 12 months, On this date, Before this date, After this date, and Specific date range, which allows the researcher to key in the month, day, and year. The default is All dates. Users can also check the box options for retrieving full-text articles or scholarly articles (including peer-reviewed journals).

   The Advanced Search presents three drop boxes for searching within specific fields, separated by Boolean operator drop boxes with the options of AND, OR, AND NOT, WITHIN 3 (words), and PRE/1 (to find words within x words in a field). More sophisticated operators are available by clicking Search Tips or Help. The fields to search are the default Citation and Abstract, Citation and article text, Abstract only, Article text, Article title, Article type, Author, Classification code, Company, Image caption, Location, NAICS code, Person, Product name, Publication title, and Subject. The Search Tips section helps to further understand the search logic of the database. Guides offer more information on truncation symbols and wildcard characters (? and *), further Boolean connection operators to use (AND, NOT, WITHIN, NOT WITHIN, etc.),

Figure 6-39. ABI/Inform Advanced Search Screen

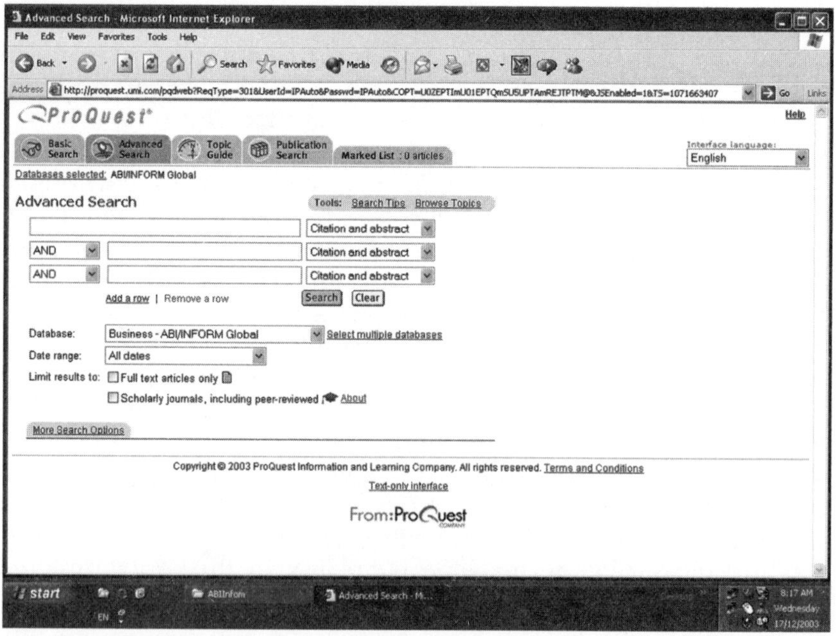

Image published with permission of ProQuest Information and Learning Company. Further reproduction is prohibited without permission.

Search field syntax (AU(Smith) for author), Stop words (ignored words like *a, the,* and so on), and provides Example searches to further assist the user. All date ranges available for the Basic Search are presented as well as the option to narrow by choosing the Scholarly journals check box. The Advanced Search is geared toward precision searching, whereas the basic engine is useful for "free text searching" (looking for general research ideas). This is recommended for the seasoned researcher or someone who already knows exactly what they are looking for, and is recommended for retrieving the best results.

The Publication Search is a convenient way to look for a specific journal or news article. The user has the option to search by the publication name, or browse an alphabetical listing of titles in addition to retrieving a Show All list. Publications that are available in full text are indicated next to the titles, including a useful indicator for full-text date range coverage and whether the information is current or delayed. When the user clicks on a hypertext title, a page of links appears, with each link representing a volume and issue number. When the user selects a link, the table of contents and list of articles for that particular volume and issue are displayed. The most recent update of ABI/Inform features the ability to perform a Search Within Publication that also provides a link to Publication Information of the particular title.

Figure 6-40. ABI/Inform Search Results List

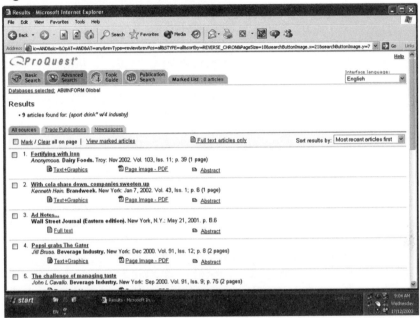

Image published with permission of ProQuest Information and Learning Company. Further reproduction is prohibited without permission.

4. **Highlights of Other Web Features**. The Topic Guide offers an alternative to the "keywords-and-search-box" style of article searching. Topic Guide presents a hierarchy of hyperlinked business-related topics and subtopics. The interface initially shows six main topic areas: Business & Industry, Computers & Internet, Economics & Trade, Environment, Government & Law, and Social Issues & Policy. When the user clicks on a selection, another group of hyperlinked subtopics appears. These are then divided four more times where the user gets a View Articles link.

The Results List offers a variety of options to view an article, depending on the availability and license that ProQuest has with the publisher. These are Full text, Text + Graphics (which has plug-ins of pictures, tables, and more, with the option to enlarge), and Page Image—PDF and Abstract only. Once you have finished selecting articles, the Marked List button takes you to a display of the articles you have selected and offers the ability to print your bibliography, e-mail marked articles, or export the citations into a variety of bibliographic management program formats. Each article also has a link to "Show options for finding similar articles," which will open a section to click boxes with subjects, classification codes, locations, and article types for reperforming a search to look for even more results.

5. **Special Add-On Features.** ProQuest offers a special add-on feature to the ABI/Inform database providing links to Hoover's company information directly from the article text. These links are easily recognizable with the company name highlighted in blue with a small ⓘ in front of each. Selecting the link opens a window displaying the brief company fact sheet, including the overview, key numbers, key people, rankings, and competitor company links to other Intellidocs records. The navigation bar allows the user to access in-depth information and includes further links to Products & Operations and Subsidiaries & Affiliates.

SOURCE EVALUATION: If your organization is interested in purchasing the "Rolls Royce" of business journal databases, ABI/Inform is the database for you. ABI/Inform offers precision searching, daily content updates, superior technical service, archival content, and tools that respond to the changing technological needs of its customers. In June 2003, ProQuest publicized the addition of new content, including news from the *Wall Street Journal* and SAGE Publications. A separate news release announced an improved interface design for the database, which has significantly improved usability. Options are logical and organized conveniently under main buttons, allowing the user to quickly identify the location of features. After every performed query, an indication that the database is "searching" is displayed prominently.

Depending upon the type of institution and needs of its users, all environments may not need the high-powered features of ABI/Inform. ABI offers superior indexing and a search engine with more options than its competitors, but that comes at a price. A general cost analysis for a mid-to-large-sized academic institution suggests that an annual subscription price of ABI/Inform costs 35–45 percent more than a similar contract with its main competitor, EBSCO's Business Source Premier. ABI/Inform is considered an essential source for universities and colleges that have a business school. If an organization can afford the product, it is certainly one of the most sophisticated and reliable sources for current, full-text news content and business literature on the market.

SOURCE VALUE RATING: All of the data source reviewers were asked to rate each source on the basis of the following eight categories, using "10" as the highest rating and "1" as the lowest ("80" being a perfect score):

1. Relative cost-to-value:	6
2. Relative timeliness of data:	10
3. Relative comprehensiveness of data:	8
4. Ease of use:	10
5. Search options available:	10
6. Level of support services:	9
7. Level of training offered:	9
8. Amount/kinds of special services offered:	10
Total Rating:	72

SOURCE REVIEWS:

Chapman, K. 2002. Full-Text Database Support for Scholarly Research in Finance. *Journal of Business & Finance Librarianship* 7: 35–44. Compares three business journal databases—ABI/Inform, Business Source Premier, and General BusinessFile—to determine the quality of finance coverage in the content. ABI/Inform is the writer's pick, providing the most comprehensive coverage, with 76 percent of the articles, 35.9 percent of which are in full text.

Golderman, Gail and Bruce Connolly. 2003. E-reviews: Getting Down to Business. *NetConnect* (Winter): 38–43. Provides a summary of ABI/Inform with an overview of the different available variations of the product's content. A useful comparison of this and other business information products is provided.

O'Leary, Mick. 2001. Big Databases Pose Big Questions. *Online* (May 25): 82–86. Comparison and review of "mega databases" created by Gale Group, ProQuest, EBSCO, and LexisNexis. This article argues that quantity does not guarantee quality. The author writes about "jumbo-sized" databases that are too big and costly. The source mentions ABI's focus on archived information.

Shigo, Kimberly. 2003. Proquest Completes Digital Archive, Adds Content to ABI/Inform, Changes Interface. *Computers in Libraries* (June): 60. Details ProQuest Information and Learning's announcement of content addition from the *Wall Street Journal* and SAGE Publications. Information about the ABI/Inform new interface launch in July 2003 is also discussed.

CONTRIBUTOR NAME: Jen Venable / Patricia A. Watkins / Tanja Harrison

AFFILIATION: Purdue University / Thunderbird School of International Management / Acadia University

USEFUL TIPS

- Use the Basic Search module when executing keyword and subject searches.
- Use the Advanced Search module for more precision searching and when you know the publication title, author, or article title.
- Use the Publication Search module when you are interested in browsing a particular journal volume or want quick access to a particular volume and issue.

LEXISNEXIS

ALTERNATE/PREVIOUS DATA SOURCE NAMES: LexisNexis

SERVICE/PORTAL NAME: *http://www.lexisnexis.com, http://www.nexis.com*

SOURCE DESCRIPTION: LexisNexis provides information services to a broad spectrum of the legal, business, government, financial, and academic communities, providing access to thirty-six thousand sources of current and historic publications and materials in the areas of law, science/medicine, finance, news, international news, and public records from more than thirty-one thousand database sources. Its flagship Web-based product for business professionals is nexis.com.

When introduced in 1980, Nexis, as it was then called, offered several magazines and newspapers as well as the Reuters and Associated Press newswires. Several years later the New York Times Information Service and its INFOBANK library were added to

Nexis, which remains the only place to search the full text of the *New York Times* back to 1980. Also added during this period was the LEXPAT service, with more than 650,000 patents issued since January 1, 1975. The majority of the material is full text, even in the older files. In the two decades since its inception, Nexis has evolved into a comprehensive collection of U.S. and international business information sources (in multiple languages) that includes current and archived news, newspapers, broadcast transcripts from major networks, wire services, magazines, and trade journals.

PRICING: Cost is an important factor to consider when performing online research. LexisNexis has supplemented its original monthly subscription-based approach by adding a number of new purchasing options. Large companies, law firms, or academic institutions almost exlusively contract for deeply discounted flat-rate subscriptions that are negotiated based on the number of users, types of materials searched, and other customization. Small firms often purchase reduced-rate packages of legal materials through their bar associations, and individual users may purchase short-term packages for a day, week, or month, and download as much as they want during the lifetime of the package. Another approach provides "pay-as-you-go" access, and prices vary for document viewing. Spokespeople for LexisNexis stress the flexibility of their purchase plans. Complete descriptions of nonsubscription plans, and lists of files or titles available under either of the plans, can be toured by clicking on the link titled "Nonsubscribers: Find a product that's right for you!," which is found in the upper left corner of the main LexisNexis home page (*http://www.lexisnexis.com*). Contacting a sevice representative is strongly suggested.

SOURCE CONTENT: LexisNexis at nexis.com offers a variety of different search methods to meet different types of information needs. Several search approaches are presented under the following categories:

- **Quick Search.** The Quick Search allows for simple queries across a combination of file types simultaneously. The content searched is noted as being from a "popular selection of sources," and the source drop-down menu offers choices such as News and Company Sources, News Sources, Legislative Sources, Company Sources, and Web Sources. There is also the ability to narrow a search by date, with a drop-down box including Today and Previous 60 Days, Week, Month, 60 Days, 90 Days, Six Months, Year, and Two Years.

A brief record result list is displayed with full-text availability. The option to change to full text is tabbed at the top of the list. Users can mark records, display tagged items, and print, e-mail, or download the records. The option to edit a search, create a new search, or search within results is available at the top of the screen. If the search has company-related information, the results screen presents a Company Navigation Panel for access to a LexisNexis Company Dossier Snapshot and report.

- **Power Search.** The Power Search is the default search tab and helps to sift through the full text of more than three billion documents in more than thirty-six thousand individual publications or sources. Both the Quick and Power option requires the user to first select a source before entering the search statement. The Find More Sources link takes the user to the Source Directory, a link to Popular Sources and the option search for a title under Find a Source.

  Power Search allows for sophisticated search strategy construction using Boolean logic, more date restriction options, the option to sort by date or relevance, and the help of an index. The center section of the Power Search page is where the actual search is constructed. The results list options for Quick Search are also available within the Power Search lists of sources, as is the Company Navigation Panel, but additional tools to change the sorting by date or relevance is provided, as is the option to view the information differently with Expanded List (which gives an example of sentences where your terms appear in context of the article), KWIC for a keyword in context view, and Custom to allow the manipulation of viewing with various field selections.

  Experienced searchers will want to take advantage of the invaluable Index tool. When one enters a search term, such as *derivatives,* for example, four broad categories and six company names using the word appear in the index box, with buttons that will add them to the search strategy constructed previously. Clicking the categories displays definitions and possible broader search terms. The tool may not be necessary for every search, but it is helpful when dealing with unfamiliar terms or for a precise search strategy.

- **Subject Directory.** The Subject Directory is always available for easy access underneath the Quick and Power Search interfaces. The list of thirty-six categories provides brief examples under each heading for easy identification. Once a category is chosen, the request is searched against the database and provides article results with further clickable subcategories to refine the search

Figure 6-41. LexisNexis Power Search Showing the Index Tool

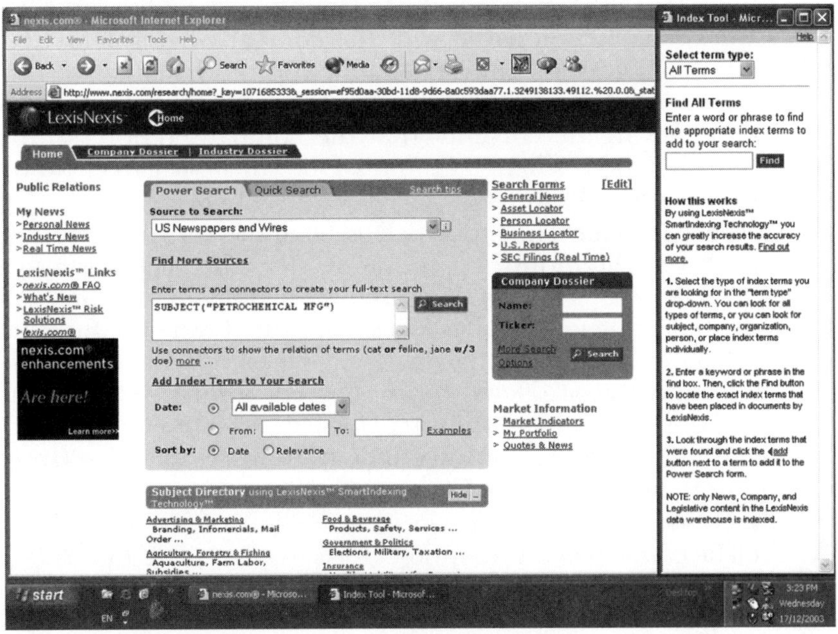

Reprinted with the permission of LexisNexis. LexisNexis is a trademark of Reed Elsevier Properties, Inc. Used with permission of LexisNexis.

again. There are more than twelve hundred topics in the Subject Directory.

- **Company Dossier.** The Company Dossier tool to the right of the main interface provides a convenient way to quickly locate companies by name or ticker symbol. Additional search options for company information are available under the link to the top left of the screen with the same name, including Company Type, DUNS Number, Business Description, and various location limiters. The amount of information retrieved will vary depending on whether the company is publicly or privately held. A sample search on a major U.S. corporation yields a lengthy report consisting of a Company Snapshot (including stock information and key people), In the News (recent articles mentioning the company, chosen by Top Publication, Topic, or Region), Business Information (from Hoover's Company Profiles), Financial Information (summary of yearly and detailed financials from Disclosure), Legal Information, Intellectual Property Information, References, and the option to build a Custom Report with various fields to choose from. Nexis.com offers a large quantity of non-U.S. data, and dossier reports are available from several highly respected sources.

A useful feature accessible from the Company Dossier is the Company Compare link. As many as five additional companies may be compared with the company being searched. Assets, liabilites, income statement, and ratio analysis is compared for companies that are listed on one of the U.S. stock exchanges in the currency that the company reports to the Securities and Exchange Commission. The table can be downloaded in Excel format.

- **Industry Dossier.** The Industry Dossier allows the user to search by terms in the industry name or by SIC code. There is also a useful Browse Industry Hierarchy available to explore. An Industry Snapshot includes a brief Industry Overview, Industry Aggregates and Ratio Analysis, Top Companies, Ratio Components, and Recent News stories. Further information is available from the left-hand Industry Dossier navigation box, including Mergers, Legislative Information, Industry Revenue (from Integra), and Economic Census reports.

- **My News.** This link is at the the top left of the main page interface and has three options for selection. The first is Personal News, which offers search strategies created by the user to monitor topics of choice in the news. These can be created by using Power Search or other search options using keywords, phrases, or a more sophisticated search string. Results can be selected to provide regular updates about specific topics of interest delivered via e-mail. Real Time News functions in a similar manner. After entering your e-mail address, the user is prompted to create search terms or strategies to retrieve articles from the newswires, which are updated at least hourly. After you have completed a search request, you can name your topic and select whether you prefer the results to come by e-mail alerts, in Real Time, Hourly, Every Four Hours, or Daily. After completing one search and saving this, the user will be taken to their results accumulating by topic every time they click on the Real Time News link from the main page. The Industry News link retrieves the daily economic news from sources around the globe. The blue frame to the left offers the user choices from the last two weeks to review or the option of choosing from economics-related information under the headings Economic Forecasts, Federal Reserve, Trade Balance, and Economic Monetary. Other sections include Computer News, Broadcast News, and NPR Pubwatch for sources from National Public Radio.

Figure 6-42. LexisNexis Personal News Options Page

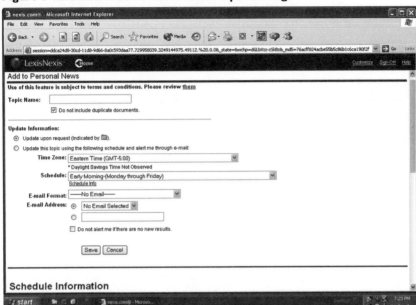

Reprinted with the permission of LexisNexis. LexisNexis is a trademark of Reed Elsevier Properties, Inc. Used with permission of LexisNexis.

- **Search Forms.** The Search Forms box on the right side of the screen provides links to guided search forms for a variety of specific searches, offering fields that may not be searchable from the Quick or Power searches. Search forms that are available include News (including General News, World News, and the *New York Times*), Company (including *US Reports*), People (including a Person Locator and various demographic forms), Government (including tracking and searching of Bills at various levels of government), Medical, Country (including profiles), Public Records (including an asset locator), Legal (including Patent searching and case law), and Markets (including MarkIntel research reports and Hoover's Industry Snapshots). The search forms offer a useful approach when the search should be limited to a specific source, as these are pre-identified in the source drop-down menu of most search forms.
- **Market Information.** The Market Information links are available under the Company Dossier box on the right side of the main screen. The Market Indicators link brings the user to a snapshot of stock indices charts, including the Dow Jones Industrial Average, NYSE Composite, NASDAQ Composite, and the S&P 500. The quotes are updated daily. The user can

search by stock symbols or company name within Quotes and News, Stock Charts, and Earnings/Forecasts. My Portfolio allows the user to customize a market portfolio, and the Quotes and News link provides quick access to the search described earlier below the Market Indicators stock chart page.

Figure 6-43. LexisNexis Market Indicators Page

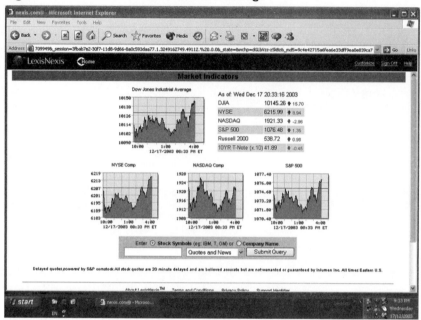

Reprinted with the permission of LexisNexis. LexisNexis is a trademark of Reed Elsevier Properties, Inc. Used with permission of LexisNexis.

Many of the desciptions of searches and features above are only a sampling of the extensive power and content that this LexisNexis product offers. The Search Tips and Help links comprehensively cover all search information, services, and features in much more detail.

SOURCE EVALUATION: As a business research tool, LexisNexis at nexis.com is an excellent product and one of the most renowned and respected sources for information in the industry. The source offers staggering amounts of information. The searchable journal, trade, and news publications along with the company, industry, and market information will be invaluable for the business researcher. The competitive intelligence professional will find the news-alerting services an important feature for keeping current with topics of interest. LexisNexis uses SmartIndexing Technology, search algorithms specially designed and monitored by information and subject experts on staff who are responsible for creating optimal access to content. Users will notice varying degrees of complexity in search methods, depending on the information need and where they are working within the source. However, navigation is fairly intuitive and the online assistance is easy to find, clearly presented, and plentiful. (1-800 Contact Us numbers are available and linked directly from the Help pages). Free training may be arranged telephonically through a link at *http://www. lexisnexis.com.* The session lasts about an hour and can be customized according to interests and level of expertise.

SOURCE VALUE RATING: All of the data source reviewers were asked to rate each source on the basis of the following eight categories, using "10" as the highest rating and "1" as the lowest ("80" being a perfect score):

1. Relative cost-to-value:	9
2. Relative timeliness of data:	10
3. Relative comprehensiveness of data:	9
4. Ease of use:	7
5. Search options available:	9
6. Level of support services:	8
7. Level of training offered:	8
8. Amount/kinds of special services offered:	10
Total Rating:	70

SOURCE REVIEWS:

Bates, Mary Ellen. 2003. Can Small Businesses Go Online? *Searcher* 11, no. 1 (January): 16. Dialog, LexisNexis, Factiva, and Northern Light are compared, mostly in terms of "by-the-drink" prices.

Choosing a Journal Database Provider: Current Options for Searching Journal Databases Online. 2003. *The Information Advisor* 15, no. 4 (April). Reviews current vendor options for searching key databases of trade and journal articles.

Lawrence, Stephanie. 2002. Natural Selection Is the Key to Software Evolution, Consult on All Proposed Changes and a Successful Program Can Be Updated to Appeal to Less Sophisticated New Users Without Alienating Savvy Old Hands. *Information World Review* (December 1): 26. Discussion of the evolution of software at LexisNexis. The author is a product manager at LexisNexis Butterworths Tolley.

Matesic, Maura. 2001. International News Sources. *Toronto Chapter SLA Courier,* Summer <*http://www.sla.org/chapter/ctor/courier/v38/v38n4a4.htm*>. Discusses international news searching on Factiva's Dow Jones Interactive, LexisNexis, and free Internet news Web sites in terms of search engine, content, and delivery method.

Russell, Roger. 2002. LexisNexis Targets Small to Midsized CPA Firms. *Accounting Today* 16, no. 4 (February 25): 22. Discusses how small and medium-sized accounting firms can use LexisNexis.

Sabroski, Suzanne. 2003. Dialog Enhances Company Profiles; LexisNexis Enhances Company Dossier. *Online* 27, no. 6 (November/December): 6. Overviews the increase of companies covered by the Company Dossier product offering.

CONTRIBUTOR NAME: Helen P. Burwell / Meryl Brodsky / Tanja Harrison

AFFILIATION: Burwell Enterprises / Consultant / Acadia University

USEFUL TIPS

- Customize the LexisNexis at nexis.com by clicking the link from the top right-hand corner of the main page to set your preferred viewing options for your start page and results pages.
- Use the Track in Personal News link at the top right-hand corner of an article results screen to set tracking options delivered to your e-mail account.
- Use the Search Forms option on the right of the main screen for precision field searching, especially when you need to search within a specific source.

U.S. CONSUMER PRODUCT SAFETY COMMISSION

ALTERNATE/PREVIOUS DATA SOURCE NAMES: CPSC

SERVICE/PORTAL NAME: *http://www.cpsc.gov*

SOURCE DESCRIPTION: According to the Web site, "The U.S. Consumer Product Safety Commission is charged with protecting the public from unreasonable risks of serious injury or death from more than 15,000 types of consumer products under the agency's jurisdiction." The U.S. Consumer Product Safety Commission (CPSC) notifies consumers through press releases, media outlets, and the Web site about product deficiencies that could bring harm to people, particularly children, or damage to property. The CPSC's focus is consumer products, such as appliances, clothing, furniture, children's products, lighting, and outdoor equipment. It does not have jurisdiction over cosmetics, food, motorized vehicles, medicine, or environmental products.

Figure 6-44. CPSC Home Page

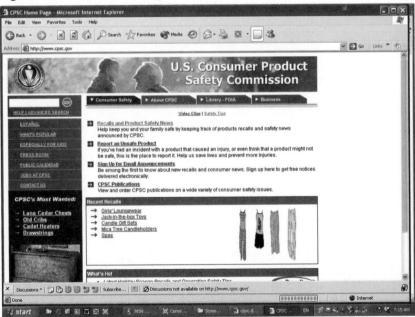

Reprinted courtesy of U.S. Consumer Product Safety Commission.

SOURCE CONTENT: The CPSC Web site was revamped in late 2003. The Web site is divided into four folders and additional categories on the left-side bar. As with all U.S. government sites, the information is provided free of charge. The site offers information to consumers about unsafe products as well as allowing consumers to report problematic products. E-mail service is available through this site to alert participants as new recalls are made.

The Web site is divided into four major folders at the top of the page:

1. **Consumer Safety.** This is the default page. It contains a list of recalled products and safety news, forms to report an unsafe product, a place to sign up for the e-mail service, and a list of the CPCS publications. It also highlights recently recalled items and has a "What's Hot" section.

   The recall page figure below provides various access points to the data. The most recent recalls from the last two months are highlighted, and then recalls are available by month and year. Other categories are product type, company, and product description, as well as six major product categories: child products, toys, household, outdoor, sports and recreation, and specialty products, plus press release number.

Figure 6-45. Search Screen for Recall Information

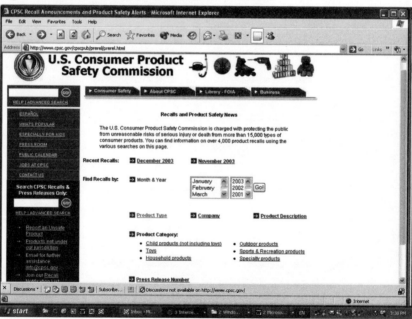

Reprinted courtesy of U.S. Consumer Product Safety Commission.

2. **About CPSC. This** includes an overview of the commission and information about the department staff, the chairman, vice

–chairman, and commissioner, and the other executive staff members. The left-side bar changes according to the folder you are displaying. On the side bar, information such as FAQs, a Guide to Public Information, a Hotline Brochure, the National Injury Information Clearinghouse, and CPSC reports and policies is available.

3. **Library—FOIA.** This section includes documents from the Freedom of Information Act, access to the National Electronic Injury Surveillance System, CPCS regulatory documents, and consumer product–related statistics.

4. **Business:** This consists of information for manufacturers, importers, distributors, and retailers such as regulations, laws, recall programs, handbooks, federal register notices, and access to a database of civil and criminal penalties browsable by company and product.

The site includes a search engine, with the basic search located prominently on the Web site and with both help and advanced search screens available. Other information listed on the left-side bar includes a link to the Spanish version of the Web site, a kids' section, press releases, a public calendar of events, jobs, and contact information.

SOURCE EVALUATION: In general, U.S. government Web sites are becoming more consistent with each other, making them more intuitive for users and thus easier to use. Side bars and folders make navigation simpler, and the small amount of repetition is useful, rather than annoying. To meet the needs of consumers much of the information is now provided in Spanish as well as English. Contact information is complete, providing both e-mails and telephone numbers, and requests are processed quickly. The E-mail Alerting service is customizable so you can receive only recalls in a certain product category such as toys or children's products, or receive additional documents such as press releases and public event information. Recall press releases are descriptive and specificIn addition, the images are large and clear, so consumers have a written physical description and an image to determine whether or not they own the affected product.

The next two figures are an example of a press release and image:

Figure 6-46. CPSC Example of Recall Press Release

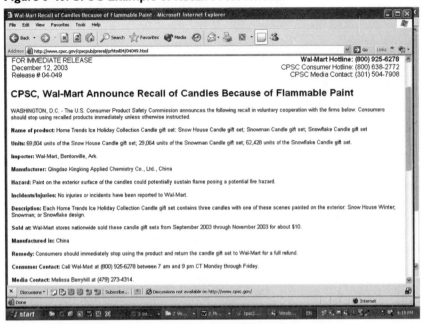

Reprinted courtesy of U.S. Consumer Product Safety Commission.

Figure 6-47. Example of Image Provided in Recall Press Releases

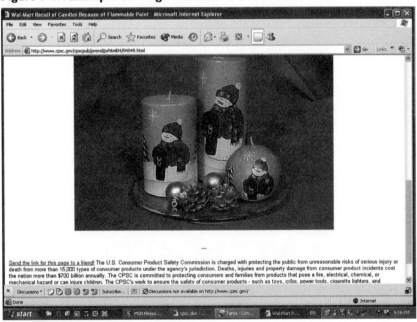

Reprinted courtesy of U.S. Consumer Product Safety Commission.

SOURCE VALUE RATING: All of the data source reviewers were asked to rate each source on the basis of the following eight categories, using "10" as the highest rating and "1" as the lowest ("80" being a perfect score):

1. Relative cost-to-value:	10
2. Relative timeliness of data:	10
3. Relative comprehensiveness of data:	10
4. Ease of use:	8
5. Search options available:	8
6. Level of support services:	8
7. Level of training offered:	8
8. Amount/kinds of special services offered:	7
Total Rating:	69

CONTRIBUTOR NAME: Jennifer Richard
AFFILIATION: Acadia University

USEFUL TIPS

• Check out the link to the newly created *http://www.recalls.gov* Web site, where all regulatory departments have pooled their information for one-stop shopping of recall information.

EPINIONS

SERVICE/PORTAL NAME: *http://www.epinions.com*

SOURCE DESCRIPTION: According to its Web site, "Epinions is the Web's premier consumer reviews platform and the most reliable source for valuable consumer insight, unbiased advice, in-depth product evaluations, and personalized recommendations." Epinions is a service of *Shopping.com, Inc.*, a leading provider of comparison shopping services. The Web site contains thousands and thousands of personal reviews of thousands and thousands of products, everything from cars to stores to wines to banks and credit cards and on and on. This site is free of charge, and reviewers are financially compensated through royalties to ensure a steady supply of consistently high-quality reviews. The site receives revenue mainly through placement of advertisements and licensing of its technology. To become a reviewer, you must be a member of Epinions and log in; there are safeguards in place to ensure quality. All reviews are signed, and the Web site has set up filters to detect profanity as well. Most of the reviews are arranged by pros, cons, a summary statement, ratings, and links to retailers and prices.

Figure 6-48. Epinions Main Page

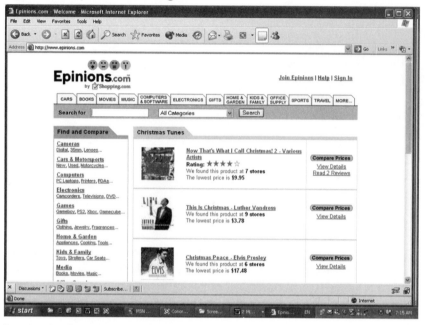

Reprinted with permission of Shopping.com.

SOURCE CONTENT: Main categories are tabbed at the top and include cars, books, movies, music, computers and software, electronics, gifts, home and garden, kids and family, office supplies, sports, travel, and more. There is a search box with the ability to limit to a particular category. A product is highlighted in the center section of the main page. There is also a list that corresponds somewhat, but not exactly, to the tabs and the top, with further examples of types of products in each category. Within each major category, there is an advanced search option, as illustrated in the figure below. Each advance search is customized to the product that you are investigating. For example, this advance search on phones has search boxes for type, brand, price, caller ID, and answering machines.

Figure 6-49. Advanced Search within a Product

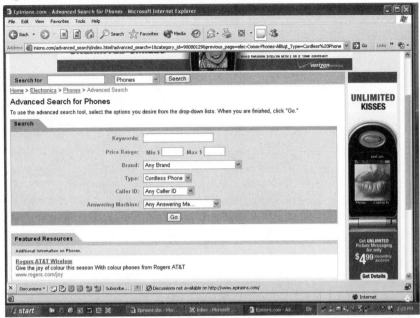

Reprinted with permission of Shopping.com.

If the search engine is not used, the product information is arranged nicely in categories, and products are subdivided by brand, price, age, by type or specific requirements, or other applicable criteria. Top items or categories are pulled out and displayed on the right side. Images are clear and accompany the majority of the products. In addition to the products listed in each category, the Web site provides links to other resources related to the product as well as a section titled Advice on the Product. In addition to product reviews, the Web site provides details about the products and links to stores affiliated with the parent company to allow you to purchase items directly from this site.

SOURCE EVALUATION: There are numerous ads on the top and side bars that can be annoying and distracting. The affiliation with the parent company Shopping.com is clearly stated up front. The display is similar to both Amazon.com and Shopping.com, making it familiar and comfortable for Web users. The number of reviews and products on this site is overwhelming; you could spend hours and hours looking for information on products you plan to purchase or have already purchased, so it can be a time trap. The reviews live up to the site's claims of being reliable, consistent,

Figure 6-50. Product Information Arranged by Category

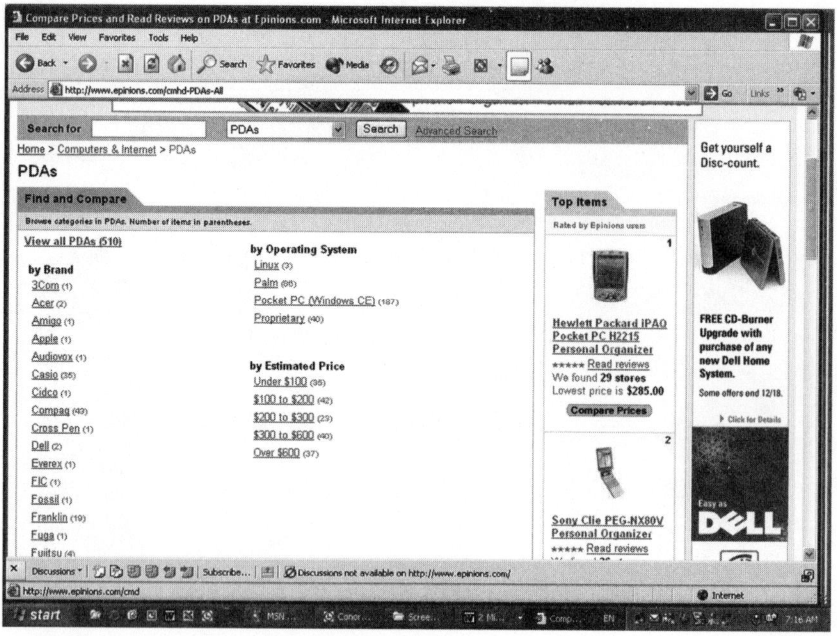

Reprinted with permission of Shopping.com.

highly opinionated, thorough, and current. For a Web site with such an enormous amount of information, the site is easy to navigate. The tabs, side bar, and search engine provide all the navigation tools needed to find your way around quickly. Though the site does not contain government statistics or other hard-core business data, it could be useful for those interested in competitive intelligence for consumer products. One other interesting fact about this Web site that is discussed in reviews and articles is the sense of community that a site like this creates, with the major focus being communication between like-minded people, rather than on the products. Users can actually get to know regular reviewers and communicate through the Web site and in person. The member center section of the site provides links to bulletin boards, chat sessions, and even meet-and-greets in various cities. Members participate in surveys and contests as well. The contact information is a bit confusing, requiring you to choose a department or person that may not fit your inquiry.

SOURCE VALUE RATING: All of the data source reviewers were asked to rate each source on the basis of the following eight categories, using "10" as the highest rating and "1" as the lowest ("80" being a perfect score):

1. Relative cost-to-value:	10
2. Relative timeliness of data:	10
3. Relative comprehensiveness of data:	10
4. Ease of use:	9
5. Search options available:	8
6. Level of support services:	6
7. Level of training offered:	6
8. Amount/kinds of special services offered:	7
Total Rating:	66

SOURCE REVIEWS:

O'Leary, Mick. 2002. Epinions Creates Top Product Community. *Information Today* (July/August): 14–15.

CONTRIBUTOR NAME: Jennifer Richard

AFFILIATION: Acadia University

USEFUL TIPS

- Set some time aside for browsing this site. You can literally spend hours and hours reading reviews.
- If you are just looking for reviews, you are not required to sign up, but if you are interested in writing reviews, you need to be a member. If this is your type of thing, Epinions is the place to do it.

PLANETFEEDBACK

ALTERNATE/PREVIOUS DATA SOURCE NAMES: Intelliseek

SERVICE/PORTAL NAME: *http://www.planetfeedback.com/consumer*

SOURCE DESCRIPTION: PlanetFeedback offers consumers an empowering forum to provide feedback based on personal shopping experiences. PlanetFeedback notes that "for every 25 people who want to give consumer feedback, only one ends up following through." The service is designed to make the follow-through easier by providing formatted business letters for the user to edit, after which PlanetFeedback sends the letter at no cost to the consumer. An individual can write letters of complaints or praise, ask a question, or offer a suggestion to the various companies listed by industry. Consumers can share warnings with each other of potential pitfalls in a company's service or product(s). Personal information is removed from the letter, and any response can be monitored from the site.

The site's FAQ section explains that PlanetFeedback pools, analyzes, and sells information submitted by consumers to companies "so they can see how they stack up compared to others in their industry." The site gives companies insight into what their customers really think about them and provides valuable information into the track records of their competitors.

Figure 6-51. PlanetFeedback's Home Page

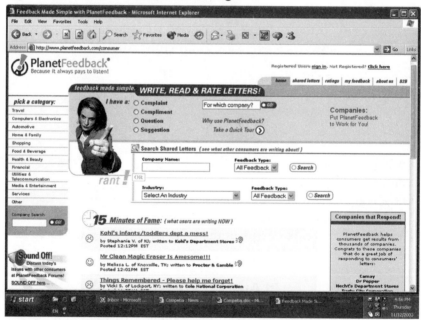

PRICING: PlanetFeedback has been a free service to consumers since its Web launch on February 17, 2000. Consumers are asked to become registered users before taking advantage of the site's various features. Basic personal information is required as well as answering a brief consumer survey. Businesses can gain market intelligence by receiving fee-based access to all shared letters by subscribing to PlanetFeedback's flagship product, BrandPulse, and other Intelliseek solutions at *http://www.intelliseek.com/solutions.asp.*

SOURCE CONTENT: The site features various ways for consumers to provide and gather feedback from fellow consumers, as well as providing the opportunity for individuals to write comments to companies. These features include the following:

1. **Write a Letter.** PlanetFeedback is all about venting. It offers two ways to find companies, either through the Search by Company feature or the Browse by Industry feature. There are four categories for a letter: a complaint, compliment, question, or suggestion. Users are then prompted to "Choose a Reason" from a drop-down menu based on a service or product (for example, Airlines have options such as Airport Check-in, Flight Scheduling, and Food Service). A five point "mood scale" is presented, from "furious" to "thrilled." One or two boxes are provided, depending on the reason for writing the letter. The first gives the opportunity to outline the details of the complaint, compliment, question, or suggestion. The second (in instances of a complaint only) is what the customer would like the company to undertake based on the problem. After answering a series of questions and selecting options for delivery, a letter is generated and PlanetFeedback sends it to the appropriate company. Personal information is optional, but it is suggested that most companies will not respond to messages without this information.

    If the search does not bring up a company from the dataset, an option for "Write it anyway" is presented and the consumer is prompted to provide as much information about the company as they can, which is then added to the PlanetFeedback database. The customer will be able to write and send a professional letter, and others will be able to find the company in the database.

2. **Shared Letters.** The PlanetFeedback service also enables users to read other letters. After every written piece of feedback, consumers are given the option of whether they would like to share their letter for others to read. Although personal information may have been attached to the letter for the company, this information can be (and some should be) removed before having the letter posted on the site. The most recent one hundred letters per company are posted to ensure currency and relevancy. Businesses can receive compiled, customized

shared letters by subscribing to PlanetFeedback's fee-based flagship product, BrandPulse.

3. **My Feedback.** The section called My Feedback can be used to gain easy access to a copy of the letter, track feedback, and monitor the status of responses and resolutions from companies. It also allows the user to resend a letter if feedback has not been received in a reasonable period of time. An In Progress–labeled letter signifies that PlanetFeedback is attempting to deliver it to the company. If the status changes, it means the letter should have been delivered. A section titled Success Stories is accessible from the home page and allows users to read customer testimonials of their experiences with companies using the PlanetFeedback service.

4. **15 Minutes of Fame.** Accessible from the home page, this feature provides a listing of selected shared letters, including the time of posting. Type of feedback is indicated by the symbols ☹ for complaints, ☺ for compliments, a ? for queries, and 💡 for suggestions. The 💬 symbol represents companies that are rated as having a good record of responding to consumers' letters.

5. **Ratings.** The Ratings section provides a "report card" of PlanetFeedback consumers' top ten best and worst rated companies, accompanied by a letter grade. One option is to search more ratings by company name or industry. Searches reveal a "letter breakdown," including percentages for the selected company or industry. A Company Report Card includes a company and industry grade, as well as averages of feedback type for the company and industry comparison. The Industry Report Card supplies an overall letter grade, rated companies included in that industry, and the top compliment and complaint percentages.

    Company and Industry Ratings are derived from the satisfaction levels reported in the letter-writing process. To be eligible for the Ratings section, a company must have received a minimum of fifty letters from PlanetFeedback registered users in the last nine months.

6. **Companies that Respond.** A brief listing on the Web site indicates which companies have a favorable response record. The link See More Companies that Respond, next to the 💬 symbol, produces a pop-up feature with an extensive alphabetical listing of companies.

7. **Sound Off!** PlanetFeedback forums are accessible under the Sound Off! link, routing users to a discussion of today's current issues. The letters are in the format of those sent to companies, which is confusing. However, this section does offer an inter-

esting aspect to the site, changing the focus to further issues beyond direct company feedback in as many varieties as there are consumer concerns.

SOURCE EVALUATION: PlanetFeedback is a success story among Internet business services. After the dot-com meltdown, its unique business strategy has emerged to combine an innovative way to make money from marketers eager to learn what consumers think of their companies and their competitors. It has also brought the power back to the consumer. Users continue to take advantage of the streamlined feedback service at no cost, better enabling them to vent, praise, question, and make suggestions to companies in various industries, including airlines, baby-food manufacturers, fast-food chains, Internet service providers, and colleges and universities.

PlanetFeedback's database is kept reasonably up-to-date. Minor criticisms include that the 15 Minutes of Fame features selected are simply a marketing technique, and that the "Sound Off!" service is somewhat cumbersome and should provide a different template than a company feedback letter form. When searching Ratings, not all companies that have received feedback in other sections of the site are included. The database content depends on the feedback from consumers and is not comprehensive.

Overall, PlanetFeedback provides a helpful service for both companies and the consumers they serve. Businesses can scan free information or investigate fee-based strategy services, such as BrandPulse for various customer data, and ExpressFeedback for Web-based tools to elicit customer opinions on a company's own Web site.

SOURCE VALUE RATING: All of the data source reviewers were asked to rate each source on the basis of the following eight categories, using "10" as the highest rating and "1" as the lowest ("80" being a perfect score):

1. Relative cost-to-value:	10
2. Relative timeliness of data:	8
3. Relative comprehensiveness of data:	7
4. Ease of use:	9
5. Search options available:	8
6. Level of support services:	8

7. Level of training offered:	7
8. Amount/kinds of special services offered:	8
Total Rating:	65

SOURCE REVIEWS:

Boehle, Sarah. Dot-com Management Grows Up. 2000. *Training* (July): 70–75. Outlines the post-dot-com Internet industry challenges and emphasizes how PlanetFeedback is cashing in on the movement toward outsourced market research innovation.

Neff, Jack. PlanetFeedback Happy to Hear Consumer Gripes. 2000. *Advertising Age* (October 2): 48–52. Describes Planet-Feedback's consumer-directed advertising campaign to increase their database of grievances, compliments, and suggestions for prospective marketers. The article highlights the company's service and business strategy.

Smith, Tom. PlanetFeedback.com Among the Fittest. 2001. *InternetWeek* (April 2): 26. Describes PlanetFeedback's market strategy in an interview with CEO Pete Blackshaw. Lists examples of companies signed to date and provides perspective on what each is looking for from the consumer-based Internet business.

CONTRIBUTOR NAME: Tanja Harrison
AFFILIATION: Acadia University

USEFUL TIPS

- Use the search function (company and/or industry) and feedback limiters to gain quick access to consumer data.
- Get a snapshot of how a company or industry stands up by using the Ratings function to generate a "report card" for company and industry comparisons.

BUREAU OF LABOR STATISTICS

ALTERNATE/PREVIOUS DATA SOURCE NAMES: Department of Labor, BLS

SERVICE/PORTAL NAME: *http://www.bls.gov*

SOURCE DESCRIPTION: According to its Web page, "The Bureau of Labor Statistics (BLS) is the principal fact-finding agency for the (United States) Federal Government in the broad field of labor economics and statistics. The BLS is an independent national statistical agency that collects, processes, analyzes, and disseminates essential statistical data to the American public, the U.S. Congress, other Federal agencies, State and local governments, business, and labor. The BLS also serves as a statistical resource to the Department of Labor."

Free of charge, the Bureau of Labor Statistics data satisfies a number of criteria, including relevance to current social and economic issues, timeliness, accuracy, and impartiality in both subject matter and presentation. The indicators provided by the BLS, including the Consumer Price Index (CPI) and the Producer Price Index (PPI), are among the major measurements of inflation.

SOURCE CONTENT: As is usual with government Web sites, the BLS site includes an almost overwhelming amount of information. This summary will deal with the main areas displayed and the information contained within these areas.

Figure 6-52. Bureau of Labor Statistics Home Page

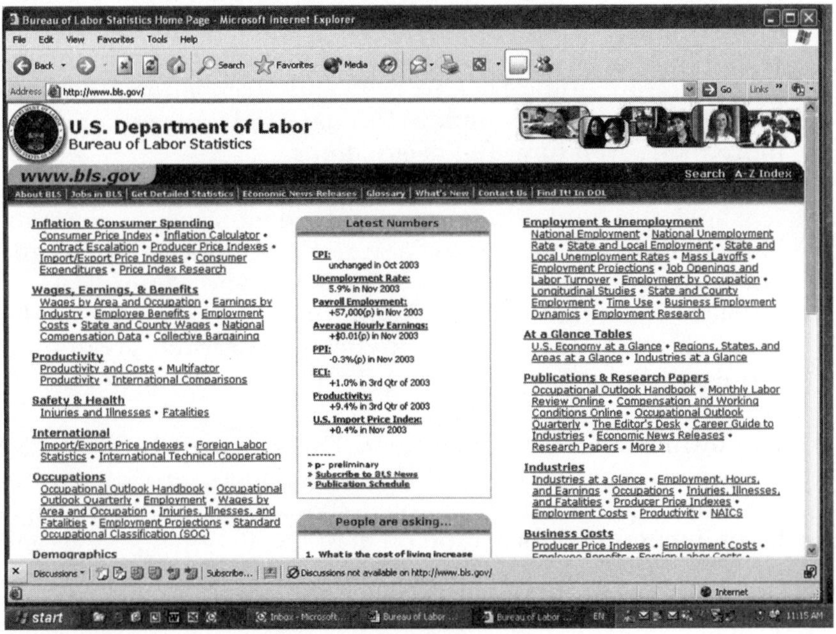

Reprinted courtesy of U.S. Bureau of Labor Statistics.

235

- **Inflation and Consumer Spending.** The main information sources in this area are the CPI, a CPI calculator, the consumer expenditure survey, the PPI, and Import/Export Price Indexes. All data is available in table format, and customized tables can be formed. Large files can be transferred using file transfer protocol (FTP). But for most users the customized tables supply the needed information.

- **Wages, Earnings, and Benefits**. Includes information on wages by area and occupation, earnings by industry, employee benefits and costs, state and county wages, national compensation data, and statistics on the collective bargaining area. As in all areas of the site, users can customize tables by using the "detailed statistics" section.

- **Productivity.** Includes productivity, costs, and international wage comparisons.

- **Safety and Health.** Consists of information on both nonfatal injuries and illnesses and fatalities, with both nationwide and participating state data. Most is available in both text and PDF formats.

- **International.** Contains Includes Import/Export Price Indexes and imports and exports searchable by Harmonized Classification systems and SITC (Standard International Trade Classifications) number.

- **Occupations.** Includes full-text access to the Occupational Outlook Handbook in a very user-friendly format. Tables are displayed separately for those with modem or slow Internet access as well as access to the Occupational Outlook Quarterly, including an archive going back to 1999 and **Occupational Employment Statistics** listing employment data and wage estimates for more than seven hundred occupations.

- **Demographics.** Demographic categories used by BLS include sex, age, race, and ethnic origin. The data by age is generally limited to people of working age, defined as sixteen years and older. Data on race generally is for blacks and whites. Data on ethnicity is confined chiefly to information on people of Hispanic origin. Areas of focus have been labor force, geographic profiles, consumer spending, and access to national longitudinal studies.

- **Employment and Unemployment.** This section provides access to employment and unemployment numbers through various reporting agencies at the national, state, county, and municipal levels, including information on mass layoffs, job openings and labor turnover, and labor projections.

- **At a Glance Tables.** Includes data for the past six months, in table format, for the main indicators: Unemployment Rate, Change in Payroll Employment, Average Hourly Earnings, Consumer Price Index, Producer Price Index, U.S. Import Price Index, Employment Cost Index, and the Productivity Index. A link is provided to annual data for ten years in table or graph format. The data is also available at the region or state level.

- **Publications and Research Papers.** Includes occupation and career guides, but perhaps most useful, it links to the online full-text edition of the *Monthly Labor Review.*

- **Industry.** This section contains information on twelve industry divisions. They are Construction, Education and Health Services, Financial Activities, Government, Information, Leisure and Hospitality, Manufacturing, Natural Resources and Mining, Other Services, Professional and Business Services, Transportation and Utilities, and Wholesale and Retail Trade. It should be noted that BLS is converting much of its sources and data from Standard Industrial Classification (SIC) to the North American Industry Classification System (NAICS) in cooperation with Canada and Mexico.

- **Geography.** This section contains many resources that are available in other sections such as employment and unemployment figures, consumer price index, and health and safety information.

- **Other Sections: BLS Information Offices & Other Statistical Sites.** These sections provide links to regional offices that provide contact information, as well as links to other federal statistical sites, such as the Census Bureau, and international sites arranged alphabetically by country.

- **Other features.** These include a comprehensive glossary, and a children's site, which also provides information for elementary school educators.

SOURCE EVALUATION: Although the sheer amount of information on this site can be overwhelming, the information is presented in a logical manner. The well-organized layout of the main page allows for the massive amount of information to be easily accessible without scrolling or having the information buried under layers of links. Some information, such as the Consumer Price Index, is available in more than one section and is therefore easily found. The At a Glance Tables section satisfies most information needs, and the ability to customize other tables is invaluable. There is also a search box, an excellent A–Z index, and a glossary. Maneuverability within the sections is not impossible, but it is much easier to return to the BLS home page (a link is available on each screen) to begin a new search. Each category, like the main page, has three consistent ready-reference sections that are very handy. They are Latest Numbers, What People Are Asking, and Regional Resources. Find It! in DOL is a nice addition, breaking down information into various categories for those who prefer to search for information that way. You can search Find It by topic, by audience, by location, by organization, by form, and by the top twenty most often requested items. Items are frequently highlighted with tags such as *updated* or *important* and *new*. The site provides a good mix of historical and current information. The dinosaur icon denotes historical information. Contact information is easy to find and gives both e-mail and telephone access to resource people, and a mailing address is at the bottom of every page.

SOURCE VALUE RATING: All of the data source reviewers were asked to rate each source on the basis of the following eight categories, using "10" as the highest rating and "1" as the lowest ("80" being a perfect score):

1. Relative cost-to-value:	10
2. Relative timeliness of data:	10
3. Relative comprehensiveness of data:	10
4. Ease of use:	7
5. Search options available:	8
6. Level of support services:	8
7. Level of training offered:	7
8. Amount/kinds of special services offered:	8
Total Rating:	68

SOURCE REVIEWS:

Webwatch [column]. 1998. *Library Journal* 123, no. 18 (November 1): 28. "Data tables download quickly and print easily. Labor demographic data with links to the full reports will be found at Economy at a Glance, Surveys and Programs, and Publications and Research Papers. Bottom Line: This site offers timely information on labor and financial demographics—a narrower mandate than the Census site."

CONTRIBUTOR NAME: Rita W. Moss / Patricia A. Watkins / Jennifer Richard

AFFILIATION: University of North Carolina–Chapel Hill / Thunderbird School of International Management / Acadia University

USEFUL TIPS

- Spend time clicking on all the data and tools.
- Make use of the e-mail alerting service for new statistical releases.
- By clicking on the detailed statistics area in each section, one can easily customize tables.

TABLEBASE

ALTERNATE/PREVIOUS DATA SOURCE NAMES: Available directly from Gale Group through the Responsive Database Services eb site or Dialog (File 93)

SERVICE/PORTAL NAME: *http://search.rdsinc.com/texis/rds/sessions/LoginForm.html*

SOURCE DESCRIPTION: TableBase is the third database produced by Responsive Database Services (RDS), Inc. This source provides direct access to tabular information from more than a thousand business sources. Sources are international in scope and include more than nine hundred journals, annual statistics reports, and public and private sector reports, and coverage goes back to 1997. Most of the sources are available in the RDS Business & Industry database. The company provides enhanced value by creating descriptive titles that aid users in finding the required data quickly and efficiently. According to the RDS promotional material, "The tables provide information such as: market share, market size, capacity, production, imports, exports, sales, product and brand rankings, forecasts, healthcare statistics and demographics." The table data, descriptive title, company name, concept term, marketing term, industry sector, product name, six-digit SIC code, and geographic location are searchable. This allows for precision searching of the exact table information, rather than keyword searching the entire document, resulting in more accurate retrieval.

Figure 6-53. TableBase Search Screen

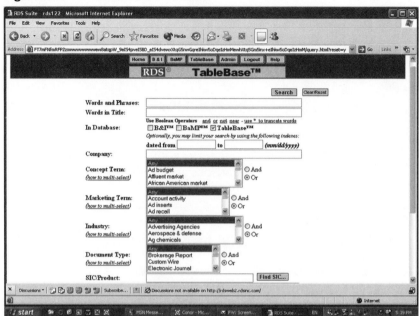

Reprinted with permission of Gale Group.

SOURCE CONTENT: Upon logging in to the product, the main screen is the search screen. The navigation across the top of the screen provides access to the RDS home page, the other two databases provided by this company, Business & Industry and Business & Management Practices, and Admin and Help.

The search screen is well organized and detailed. Brief annotations about truncation and date order are useful and do not clutter the display. The first box calls for words and phrases. This field will search the full text of the table, abstract, title, and select descriptor fields, but will not search the text accompanying the table. Boolean operators are available in this search box to facilitate more intricate search strategies. The next seven sections are controlled vocabulary choices using drop-down boxes. They are concept terms, company, marketing terms, industry, document type, SIC codes, and geographical region. Because of the number of SIC codes, they are not in a drop-down box, but do link directly from the page. At the bottom of the screen there are two source-related search options: "From a Specific Source" allows users to select a particular publication, and the "Look Up" button allows users to browse through the list of sources. Users are able to select more than one term in any of the drop-down boxes by using the control or shift key.

The results page is clear and easy to decipher. The brief display provides date, title, source, and text availability in the results list. Your search terms are highlighted in red. From this page, users are given the options of refining their search or marking documents from the list. The icon displayed in the title section links the user to the table, and the icon provided under the Text Available section links to the whole document with tables included.

Figure 6-54: Search Results Screen

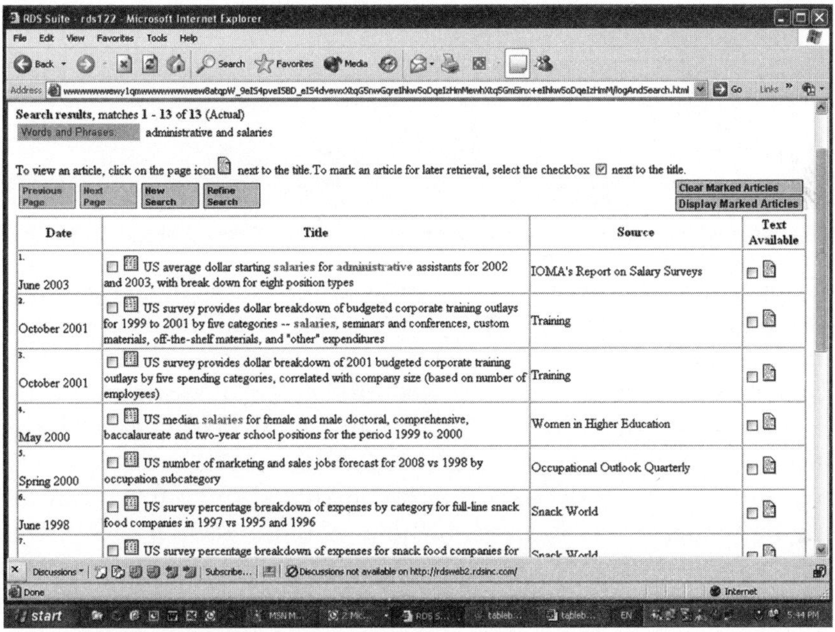

Reprinted with permission of Gale Group.

Records are well displayed with plenty of white space. The search terms are highlighted in red, but the option of turning off the highlighted terms is available. From the record screen, users can print, save, or e-mail records.

Figure 6-55. Record Display

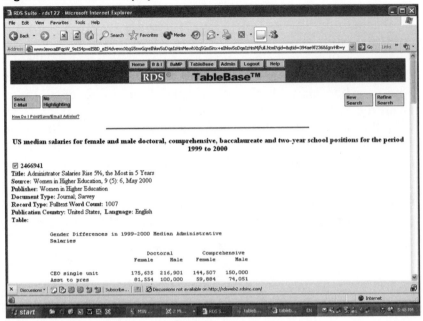

Reprinted with permission of Gale Group.

SOURCE EVALUATION: In the past, aggregator databases have often omitted table information because it is often difficult to index and display. This product fills the void created by those other products. The search screen is multifaceted, providing enough options through controlled vocabulary and keyword search boxes to satisfy novice to savvy searchers. The cost of the product is reasonable, with good discounts for academic and public libraries; perhaps this is why it seems to be a very popular choice in U.S. libraries. It is difficult to track the appropriate contact people if you don't have a subscription. Contacting your local Gale Group representative is the best way to go; once contacted they were prompt and courteous.

SOURCE VALUE RATING: All of the data source reviewers were asked to rate each source on the basis of the following eight categories, using "10" as the highest rating and "1" as the lowest ("80" being a perfect score):

1. Relative cost-to-value:	8
2. Relative timeliness of data:	8
3. Relative comprehensiveness of data:	8
4. Ease of use:	9
5. Search options available:	9
6. Level of support services:	7
7. Level of training offered:	7
8. Amount/kinds of special services offered:	7
Total Rating:	63

Source Reviews:

Mick O'Leary. 1998. TableBase Soothes Searchers' Headaches. *Information Today* (July–August).

Paula Berinstein. 1998. TableBase: numeric tables online—finally! *Online* (May–June).

Contributor Name: Jennifer Richard

Affiliation: Acadia University

USEFUL TIPS

• To become a more savvy user, check out the help options. They have well-written, detailed descriptions to help users maximize their search results.

LEXISNEXIS STATISTICAL

Alternate/Previous Data Source Names: LexisNexis Statistical Universe

Service/Portal Name: *http://web.lexis-nexis.com/statuniv*

Source Description: Through a common interface, LexisNexis Statistical allows simultaneous and unlimited searching to a world of statistical information. LexisNexis Statistical comes in two editions: Basic Edition and Research Edition. In addition, Lexis-Nexis provides Statistical Abstract and Index modules as add-on products to the Base Edition. Both options incorporate the use of

PowerTables to allow searching in the tables within documents. The Basic Edition allows searching of more than 90,000 statistical tables, with an additional 30,000 statistical tables added each year, and the Research Edition allows searching of more than 250,000 tables. According to LexisNexis, in February 2004 the total product contained more than 340,000 tables. The additional material in the Research Edition mainly comes from private sector and nonprofit organizations.

The add-on modules, which are included with the Research Edition, contain abstracts of more than two thousand international statistical publications through the Index to International Statistics, ranging from 1980 to the present; more than one thousand private and state sources back to 1983 in the Statistical Reference Index; and all of the U.S. government statistics back to 1973. Materials are updated at various intervals, some annually, some quarterly. Examples of the types of data found in these sources are income and production statistics, economic and financial indicators, cancer rates, airline fatalities, voter turnout, and educational statistics, to name only a few. Publications from 1995 to the present are available in full text, and a link directing users to your local library resources can be created for pre-1995 works. The data is provided in various formats, including gifs, text, Excel files, and PDF.

Source Content: The main section of this Web site is the search screen, as illustrated below in Figure 6-56. The search screen defaults to the PowerTables search. This search page has great options, in addition to the keyword search. The check-box limits or "breakdowns" help to narrow and optimize searches. These breakdowns are geographic, demographic, economic, and frequency of data.

The results page has two options for display: the Document List or the Table View. There are a number of options to manipulate your search at this point as well. The FOCUS option is a unique feature that allows users to search within their results list. Users can also edit the search, e-mail, or print results from this page.

There are two other options on the left-side bar. They are a link to the abstract search page, which varies slightly from the PowerTables search, and Links. The Links page provides a reasonable list of government agencies and services, university sites, and

Figure 6-56. LexisNexis Statistical Search Page

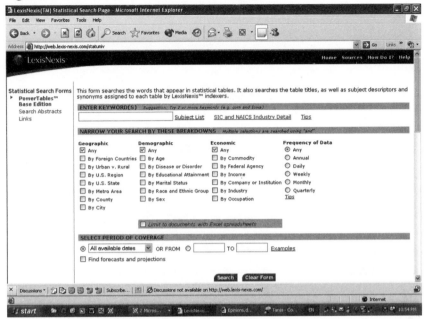

Reprinted with permission of LexisNexis. LexisNexis and FOCUS are trademarks of Reed Elsevier Properties, Inc. Used with permission of LexisNexis.

nongovernmental services with brief annotations. The other options across the top of the Web site are Sources, How Do I, and Help, which are described below:

- **Sources.** This page includes lists of the documents accessible through both the basic and the research packages. It also includes pricing information, access to a newsletter, training documents, e-mail alerts, usage statistics, brochures, and contact information.
- **How Do I.** This is basically an FAQ page. This page lists common inquiries and instructions on how to find the answers.
- **Help.** This section is divided into three areas: information about the product; primer and introductory material on statistics, including a glossary of terms; and customer support access called the LexisNexis Statistical Knowledge Basic.

Source Evaluation: This is a very good product, comprehensive with a certain amount of historical significance—thirty years' worth. In the past, tables were often left out of electronic databases or indexes, so the use of this technology to gain access to the valuable information stored in tables is crucial to this product's success. The search interface is clear and straightforward, and the

Figure 6-57. Search Results Screen

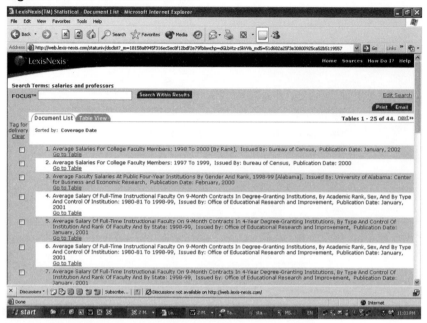

Reprinted with permission of LexisNexis. LexisNexis and FOCUS are trademarks of Reed Elsevier Properties, Inc. Used with permission of LexisNexis.

limits or "breakdowns" are easy to use. The results page is also well displayed, and the options such as printing, editing the search, and searching within results are prominent and easy to locate. However, the headings and the navigation on the rest of the site are not at all intuitive or user-friendly. The Sources page is a hodgepodge of resources with some of the materials also appearing in other sections of the Web site. Note that the option to link to the library's holdings is not quite what it seems. LexisNexis does not have the ability to link directly to sources in a library catalog or other electronic resources.

SOURCE VALUE RATING: All of the data source reviewers were asked to rate each source on the basis of the following eight categories, using "10" as the highest rating and "1" as the lowest ("80" being a perfect score):

1. Relative cost-to-value:	7
2. Relative timeliness of data:	8
3. Relative comprehensiveness of data:	8
4. Ease of use:	7

5. Search options available:	9
6. Level of support services:	7
7. Level of training offered:	9
8. Amount/kinds of special services offered:	8
Total Rating:	63

SOURCE REVIEWS:

Hurst, Jill Ann and *David M. Oldenkamp.* 2002. LexisNexis Statistical Universe. (Web Wise Ways). *Searcher* (June).

CONTRIBUTOR NAME: Jennifer Richard
AFFILIATION: Acadia University

USEFUL TIPS

- Try out the FOCUS feature. It helps you find specific terms within your search results.
- The Find More Like This feature builds a custom search screen using the subject descriptors of the specific table. The user can then decide which descriptors to use and whether or not to include additional breakdowns.

GLOBAL FINANCIAL DATA

SERVICE/PORTAL NAME: *http://www.globalfindata.com*

SOURCE DESCRIPTION: According to the Web site, "The Global Financial Database is the most complete collection of financial and economic data in the world." This product lives up to its claim, providing access to more than 6,500 historical and current data series covering more than 150 countries. This database provides long-term total return data on stocks, bonds, and bills from every major market in the world dating back to 1900. The data has been collected from numerous sources, primarily from the Internet for the current data. The historical data was gathered by converting original materials to electronic formats. Global Financial Database has purchased some of the original source data, but most of the data is obtained from public sources. The target market is people or institutions that require data pertaining to long-term historical analysis of financial markets. Their customer base consists of educational institutions, Central Banks, Wall Street investment firms, brokers, and mutual funds, as well as individuals such as investors, accountants, lawyers, and historians. Special rates are provided to educational institutions.

Figure 6-58. Global Financial Data Main Page

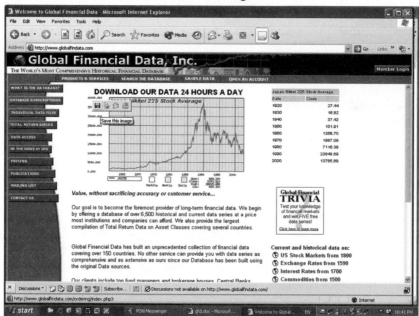

Reprinted with the permission of Global Financial Data, Inc.

The main subscription database is the Global Financial Database. It contains all 6,500 sets of data, as well as automatic downloading software, analysis software, technical indicators, and the Encyclopedia of Global Financial Markets. For more limited research needs there are subsections of the main database. Subscriptions to these databases can be acquired at a reduced cost. These subsections include the following:

1. **Long-term Financial Database.** Includes Consumer Price Indices, Wholesale Price Indices, Exchange Rates, and Futures and Commodity Prices.
2. **Interest Rate Database.** Provides Discount Rates, Eurocurrency Rates, Interbank Offer Rates, Private Discount Rates, Government Bond Yields, Corporate Bond Yields, Deposit Rates, Lending Rates, Money Market Rates, Treasury Bill Yields, Bond Prices, and Daily Interest Rates.

3. **United States Daily Stock Market Database.** Provides Dow Jones Averages, Standard & Poor's Indices, New York Stock Exchange Indices, American Stock Exchange Indices, NAS-DAQ, and Over-the-Counter Indices.

4. **Global Stock Market Database.** Contains Stock Market Indices, Total Return Indices (The Total Return Database), Stock Market Yields, and P/E Ratios.

5. **Total Return Database:** Consists of total returns on stocks, bonds, and bills for every major country in the world. This is the largest, most complete package of International Total Return Data available anywhere.

6. **Annual Database Collection:** Provides long-term financial data for the following twelve topics:
   - Government Bond Yields and Discount Rates
   - Dividend Yields and P/E Ratios
   - Total Returns on Stocks, Bonds, and Bills
   - Global Stock Market Indices
   - Capitalization, Shares Traded, and Number of Firms Listed
   - Consumer Price Indices
   - Wholesale and Producer Price Indices
   - Exchange Rates
   - Population by Country
   - Imports, Exports, and Trade Balances
   - Gross Domestic Product
   - United States Personal Income Tax Rates

7. **Dow Jones Intraday Database.** Includes the Dow Jones Industrial Average. Intraday Database includes the most extensive series of intraday data available for any index. This database provides half-hourly data back to 1987, and hourly data back to 1932. Also included are intraday data on New York Stock Exchange volume.

There are three categories of publications offered through this site as well: the GFD Encyclopedia, a number of articles written mainly by the president of the company, and detailed essays and links to a global history of currencies.

The database is fully searchable without a subscription, so you can see the data that is available before you purchase it. The search page offers the following options for searching: keyword, GFD symbol, by country, or by index category; these forty-seven index categories are then further broken down by country. The Results Page is clear and concise, giving enough information about the dataset for it to be understandable, including the GFD number, but not so much information that it clutters up the display. The record display is also clear and easy to read. The record includes the file name, a one-line description, series, country, currency, frequency information, and the number of records in the file. The Web site provides numerous files of sample data, free of charge. This data displays in the same format as the data retrieved if you have a paid subscription. The sample data illustrates the spreadsheet and graphing capabilities of this product. To graph the sample data, the graphing system has easy-to-use controls at the bottom of the page to change the dates and indicators, and to add a secondary series and conversion series. Users can plot logarithmic graphs and graph two moving averages. Descriptions of the technical indicators used for graphing are also available on the Web site.

Figure 6-59. Global Financial Search Screen

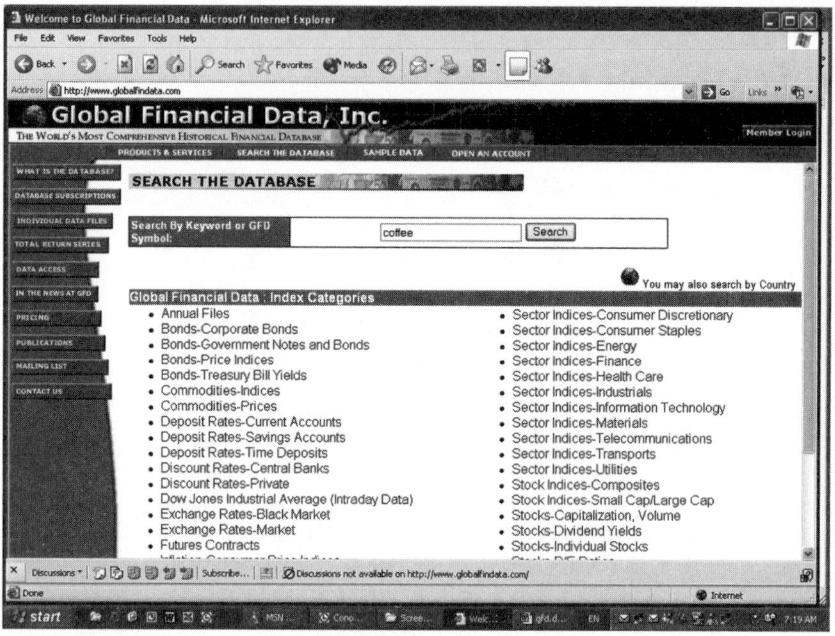

Reprinted with the permission of Global Financial Data, Inc.

SOURCE EVALUATION: Global Financial Data, Inc. is a very impressive company with a notable product. Access to the database without the full display features allows a window into the product that is not often provided by other sources. The information on the Web site is clearly displayed and well organized. Initially the search features seemed limited, but the search engine is powerful enough to be able to retrieve the data with the keyword search, and with the other indexes and geographical options, it does not seem necessary to have advanced search features on an additional screen. As for the large amounts of data available in the download files, they downloaded quickly and glitch free every time. The graphing system is simple to use, yet very powerful as an application. The subscription is a bit pricey. Full access per individual subscription is $8,000/year, though they give multiple types of subscriptions, as well as options to download individual records at a one-time cost. However, if this type of data is required for an individual or organization, this is the place to get it. Data is both historical in nature and current. This site provides more than forty datasets in the sample collection. This is definitely enough data for basic users, such as students and educators, to bookmark and make good use of this site.

SOURCE VALUE RATING: All of the data source reviewers were asked to rate each source on the basis of the following eight categories, using "10" as the highest rating and "1" as the lowest ("80" being a perfect score):

1. Relative cost-to-value:	8
2. Relative timeliness of data:	9
3. Relative comprehensiveness of data:	10
4. Ease of use:	10
5. Search options available:	8
6. Level of support services:	10
7. Level of training offered:	8
8. Amount/kinds of special services offered:	7
Total Rating:	70

CONTRIBUTOR NAME: Jennifer Richard
AFFILIATION: Acadia University

USEFUL TIPS

- Even if you cannot afford the subscription costs, this Web site is well worth bookmarking for the amount of sample data available to the general public.
- Search the database before subscribing to determine if the datasets you need are available from this source.

- Do not hesitate to contact this company by e-mail. They are friendly and respond quickly to requests.

VAULT

ALTERNATE/PREVIOUS DATA SOURCE NAMES: Vault Reports

SERVICE/PORTAL NAME: *http://www.vault.com*

SOURCE DESCRIPTION: Employment anxiety has increased in the last decade, and as a result, employment Web sites have seen a huge jump in popularity. Vault has become one of the most reputable employment sites on the Web today. Designed for employers, employees, and job seekers, it offers a valuable insiders' guide to the business world. For the competitive intelligence professional, job and employee message board postings can supply vast amounts of information and insight into developments in the structures of its competitors.

Figure 6-60. The Vault Home Page

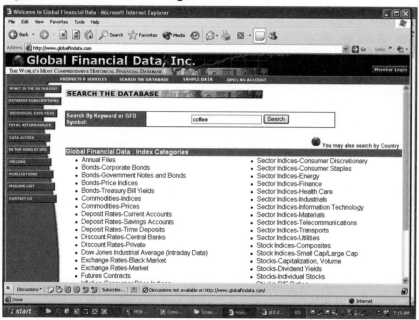

Reprinted with the permission of Vault, Inc.

PRICING: The basic membership to Vault is free, but a new fee-based service, the Vault Gold Membership, offers enhanced career and information services, including employer snapshots, detailed employer surveys, salary information, access to message board and newsletter archives, and savings on Vault guides and resume/career services. The Gold Membership is available for individual and corporate/institutional users. Individual subscriptions range from $41.70 for six months to $142.20 for three years. Corporate rates range from $1,194 for a six-month subscription to $3,564 for three years.. The longer the subscription, the more the customer saves in membership fees.

SOURCE CONTENT: The Vault site is divided into various sections to meet the information needs of its users. Accessible from the top frame are the following choices:

1. **Industries.** This page takes the user to a browsable page with links to industries broken down by subcategories. Selecting a choice presents further options and features, including employer surveys, industry profiles, job descriptions, workplace culture, top interview questions, links to current position postings in the area, and advice on starting a career in a particular industry. Much of the industry information, including profiles and employer surveys, are available only with a Gold Membership.

2. **Career Topics.** This feature includes tools to assist in selecting a career path and getting advice for admission into educational institutions. Other career topics include career change, diversity, entrepreneurship, internships, salaries, compensation, and a workplace "guide to making the most of your time on the job." Many of the full-text topics feature excerpts from Vault Guides.

3. **Companies.** The Company Research page provides a number of features to explore information about companies. Users can choose to browse alphabetically or search by company name. A quick search for companies is always available from a query box at the top of the site. There is also a Power Search for more precision searching. Searchable fields include industry, city, state, country, company type, numbers of employees, and company revenue. Company statistics, message board mentions, and brief snapshots are available with a regular membership; more detailed snapshots and surveys are available with a Gold Membership.

4. **For Employers.** This highlighted link brings hiring personnel to a page designed specifically for managers and human resource professionals. Employers can subscribe to a free HR newsletter, read daily features on workplace topics, link

Figure 6-61. Vault Brief Company Snapshot Example

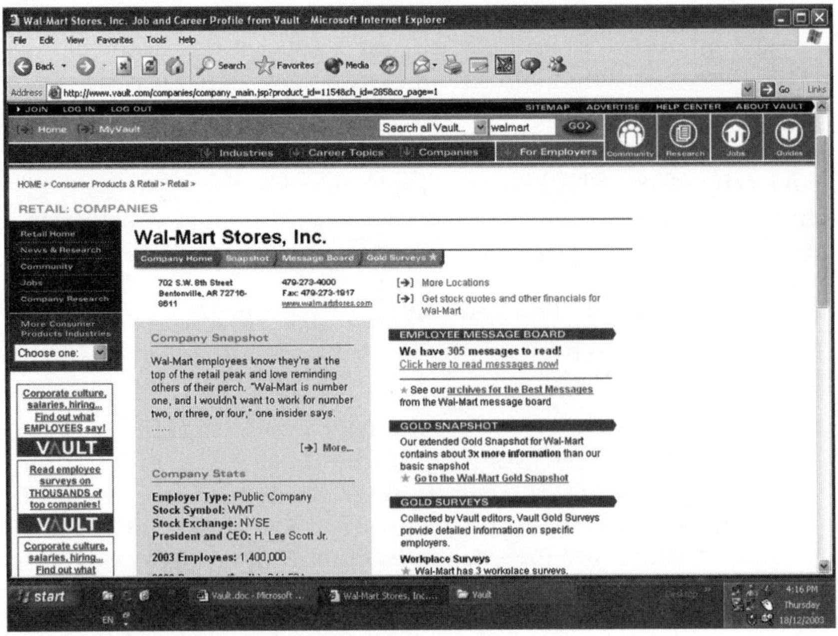

Reprinted with the permission of Vault, Inc.

directly to the recruiting message board, and post job offerings. Posting jobs is offered on an individual or unlimited subscription basis to Corporate Gold Members. Posting internship positions is a free service.

5. **Community.** Job message boards are one of the more popular features of the Vault Web site. Job seekers can gain valuable insight on potential employers, and the boards can provide the reader with lively discussions on a variety of topics to get an inside look into a company and its employees. Messages are arranged chronologically by topic to the left, including clickable discussion threads, and the message is displayed on the right-hand side of the screen. Archived messages more than sixty days old are restricted to viewing by Gold Members.

6. **Research.** The Research link provides the user with access to a variety of information offered on the Vault site collected in one place. Users can perform searches for companies with the functions available under the Companies link. There is also easy access to company snapshots, employer surveys, occupational profiles and industry overviews (available to Gold Member subscribers), and the ability to search various free newsletters offered by Vault, as well as Education Center and Guidebook links. News and Research is always searchable from the search box at the top of the Vault site.

7. **Jobs.** The job link offers the user a searchable Vault Job Board for employment postings. Fields for searching include location and function (the type and area of the desired job). An option to search jobs by keyword is also presented. The quick-search box is also available for searching jobs at the top of the Vault site. Results matching the search criteria lead to a brief information screen, including the date posted. Selecting the Job Title link takes the member to the full ad.

8. **Guides.** Published since 1997, the Vault Career Guides can be purchased from this link. All guides are available in either print or online in PDF format, with discounted rates if purchased in bulk. The recently published guides to various industries in 2003 were given favorable reviews by *Choice* magazine.

More information is available on the left frame of the main page, offering quick access links for job seekers (including a Job Search Survival guide and Expert Resume Review) and employers (including a free HR newsletter sign-up option). There is also convenient, alphabetical access to the industry pages, education starting points, and other career topics. The Help Center link has useful FAQs for descriptions and use of the variety of sections on the site.

"My Vault" is a special feature that allows users to customize and personalize their experience with Vault. It allows members to receive free e-mailed job postings that match their interests and biweekly job alerts for posted Vault board positions. It also allows the opportunity to network with other members for the "inside scoop" and career advice, and to keep track of postings in My Messages.

SOURCE EVALUATION: Outsourcing, downsizing, mergers, acquisitions, restructuring—all are realities in today's business environment. Skilled employees in lucrative industries are indispensable, and employers know they must attract and retain talented staff in this volatile job market. For job seekers and recruiters alike, Vault provides valuable tools and has been called "the most trusted name in career information."

As a Web "water cooler" site, Vault is professionally presented and is an excellent source for employment-related information. Following the trend of increasing fee-based Internet services, many of the more detailed features are available only with a Gold Membership. Paid access is indicated appropriately throughout the site with yellow stars next to each "Gold" link to more information. However, the enhanced membership is relatively inexpensive for the value, and free members should get enough information from their regular access to decide whether to invest. Privacy concerns Vault, and they use what is called Single Blind E-mail, which never displays an e-mail address on the site or in the messages sent to you by other Vault members in the Community. Instead, all e-mail goes through the Vault system and addresses are viewable only if the member responds. Your e-mail address will be displayed only if you choose to respond to someone, either from a message board posting or by searching the membership directory.

For competitive intelligence professionals, Vault is recommended. They will find various sources for employment insights, including valuable information on message boards, job ads, and employer and employee surveys while remaining anonymous. Other similar sites to try are Wetfeet (*http://www.wetfeet.com*) and Yahoo! HotJobs (*http://hotjobs.yahoo.com*).

SOURCE VALUE RATING: All of the data source reviewers were asked to rate each source on the basis of the following eight categories, using "10" as the highest rating and "1" as the lowest ("80" being a perfect score):

1. Relative cost-to-value:	9
2. Relative timeliness of data:	8
3. Relative comprehensiveness of data:	7
4. Ease of use:	9
5. Search options available:	9
6. Level of support services:	8
7. Level of training offered:	8
8. Amount/kinds of special services offered:	9
Total Rating:	67

SOURCE REVIEWS: Various Vault Career Guides, published in 2002 and 2003, are reviewed together in the December 2003 issue of *Choice* magazine. Also see the following:

Cohen, Adam. 2000. Click Here for a Hot Rumor About Your Boss. *Time* (September 11): 48. Describes the trend of "virtual water cooler" sites and provides examples of real-life companies that could have been affected by information posted on Vault.com.

Etzel, Barbara. 2001. On the Job Front, Bankers Look to Web, New Priorities. *The Investment Dealers Digest: IDD* (April 16):

1. With increasing job uncertainty in many industries, this article discusses the gaining popularity of job-related Web sites and highlights Vault.com.

CONTRIBUTOR NAME: Tanja Harrison

AFFILIATION: Acadia University

USEFUL TIPS

- Visit the Help Center link first, in the top right-hand corner of the site, for an overview of all features, products, services and membership pricing.
- Use the Power Search for better-defined results when researching companies.
- Use Search the Boards keyword search option to sift through message titles and text for specific topics.

Appendix

The source listings and source value rating surveys provided in this appendix are, by nature, very time sensitive and will certainly be dated to some extent at publication. Here is a brief overview of the origin of each appendix.

A. **Directory of Online Business Data Sources:** All of the data sources (databases) that are referred to in this volume and/or other volumes in the Business Research Solutions Series are listed alphabetically by name with the name of the publisher immediately underneath. The contact information is often slanted to public relations rather than sales or support, but each publisher handles outside queries in a different fashion.

B. **Directory of Online Business Data Publishers:** All of the publishers of business data sources are listed by publisher name in this directory followed by the names of the data sources (databases) that are owned and distributed by that publisher. The contact information that follows is identical to the first directory discussed above.

C. **Business Data Source Rating Survey:** This presentation of source ratings is in the same form as the survey in Chapter Six but has been extended to include *all* 119 business data sources covered in *all* volumes of the Business Research Solutions Series. The reader is cautioned, again, that these ratings reflect only the opinions of the contributor/reviewer and should not be viewed as the results of a large-scale national survey. Please also refer to the data source ratings section in the introduction to Chapter Six of this volume.

D. **Contributor Biographies:** The biographies of contributors to all the volumes in the series are included to the extent that was possible. Much of the credit for the problems and solutions and the data source reviews goes to the creative group of experts.

Appendix A: Directory of Online Business Data Sources

10k Wizard
> *10k Wizard Technology LLC*
> Elise Soyza
> Director, Marketing
> elise@10kwizard.com
> (214) 800-4565
> 1950 Stemmons Freeway,
> Suite 7016
> Dallas, TX 75207

ABI/Inform
> *ProQuest, Inc.*
> Tina Creguer
> Marketing/Communications
> Director
> tina.creguer@il.proquest.com
> (800) 521-0600 x3805
> 300 N. Zeeb Road, P.O. Box 1346
> Ann Arbor, MI 48106

Accounting & Tax Database
> *ProQuest, Inc.*
> Tina Creguer
> Marketing/Communications
> Director
> tina.creguer@il.proquest.com
> (800) 521-0600 x3805
> 300 N. Zeeb Road, P.O. Box 1346
> Ann Arbor, MI 48106

Accurint
> *Seisint, Inc.*
> Cathy Demarco
> cdemarco@accurint.com
> (561) 893-8008
> 6601 Park of Commerce
> Boulevard
> Boca Raton, FL 33487

Adweek
> *VNU eMedia*
> Deborah Patton
> Media Relations
> Dpatton@vnubusinessmedia.com
> (646) 654-5755
> 770 Broadway, 7th Floor
> New York, NY 10003

AICPA
> *American Institute of Certified Public*
> *Accountants*
> Edward J. Novack
> Product Marketing Director
> edward.novack@CPA2Biz.com
> (201) 521-5714
> 1211 Avenue of the Americas
> New York, NY 10036

Alacra
> *Alacra, Inc.*
> Carol Ann Thomas
> Marketing Manager
> carolann.thomas@alacra.com
> (212) 804-1541
> 88 Pine Street, 3rd Floor
> New York, NY 10005

BigCharts
> *MarketWatch.com, Inc.*
> 123 North 3rd Street
> Minneapolis, MN 55401

Bloomberg Professional

Bloomberg L.P.
　Leslie Van Ordsdel
　Bloomberg Professional
　Product Training
　lvanorsdel@bloomberg.net
　(212) 318-2244
　499 Park Avenue
　New York, NY 10022

Bondtrac

Bondtrac, Inc.
　Dan Powers
　President
　dan.powers@bondtrac.com
　(800) 555-6864
　210 Park Avenue, Suite 2200
　Oklahoma City, OK 73102

Brandweek

VNU eMedia
　Deborah Patton
　Media Relations
　Dpatton@vnubusinessmedia.com
　(646) 654-5755
　770 Broadway, 7th Floor
　New York, NY 10003

Briefing.com

Briefing.com
　Cassandra Bayna
　Media Relations
　cbayna@briefing.com
　(312) 670-4463 x232
　401 N. Michigan Avenue,
　Suite 1680
　Chicago, IL 60611

Budget and Economic Outlook

U.S. Congressional Budget Office
　William J. Gainer
　Associate Director for
　Management
　(202) 226-2600
　Ford House Office Building,
　4th Floor
　Second and D Streets SW
　Washington, DC 20515

Bureau of Economic Analysis (BEA)

U.S. Bureau of Economic Analysis
　Larry R. Moran
　Media contact
　LARRY.MORAN@BEA.GOV
　(202) 606-9691
　1441 L Street NW
　Washington, DC 20230

Bureau of Labor Statistics

U.S. Bureau of Labor Statistics
　Katharine G. Abraham
　Commissioner
　blsdata_staff@bls.gov
　(202) 606-7800
　2 Massachusetts Avenue, NE
　Washington, DC 20212

Bureau of the Census

U.S. Census Bureau
　Stephen Buckner
　Media contact
　stephen.l.buckner@census.gov
　(301) 763.2135
　U.S. Census Bureau
　Washington, DC 20233

**Bureau of the Public Debt online:
Treasury Bills, Notes, and Bonds**

U.S. Bureau of the Public Debt
　Van Zeck
　Commissioner
　OAdmin@bpd.treas.gov
　Bureau of the Public Debt
　200 3rd Street
　Parkersburg, WV 26106

Business & Industry

Thomson Learning
　Jennifer Bernardelli
　Product Manager, Thomson/Gale
　jennifer.bernardelli@thomson.com
　(800) 877-4253 x1514
　Gale Group
　27500 Drake Road
　Farmington Hills, MI 48331

Business Dateline

ProQuest, Inc.
Tina Creguer
Marketing/Communications
Director
tina.creguer@il.proquest.com
(800) 521-0600 x3805
300 N. Zeeb Road, P.O. Box 1346
Ann Arbor, MI 48106

Business Wire

Business Wire, Inc.
Sandy Malloy
Senior Information Specialist
sandy.malloy@businesswire.com
(415) 986-4422 x512
44 Montgomery Street,
39th Floor
San Francisco, CA 94104

CBS MarketWatch

MarketWatch.com, Inc.
Dan Silmore
Director, Public Relations
dsilmore@marketwatch.com
(415) 733-0534
KPIX Building
825 Battery Street, 3rd Floor
San Francisco, CA 94111

CCH Tax Research Network

CCH Incorporated
Leslie Bonacum
Media Relations
bonacuml@cch.com
(847) 267-7153
2700 Lake Cook Road
Riverwoods, IL 60015

CEOExpress

CEOExpress Company
Patricia Pomerleau
President/CEO
patpom@ceoexpressmail.com
(617) 482-1200
470 Atlantic Avenue, 4th Floor
Boston, MA 02210

Chilling Effects

Electronic Frontier Foundation
Wendy Seltzer
Founder
wendy@seltzer
Electronic Frontier Foundation
454 Shotwell Street
San Francisco, CA 94110

CI Resource Index

CISeek.com
http://www.bidigital.com/ci/

CLAIMS/U.S. Patents

IFI Claims Patent Services
Jim Brown
Customer Service
(302) 633-7200
3202 Kirkwood Highway,
Suite 203
Wilmington, DE 19808

Closed-End Fund Center

Mutual Fund Educational Association
Brian M. Smith
Media contact
bsmith@cefa.com
(816) 413-8900
P.O. Box 28037
Kansas City, MO 64188

Competia

Competia, Inc.
Elaine Boroff
(514) 270-5222
1250 Rene Levesque West,
Suite 2200
Montreal, Quebec
H3B 4W8, Canada

Corporate Affiliations

LexisNexis
Judi Schultz
Senior Public Relations Manager
judith.schultz@lexisnexis.com
(937) 865-7942
LexisNexis Group
P.O. Box 933
Dayton, OH 45401

CorporateInformation
Winthrop Corporation
Eugene Helm
EHelm@wisi.com
(800) 232-0013

Country Data
PRS Group, Inc., The
Adrian Shute
Vice President Marketing/
Public Relations
ashute@prsgroup.com
(315) 431-0511
6320 Fly Road, Suite 102, P.O.
Box 248
East Syracuse, NY 13057

CyberAlert
CyberAlert, Inc.
Joel Crosley
Director, Business Development
jcrosley@CyberAlert.com
(800) 461-7353
Foot of Broad Street
Stratford, CT 06615

D&B—Dun's Electronic Business Directory
Dun & Bradstreet, Inc.
Julie C. Hiner
Public Relations, U.S.
hinerj@dnb.com
(973) 921-5608
One Diamond Hill Road
Murray Hill, NJ 07974

D&B—Dun's Financial Records Plus
Dun & Bradstreet, Inc.
Julie C. Hiner
Public Relations, U.S.
hinerj@dnb.com
(973) 921-5608
One Diamond Hill Road
Murray Hill, NJ 07974

D&B—Dun's Market Identifiers
Dun & Bradstreet, Inc.
Julie C. Hiner
Public Relations, U.S.
hinerj@dnb.com
(973) 921-5608
One Diamond Hill Road
Murray Hill, NJ 07974

D&B Key Business Ratios (KBR) on the Web
Dun & Bradstreet, Inc.
Julie C. Hiner
Public Relations, U.S.
hinerj@dnb.com
(973) 921-5608
One Diamond Hill Road
Murray Hill, NJ 07974

D&B Million Dollar Database
Dun & Bradstreet, Inc.
Julie C. Hiner
Public Relations, U.S.
hinerj@dnb.com
(973) 921-5608
3 Sylvan Way
Parsippany, NJ 07054

DailyStocks.com
DailyStocks, Inc.
info@dailystocks.com
New York, NY 10006

Datamonitor Market Research
Datamonitor/Reuters
info@datamonitor.com
106 Baker Street
London W1M 1LA, UK

Derwent Patents Citation Index
Derwent Information
sales@derwentus.com
(703) 706-4220
14 Great Queen Street
London WC2B 5DF, UK

Dialog

Thomson Legal & Regulatory
Sandy Scherer
Director, Corporate Communications, Dialog
sandy.scherer@dialog.com
(919) 461-7354
The Dialog Corporation
11000 Regency Parkway, Suite 10
Cary, NC 27511

Disclosure Database

Thomson Financial
Kerri Shepherd
Manager, Public Relations
kerri.shepherd@tfn.com
(646) 822-2077
195 Broadway, 8th Floor
New York, NY 10007

Economic Indicators

Council of Economic Advisors
wwwadmin@gpo.gov
(888) 293-6498
Office of Electronic Information
Dissemination Services
732 N. Capitol Street
Washington, DC 20402

Economy.com

Economy.com, Inc.
Monica Mercurio
Director, Customer Service
mmercurio@economy.com
(610) 241-3362
600 Willowbrook Lane
West Chester, PA 19382

EIU ViewsWire

Economist Intelligence Unit
Jisla Escoto
Senior Contract Administrator
jislaescoto@eiu.com
(212) 554-0600
111 West 57th Street
New York, NY 10019

Encyclopedia of Associations (EA)

Thomson Learning
Jennifer Bernardelli
Product Manager, Thomson/Gale
jennifer.bernardelli@thomson.com
(800) 877-4253 x1514
Gale Group
27500 Drake Road
Farmington Hills, MI 48331

Epinions

Shopping.com
Michele Husak
Senior Manager, Public Relations
Michele@shopping.com
(650) 616-6518
8000 Marina Boulevard,
5th Floor
Brisbane, CA 94005

EventLine

Elsevier Science B.V.
Eric Merkel-Sobotta
Director, Corporate Relations
PressOffice@elsevier.com
31 20 485-2994
P.O. Box 211
NL-1000 AE Amsterdam,
Netherlands

Experian Business Credit Profiles

Experian
Donald Girard
Public Relations Director
donald.girard@experian.com
(714) 830-5647
505 City Parkway W, 3rd Floor
Orange, CA 92868

Factiva

Factiva
Gina Giamanco
Global Public Relations
gina.giamanco@factiva.com
(609) 627-2342
105 Madison Avenue, 10th Floor
New York, NY 10016

FactSet
FactSet Data Systems, Inc.
Betsy Fischer
Media Relations
efischer@factset.com
(203) 863-1500
One Greenwich Plaza
Greenwich, CT 06830

Fastcase
Fastcase, Inc.
Edward Walters
Media Relations
ed.walters@fastcase.com
(202) 466-5920
1916 Wilson Boulevard, Suite 302
Arlington, VA 22201

Federal Reserve Board
U.S. Board of Governors, Federal Reserve System
Jennifer J. Johnson
Secretary
(202) 452-3000
20th Street and Constitution Avenue NW
Washington, DC 20551

Financial Accounting Research System (FARS)
Financial Accounting Standards Board
Ron Guerrette
Vice President, Publishing
rpguerrette@f-a-f.org
(203) 847-0700 x237
FASB Research Systems
401 Merritt 7, P.O. Box 5116
Norwalk, CT 06856

Financial Accounting Standards Board (FASB)
Financial Accounting Standards Board
Sheryl L. Thompson
Public Relations Manager
slthompson@f-a-f.org
(203) 847-0700
401 Merritt 7, P.O. Box 5116
Norwalk, CT 06856

Financial Forecast Center
Institute of Business Forecasting
ibf@ibf.org
(516) 504-7576
P.O. Box 670159
Flushing, NY 11367

Financial Times
Financial Times Electronic Publishing
Gregory Roth
Public Relations Manager, U.S.
Gregory.Roth@ft.com
44 171 8257777
Fitzroy House
13-17 Epworth Street
London EC2A 4DL, UK

FindLaw
Thomson Legal & Regulatory
(650) 210-1900
1235 Pear Avenue, Suite 111
Mountain View, CA 94043

First Research
First Research, Inc.
Bobby Martin
bmartin@firstresearch.com
(888) 331-2275 x1

FreeEDGAR
EDGAR Online, Inc.
Jay Sears
Senior Vice President, Business & Strategy Development
sears@edgar-online.com
(203) 852-5669
50 Washington Street, 9th Floor
Norwalk, CT 06854

Gale Group Business A.R.T.S.
Thomson Learning
Jennifer Bernardelli
Product Manager, Thomson/Gale
jennifer.bernardelli@thomson.com
(800) 877-4253 x1514
Gale Group
27500 Drake Road
Farmington Hills, MI 48331

Gale Group New Product Announcements/Plus (NPA/Plus)
Thomson Learning
Jennifer Bernardelli
Product Manager, Thomson/Gale
jennifer.bernardelli@thomson.com
(800) 877-4253 x1514
Gale Group
27500 Drake Road
Farmington Hills, MI 48331

Gale Group Newsletter Database
Thomson Learning
Jennifer Bernardelli
Product Manager, Thomson/Gale
jennifer.bernardelli@thomson.com
(800) 877-4253 x1514
Gale Group
27500 Drake Road
Farmington Hills, MI 48331

Gale Group Trade & Industry Database
Thomson Learning
Jennifer Bernardelli
Product Manager, Thomson/Gale
jennifer.bernardelli@thomson.com
(800) 877-4253 x1514
Gale Group
27500 Drake Road
Farmington Hills, MI 48331

Global Financial Data
Global Financial Data, Inc.
Bryan Taylor
btaylor@globalfindata.com
(877) 328-2999
784 Fremont Villas
Los Angeles, CA 90042

Global Insight
Global Insight, Inc.
Ken McGill
ken.mcgill@globalinsight.com
(610) 490-2644
1000 Winter Street, Suite 4300N
Waltham, MA 02451

GPO Access
Superintendent of Documents, U.S. Government Printing Office
gpoaccess@gpo.gov
(888) 293-6498
U.S. Government Printing Office
732 North Capitol Street, NW
Washington, DC 20401

Hoover's Online
Dun & Bradstreet, Inc.
Lisa Glass
Public Relations Manager
lglass@hoovers.com
(512) 374-4662
5800 Airport Boulevard
Austin, TX 78752

INPADOC/Families and Legal Status
European Patent Office
Elena Sereix
Database Online Services
maes@epo.e-mail.com
(431) 521 26 40 51
Information Service
Schottenfeldgasse 29 Postfach 82
A-1072 Vienna, Austria

Internal Revenue Service: The Digital Daily
Internal Revenue Service, Department of the Treasury
Robert E. Wenzel
Commissioner
1111 Constitution Avenue NW, Room 1552
Washington, DC 20224

International Accounting Standards Board
International Accounting Standards Board
Tom Seidenstein
Media contact
tseidenstein@iasb.org.uk
44 20 7246 6410
30 Cannon Street
London EC4M 6XH, UK

Investext
Thomson Financial
Kerri Shepherd
Manager, Public Relations
kerri.shepherd@tfn.com
(646) 822-2077
195 Broadway, 8th Floor
New York, NY 10007

IPO Express
EDGAR Online, Inc.
Jay Sears
Senior Vice President, Business
& Strategy Development
sears@edgar-online.com
(203) 852-5669
50 Washington Sreet, 9th Floor
Norwalk, CT 06854

IPO.com
IPO Group, Inc.
DeWayne Martin
Publisher
dmartin@ipo.com
(212) 918-4510
48 Wall Street, Suite 1100
New York, NY 10005

KnowX
ChoicePoint Asset Company
Jane Rafedie
jane.rafeedie@choicepoint.com
(404) 541-0300

Law Digest
LexisNexis
Judi Schultz
Senior Public Relations Manager
judith.schultz@lexisnexis.com
(937) 865-7942
LexisNexis Group
P.O. Box 933
Dayton, OH 45401

Lawyers.com
LexisNexis
Judi Schultz
Senior Public Relations Manager
judith.schultz@lexisnexis.com
(937) 865-7942
LexisNexis Group
P.O. Box 933
Dayton, OH 45401

Legal Information Institute (LII)
*Legal Information Institute/Cornell
Law School*
Thomas R. Bruce and
Peter W. Martin
Co-Directors
lii@lii.law.cornell.edu
Cornell Law School
Myron Taylor Hall
Ithaca, NY 14853

LexisNexis
LexisNexis
Judi Schultz
Senior Public Relations Manager
judith.schultz@lexisnexis.com
(937) 865-7942
LexisNexis Group
P.O. Box 933
Dayton, OH 45401

LexisNexis (Public Records)
LexisNexis
Judi Schultz
Senior Public Relations Manager
judith.schultz@lexisnexis.com
(937) 865-7942
LexisNexis Group
P.O. Box 933
Dayton, OH 45401

LexisNexis Statistical
LexisNexis
Judi Schultz
Senior Public Relations Manager
judith.schultz@lexisnexis.com
(937) 865-7942
LexisNexis Group
P.O. Box 933
Dayton, OH 45401

lexisONE

LexisNexis
Judi Schultz
Senior Public Relations Manager
judith.schultz@lexisnexis.com
(937) 865-7942
LexisNexis Group
P.O. Box 933
Dayton, OH 45401

Lipper Horizon

Reuters
Camilla Altamura
Media Relations Manager
Camilla.Altamura@lipper.
reuters.com
(877) 955-4773
3 Times Square, 17th Floor
New York, NY 10036

Litigation Stock Report

Thomson Media
Paul E. McGowan
Editor-in-Chief
pmcgowan@lsrmail.com
(804) 282-7026
P.O. Box 18322
Richmond, VA 23226

LIVEDGAR

Global Securities Information, Inc.
Bob Brooks
Marketing/Public Relations
Director
bbrooks@gsionline.com
(202) 628-1155
419 7th Street NW, Suite 300
Washington, DC 20004

LLRX.com

Law Library Resource Xchange LLC
Sabrina Pacifici
President/CEO
spacific@earthlink.net

Loislaw

Aspen Publishers
Marc Jennings
Publisher
marc.jennings@
aspenpublishers.com
(646) 728-3001 x423
1185 Avenue of the Americas
New York, NY 10036

Market Share Reporter

Thomson Learning
Jennifer Bernardelli
Product Manager, Thomson/Gale
jennifer.bernardelli@thomson.com
(800) 877-4253 x1514
Gale Group
27500 Drake Road
Farmington Hills, MI 48331

MarketResearch.com

MarketResearch.com, Inc.
Robert Granader
CEO
rgranader@marketresearch.com
(301) 468-3650 x216
11810 Parklawn Drive
Rockville, MD 20852

Markets & Industry Library on LexisNexis

LexisNexis
Judi Schultz
Senior Public Relations Manager
judith.schultz@lexisnexis.com
(937) 865-7942
LexisNexis Group
P.O. Box 933
Dayton, OH 45401

MarkMonitor

MarkMonitor, Inc.
Elisa Cooper
Director of Marketing
elisa.cooper@markmonitor.com
(208) 389-5779
12438 W. Bridge Street, Suite 100
Boise, ID 83713

Mergent Online
Mergent FIS, Inc.
Kimberly Pile
Human Resources
hr@mergent.com
(800) 342-5647
60 Madison Avenue, 6th Floor
New York, NY 10010

MindBranch
MindBranch, Inc.
Sharon Oakes
Director, Marketing
soakes@mindbranch.com
(413) 458-7673
160 Water Street
Williamstown, MA 01267

Morningstar
Morningstar, Inc.
Martha Conlon Moss
Corporate Communications
martha.moss@morningstar.com
(312) 696-6050
225 W. Wacker Drive
Chicago, IL 60606

MSN Money
Microsoft Corporation
Microsoft Corporation
One Microsoft Way
Redmond, WA 98052

Multex Fundamentals
Multex, Inc.
Samantha Topping
Media contact
stopping@multex.com
(917) 294-0329
100 William Street, 7th Floor
New York, NY 10038

National Law Library
Juri Search
Satish Sheth
President
ssheth@jurisearch.com
(877) 484-7529
4301 Windfern Road, Suite 200
Houston, TX 77041

News on LexisNexis
LexisNexis
Judi Schultz
Senior Public Relations Manager
judith.schultz@lexisnexis.com
(937) 865-7942
LexisNexis Group
P.O. Box 933
Dayton, OH 45401

OneSource
OneSource Information Services
Ed Hutchinson
Director, Public Relations
Edward_Hutchinson@
onesource.com
(978) 318-4300
300 Baker Avenue, Suite 303
Concord, MA 01742

PatentWeb
Information Holdings, Inc. (MicroPatent)
Laura Gaze
Marketing/Communications
Director
lgaze@micropatent.com
(203) 466-5055 x205
MicroPatent USA
250 Dodge Avenue
East Haven, CT 06512

PatSearch FullText
Information Holdings, Inc. (MicroPatent)
Laura Gaze
Marketing/Communications
Director
lgaze@micropatent.com
(203) 466-5055 x205
MicroPatent USA
250 Dodge Avenue
East Haven, CT 06512

PlanetFeedback
Intelliseek, Inc.
Sue MacDonald
smacdonald@intelliseek.com
(800) 333-3222
1128 Main Street
Cincinnati, OH 45210

Profound
Thomson Legal & Regulatory
Sandy Scherer
Director, Corporate Communications, Dialog
sandy.scherer@dialog.com
(919) 461-7354
The Dialog Corporation
11000 Regency Parkway, Suite 10
Cary, NC 27511

PROMT
Thomson Learning
Jennifer Bernardelli
Product Manager, Thomson/Gale
jennifer.bernardelli@thomson.com
(800) 877-4253 x1514
Gale Group
27500 Drake Road
Farmington Hills, MI 48331

Reuters Business Insight
Datamonitor/Reuters
info@datamonitor.com
106 Baker Street
London W1M 1LA, UK

RMA's Annual Statement Studies
Risk Management Association, The
Kathleen Beans
Public Relations Manager/
Senior Writer
kbeans@rmahq.org
(215) 446-4095
1650 Market Street, Suite 2300
Philadelphia, PA 19103

SAEGIS
Thomson Legal & Regulatory
Scott Rutherford
Senior Marketing Communications Specialist
Scott.Rutherford@t-t.com
(617) 376-7667
Thomson & Thomson
500 Victory Road
North Quincy, MA 02171

SDC Platinum
Thomson Financial
Kerri Shepherd
Manager, Public Relations
kerri.shepherd@tfn.com
(646) 822-2077
195 Broadway, 8th Floor
New York, NY 10007

SEDAR
CDS, Inc.
Dan Barsi
dbarsi@cds.ca
(416) 365-3788
85 Richmond Street West
Toronto, Ontario
M5H 2C9, Canada

SmartMoney
Dow Jones & Company, Inc. & Hearst Communications, Inc.
Amy Knapp
Public Relations
aknapp@smartmoney.com
(212) 649-2765
250 W. 55th Street, 10th Floor
New York, NY 10019

Standard & Poor's NetAdvantage
McGraw-Hill
Burt Shulman
Vice President, Marketing
Services & Publishing
burt_shulman@
standardandpoors.com
(212) 438-1288
55 Water Street
New York, NY 10041

TableBase
Thomson Learning
Jennifer Bernardelli
Product Manager, Thomson/Gale
jennifer.bernardelli@thomson.com
(800) 877-4253 x1514
Gale Group
27500 Drake Road
Farmington Hills, MI 48331

The Virtual Chase
Ballard Spahr Andrews & Ingersoll LLP
Genie Tyburski
Web Manager, The Virtual Chase
tyburski@virtualchase.com
(215) 665-8500
1735 Market Street, 51st Floor
Philadelphia, PA 19103

The Wall Street Transcript
The Wall Street Transcript
Andrew Pickup
CEO/Publisher
pickup@twst.com
(212) 952-7437
67 Wall Street, 16th Floor
New York, NY 10005

TheStreet.com
TheStreet.com
Wendy Tullo
Media contact
wendy.tullo@thestreet.com
(212) 321-5000
14 Wall Street
New York, NY 10005

Thomas Register
Thomas Publishing Company
Ruth Hurd
Publisher
RHURD@trpublication.com
(212) 290-7277
TR User Services
Five Penn Plaza, 12th floor
New York, NY 10001

Thomas: Legislative Information on the Internet
Library of Congress
thomas@loc.gov
(202) 707-5000
101 Independence Avenue, SE
Washington, DC 20540

Thomson Analytics
Thomson Financial
Kerri Shepherd
Manager, Public Relations
kerri.shepherd@tfn.com
(646) 822-2077
195 Broadway, 8th Floor
New York, NY 10007

Thomson Research
Thomson Financial
Kerri Shepherd
Manager, Public Relations
kerri.shepherd@tfn.com
(646) 822-2077
195 Broadway, 8th Floor
New York, NY 10007

Trademark Applications and Registrations Retrieval (TARR)
U.S. Patent and Trademark Office
James E. Rogan
Director
usptoinfo@uspto.gov
(800) 786-9199
General Information Services
Division
Crystal Plaza 3, Room 2C02
Washington, DC 20231

Trademark Electronic Search System (TESS)
U.S. Patent and Trademark Office
James E. Rogan
Director
usptoinfo@uspto.gov
(800) 786-9199
General Information Services
Division
Crystal Plaza 3, Room 2C02
Washington, DC 20231

Trademark.com
Information Holdings, Inc. (MicroPatent)
Laura Gaze
Marketing/Communications
Director
lgaze@micropatent.com
(203) 466-5055 x205
250 Dodge Avenue
East Haven, CT 06512

TRADEMARKSCAN
Thomson Legal & Regulatory
Scott Rutherford
Senior Marketing Communications Specialist
Scott.Rutherford@t-t.com
(617) 376-7667
Thomson & Thomson
500 Victory Road
North Quincy, MA 02171

U.S. Consumer Product Safety Commission
U.S. Consumer Product Safety Commission
info@cpsc.gov
(301) 504-6816
4330 East-West Highway
Bethesda, Maryland 20814

U.S. Copyright Office
U.S. Copyright Office, Library of Congress
Marybeth Peters
Register of Copyrights
101 Independence Avenue, SE
Washington, DC 20559

U.S. Copyrights
Thomson Legal & Regulatory
Sandy Scherer
Director, Corporate Communications, Dialog
sandy.scherer@dialog.com
(919) 461-7354
The Dialog Corporation
11000 Regency Parkway, Suite 10
Cary, NC 27511

U.S. Patents Fulltext
Thomson Legal & Regulatory
Sandy Scherer
Director, Corporate Communications, Dialog
sandy.scherer@dialog.com
(919) 461-7354
The Dialog Corporation
11000 Regency Parkway, Suite 10
Cary, NC 27511

U.S. Securities and Exchange Commission
U.S. Securities and Exchange Commission
Harvey L. Pitt
Chairman
help@sec.gov
(202) 942-7040
Office of Investor Education and Assistance
450 Fifth Street, NW
Washington, DC 20549

USADATA
USADATA, Inc.
Dominic LeClaire
Director of Marketing
dleclaire@usadata.com
(212) 679-1411 x222
292 Madison Avenue, 3rd Floor
New York, NY 10017

USPTO
U.S. Patent and Trademark Office
James E. Rogan
Director
usptoinfo@uspto.gov
(800) 786-9199
Office of Electronic Information Products
Crystal Plaza 3, Suite 441
Washington, DC 20231

Value Line

Value Line
David Henigson
dhenigson@valueline.com
(212) 907-1500
Institutional Services
220 E. 42nd Street
New York, NY 10017

Vault

Vault, Inc.
Mark Oldman
mark@vault.com

VersusLaw

VersusLaw, Inc.
Jim Corbett
Vice President, Business
Development
jcorbett@versuslaw.com
(888) 377-8752 x3024
2613 - 151st Place NE
Redmond, WA 98052

Wall Street City ProStation

Telescan, Inc.
Dan Olson
Media contact
dan@investools.com
(281) 588-9700
5959 Corporate Drive,
Suite LL250
Houston, TX 77036

Wall Street Journal (WSJ)

Dow Jones & Company, Inc.
Aaron Bedy
aaron.bedy@dowjones.com
(609) 520-7889
P.O. Box 300
Princeton, NJ 08543

Westlaw

Thomson Legal & Regulatory
Ruth Orrick
Senior Vice President, Corporate Communications
ruth.orrick@westgroup.com
(651) 687-4099
West Group
610 Opperman Drive
Eagan, MN 55123

White House Economic Statistics Briefing Room

White House, The
feedback@whitehouse.gov
(202) 456-1414
1600 Pennsylvania Avenue, NW
Washington, DC 20500

Yahoo! Bond Center

Yahoo! Inc.
Chris Castro
Chief Communications Officer,
Senior Vice President
(408) 349-3300
701 First Avenue
Sunnyvale, CA 94089

Yahoo! Finance

Yahoo! Inc.
Chris Castro
Chief Communications Officer,
Senior Vice President
(408) 349-3300
701 First Avenue
Sunnyvale, CA 94089

Zacks

Zacks Investment Research
support@zacks.com
(800) 767-3771
155 N. Wacker Drive
Chicago, IL 60606

Appendix B: Directory of Online Business Data Source Publishers

10k Wizard Technology LLC
10k Wizard
Elise Soyza
Director, Marketing
elise@10kwizard.com
(214) 800-4565
1950 Stemmons Freeway,
Suite 7016
Dallas, TX 75207

Alacra, Inc.
Alacra
Carol Ann Thomas
Marketing Manager
carolann.thomas@alacra.com
(212) 804-1541
88 Pine Street, 3rd Floor
New York, NY 10005

American Institute of Certified Public Accountants
AICPA
Edward J. Novack
Product Marketing Director
edward.novack@CPA2Biz.com
(201) 521-5714
1211 Avenue of the Americas
New York, NY 10036

Aspen Publishers
Loislaw
Marc Jennings
Publisher
marc.jennings@
aspenpublishers.com
(646) 728-3001 x423
1185 Avenue of the Americas
New York, NY 10036

Ballard Spahr Andrews & Ingersoll LLP
The Virtual Chase
Genie Tyburski
Web Manager, The Virtual Chase
tyburski@virtualchase.com
(215) 665-8500
1735 Market Street, 51st Floor
Philadelphia, PA 19103

Bloomberg L.P.
Bloomberg Professional
Leslie Van Ordsdel
Bloomberg Professional Product
Training
lvanorsdel@bloomberg.net
(212) 318-2244
499 Park Avenue
New York, NY 10022

Bondtrac, Inc.
Bondtrac
Dan Powers
President
dan.powers@bondtrac.com
(800) 555-6864
210 Park Avenue, Suite 2200
Oklahoma City, OK 73102

Briefing.com
Briefing.com
Cassandra Bayna
Media Relations
cbayna@briefing.com
(312) 670-4463 x232
401 N. Michigan Avenue,
Suite 1680
Chicago, IL 60611

Business Wire, Inc.
Business Wire
Sandy Malloy
Senior Information Specialist
sandy.malloy@businesswire.com
(415) 986-4422 x512
44 Montgomery Street, 39th Floor
San Francisco, CA 94104

CCH Incorporated
CCH Tax Research Network
Leslie Bonacum
Media Relations
bonacuml@cch.com
(847) 267-7153
2700 Lake Cook Road
Riverwoods, IL 60015

CDS, Inc.
SEDAR
Dan Barsi
dbarsi@cds.ca
(416) 365-3788
85 Richmond Street West
Toronto, Ontario
M5H 2C9, Canada

CEOExpress Company
CEOExpress
Patricia Pomerleau
President/CEO
patpom@ceoexpressmail.com
(617) 482-1200
470 Atlantic Avenue, 4th Floor
Boston, MA 02210

ChoicePoint Asset Company
KnowX
Jane Rafedie
jane.rafeedie@choicepoint.com
(404) 541-0300

CISeek.com
CI Resource Index
http://www.bidigital.com/ci/

Competia, Inc.
Competia
Elaine Boroff
(514) 270-5222
1250 Rene Levesque West,
Suite 2200
Montreal, Quebec
H3B 4W8, Canada

Council of Economic Advisors
Economic Indicators
wwwadmin@gpo.gov
(888) 293-6498
Office of Electronic Information
Dissemination Services
732 N. Capitol Street
Washington, DC 20402

CyberAlert, Inc.
CyberAlert
Joel Crosley
Director, Business Development
jcrosley@CyberAlert.com
(800) 461-7353
Foot of Broad Street
Stratford, CT 06615

DailyStocks, Inc.
DailyStocks.com
info@dailystocks.com
New York, NY 10006

Datamonitor/Reuters
Datamonitor Market Research
Reuters Business Insight
info@datamonitor.com
106 Baker Street
London W1M 1LA, UK

Derwent Information
Derwent Patents Citation Index
sales@derwentus.com
(703) 706-4220
14 Great Queen Street
London WC2B 5DF, UK

Dow Jones & Company, Inc.
Wall Street Journal (WSJ)
Aaron Bedy
aaron.bedy@dowjones.com
(609) 520-7889
P.O. Box 300
Princeton, NJ 08543

Dow Jones & Company, Inc. & Hearst Communications, Inc.
SmartMoney
Amy Knapp
Public Relations
aknapp@smartmoney.com
(212) 649-2765
250 W. 55th Street, 10th Floor
New York, NY 10019

Dun & Bradstreet, Inc.
D&B—Dun's Electronic Business Directory
D&B—Dun's Financial Records Plus
D&B—Dun's Market Identifiers
D&B Key Business Ratios (KBR) on the Web
D&B Million Dollar Database
Julie C. Hiner
Public Relations, U.S.
hinerj@dnb.com
(973) 921-5608
3 Sylvan Way
Parsippany, NJ 07054

Hoover's Online
Dun & Bradstreet, Inc.
Lisa Glass
Public Relations Manager
lglass@hoovers.com
(512) 374-4662
5800 Airport Boulevard
Austin, TX 78752

Economist Intelligence Unit
EIU ViewsWire
Jisla Escoto
Senior Contract Administrator
jislaescoto@eiu.com
(212) 554-0600
111 West 57th Street
New York, NY 10019

Economy.com, Inc.
Economy.com
Monica Mercurio
Director, Customer Service
mmercurio@economy.com
(610) 241-3362
600 Willowbrook Lane
West Chester, PA 19382

EDGAR Online, Inc.
FreeEDGAR
IPO Express
Jay Sears
Senior Vice President, Business & Strategy Development
sears@edgar-online.com
(203) 852-5669
50 Washington Sreet, 9th Floor
Norwalk, CT 06854

Electronic Frontier Foundation
Chilling Effects
Wendy Seltzer
Founder
wendy@seltzer
Electronic Frontier Foundation
454 Shotwell Street
San Francisco, CA 94110

Elsevier Science B.V.
EventLine
Eric Merkel-Sobotta
Director, Corporate Relations
PressOffice@elsevier.com
31 20 485-2994
P.O. Box 211
NL-1000 AE Amsterdam, Netherlands

European Patent Office
INPADOC/Families and Legal Status
Elena Sereix
Database Online Services
maes@epo.e-mail.com
(431) 521 26 40 51
Information Service
Schottenfeldgasse 29 Postfach 82
A-1072 Vienna, Austria

Experian

Experian Business Credit Profiles
Donald Girard
Public Relations Director
donald.girard@experian.com
(714) 830-5647
505 City Parkway W, 3rd Floor
Orange, CA 92868

Factiva

Factiva
Gina Giamanco
Global Public Relations
gina.giamanco@factiva.com
(609) 627-2342
105 Madison Avenue, 10th Floor
New York, NY 10016

FactSet Data Systems, Inc.

FactSet
Betsy Fischer
Media Relations
efischer@factset.com
(203) 863-1500
One Greenwich Plaza
Greenwich, CT 06830

Fastcase, Inc.

Fastcase
Edward Walters
Media Relations
ed.walters@fastcase.com
(202) 466-5920
1916 Wilson Boulevard, Suite 302
Arlington, VA 22201

Financial Accounting Standards Board

*Financial Accounting Research System
(FARS)*
Ron Guerrette
Vice President, Publishing
rpguerrette@f-a-f.org
(203) 847-0700 x237
FASB Research Systems
401 Merritt 7, P.O. Box 5116
Norwalk, CT 06856

*Financial Accounting Standards Board
(FASB)*
Sheryl L. Thompson
Public Relations Manager
slthompson@f-a-f.org
(203) 847-0700
401 Merritt 7, P.O. Box 5116
Norwalk, CT 06856

Financial Times Electronic Publishing

Financial Times
Gregory Roth
Public Relations Manager, U.S.
Gregory.Roth@ft.com
44 171 8257777
Fitzroy House
13-17 Epworth Street
London EC2A 4DL, UK

First Research, Inc.

First Research
Bobby Martin
bmartin@firstresearch.com
(888) 331-2275 x1

Global Financial Data, Inc.

Global Financial Data
Bryan Taylor
btaylor@globalfindata.com
(877) 328-2999
784 Fremont Villas
Los Angeles, CA 90042

Global Insight, Inc.

Global Insight
Ken McGill
ken.mcgill@globalinsight.com
(610) 490-2644
1000 Winter Street, Suite 4300N
Waltham, MA 02451

Global Securities Information, Inc.
LIVEDGAR
Bob Brooks
Marketing/Public Relations
Director
bbrooks@gsionline.com
(202) 628-1155
419 7th Street NW, Suite 300
Washington, DC 20004

IFI Claims Patent Services
CLAIMS/U.S. Patents
Jim Brown
Customer Service
(302) 633-7200
3202 Kirkwood Highway,
Suite 203
Wilmington, DE 19808

**Information Holdings, Inc.
(MicroPatent)**
PatentWeb
PatSearch FullText
Trademark.com
Laura Gaze
Marketing/Communications
Director
lgaze@micropatent.com
(203) 466-5055 x205
250 Dodge Avenue
East Haven, CT 06512

Institute of Business Forecasting
Financial Forecast Center
ibf@ibf.org
(516) 504-7576
P.O. Box 670159
Flushing, NY 11367

Intelliseek, Inc.
PlanetFeedback
Sue MacDonald
smacdonald@intelliseek.com
(800) 333-3222
1128 Main Street
Cincinnati, OH 45210

**Internal Revenue Service, Department
of the Treasury**
*Internal Revenue Service: The Digital
Daily*
Robert E. Wenzel
Commissioner
1111 Constitution Avenue NW,
Room 1552
Washington, DC 20224

**International Accounting Standards
Board**
*International Accounting
Standards Board*
Tom Seidenstein
Media contact
tseidenstein@iasb.org.uk
44 20 7246 6410
30 Cannon Street
London EC4M 6XH, UK

IPO Group, Inc.
IPO.com
DeWayne Martin
Publisher
dmartin@ipo.com
(212) 918-4510
48 Wall Street, Suite 1100
New York, NY 10005

Juri Search
National Law Library
Satish Sheth
President
ssheth@jurisearch.com
(877) 484-7529
4301 Windfern Road, Suite 200
Houston, TX 77041

Law Library Resource Xchange LLC
LLRX.com
Sabrina Pacifici
President/CEO
spacific@earthlink.net

Legal Information Institute/Cornell Law School
Legal Information Institute (LII)
Thomas R. Bruce and
Peter W. Martin
Co-Directors
lii@lii.law.cornell.edu
Cornell Law School
Myron Taylor Hall
Ithaca, NY 14853

LexisNexis
Corporate Affiliations
Law Digest
Lawyers.com
LexisNexis
LexisNexis (Public Records)
LexisNexis Statistical
lexisONE
Markets & Industry Library on Lexis-Nexis
News on LexisNexis
Judi Schultz
Senior Public Relations Manager
judith.schultz@lexisnexis.com
(937) 865-7942
LexisNexis Group
P.O. Box 933
Dayton, OH 45401

Library of Congress
Thomas: Legislative Information on the Internet
thomas@loc.gov
(202) 707-5000
101 Independence Avenue, SE
Washington, DC 20540

MarketResearch.com, Inc.
MarketResearch.com
Robert Granader
CEO
rgranader@marketresearch.com
(301) 468-3650 x216
11810 Parklawn Drive
Rockville, MD 20852

MarketWatch.com, Inc.
BigCharts
123 North 3rd Street
Minneapolis, MN 55401
CBS MarketWatch
Dan Silmore
Director, Public Relations
dsilmore@marketwatch.com
(415) 733-0534
KPIX Building
825 Battery Street, 3rd Floor
San Francisco, CA 94111

MarkMonitor, Inc.
MarkMonitor
Elisa Cooper
Director of Marketing
elisa.cooper@markmonitor.com
(208) 389-5779
12438 W. Bridge Street, Suite 100
Boise, ID 83713

McGraw-Hill
Standard & Poor's NetAdvantage
Burt Shulman
Vice President, Marketing Services & Publishing
burt_shulman@standardandpoors.com
(212) 438-1288
55 Water Street
New York, NY 10041

Mergent FIS, Inc.
Mergent Online
Kimberly Pile
Human Resources
hr@mergent.com
(800) 342-5647
60 Madison Avenue, 6th Floor
New York, NY 10010

Microsoft Corporation
MSN Money
Microsoft Corporation
One Microsoft Way
Redmond, WA 98052

MindBranch, Inc.
MindBranch
Sharon Oakes
Director, Marketing
soakes@mindbranch.com
(413) 458-7673
160 Water Street
Williamstown, MA 01267

Morningstar, Inc.
Morningstar
Martha Conlon Moss
Corporate Communications
martha.moss@morningstar.com
(312) 696-6050
225 W. Wacker Drive
Chicago, IL 60606

Multex, Inc.
Multex Fundamentals
Samantha Topping
Media contact
stopping@multex.com
(917) 294-0329
100 William Street, 7th Floor
New York, NY 10038

Mutual Fund Educational Association
Closed-End Fund Center
Brian M. Smith
Media contact
bsmith@cefa.com
(816) 413-8900
P.O. Box 28037
Kansas City, MO 64188

OneSource Information Services
OneSource
Ed Hutchinson
Director, Public Relations
Edward_Hutchinson@
onesource.com
(978) 318-4300
300 Baker Avenue, Suite 303
Concord, MA 01742

ProQuest, Inc.
ABI/Inform
Accounting & Tax Database
Business Dateline
Tina Creguer
Marketing/Communications
Director
tina.creguer@il.proquest.com
(800) 521-0600 x3805
300 N. Zeeb Road, P.O. Box 1346
Ann Arbor, MI 48106

PRS Group, Inc., The
Country Data
Adrian Shute
Vice President Marketing/
Public Relations
ashute@prsgroup.com
(315) 431-0511
6320 Fly Road, Suite 102,
P.O. Box 248
East Syracuse, NY 13057

Reuters
Lipper Horizon
Camilla Altamura
Media Relations Manager
Camilla.Altamura@
lipper.reuters.com
(877) 955-4773
3 Times Square, 17th Floor
New York, NY 10036

Risk Management Association, The
RMA's Annual Statement Studies
Kathleen Beans
Public Relations Manager/
Senior Writer
kbeans@rmahq.org
(215) 446-4095
1650 Market Street, Suite 2300
Philadelphia, PA 19103

Seisint, Inc.
Accurint
Cathy Demarco
cdemarco@accurint.com
(561) 893-8008
6601 Park of Commerce
Boulevard
Boca Raton, FL 33487

Shopping.com
Epinions
Michele Husak
Senior Manager, Public Relations
Michele@shopping.com
(650) 616-6518
8000 Marina Boulevard,
5th Floor
Brisbane, CA 94005

Superintendent of Documents, U.S. Government Printing Office
GPO Access
gpoaccess@gpo.gov
(888) 293-6498
U.S. Government Printing Office
732 North Capitol Street, NW
Washington, DC 20401

Telescan, Inc.
Wall Street City ProStation
Dan Olson
Media contact
dan@investools.com
(281) 588-9700
5959 Corporate Drive,
Suite LL250
Houston, TX 77036

The Wall Street Transcript
The Wall Street Transcript
Andrew Pickup
CEO/Publisher
pickup@twst.com
(212) 952-7437
67 Wall Street, 16th Floor
New York, NY 10005

TheStreet.com
TheStreet.com
Wendy Tullo
Media contact
wendy.tullo@thestreet.com
(212) 321-5000
14 Wall Street
New York, NY 10005

Thomas Publishing Company
Thomas Register
Ruth Hurd
Publisher
RHURD@trpublication.com
(212) 290-7277
TR User Services
Five Penn Plaza, 12th floor
New York, NY 10001

Thomson Financial
Disclosure Database
Investext
SDC Platinum
Thomson Analytics
Thomson Research
Kerri Shepherd
Manager, Public Relations
kerri.shepherd@tfn.com
(646) 822-2077
195 Broadway, 8th Floor
New York, NY 10007

Thomson Learning
Business & Industry
Encyclopedia of Associations (EA)
Gale Group Business A.R.T.S.
*Gale Group New ProductAnnouncements/
Plus (NPA/Plus)*
Gale Group Newsletter Database
Gale Group Trade & Industry Database
Market Share Reporter
PROMT
TableBase
Jennifer Bernardelli
Product Manager, Thomson/Gale
jennifer.bernardelli@thomson.com
(800) 877-4253 x1514
Gale Group
27500 Drake Road
Farmington Hills, MI 48331

Thomson Legal & Regulatory
Dialog
Profound
U.S. Copyrights
U.S. Patents Fulltext
Sandy Scherer
Director, Corporate Communications, Dialog
sandy.scherer@dialog.com
(919) 461-7354
The Dialog Corporation
11000 Regency Parkway, Suite 10
Cary, NC 27511
FindLaw
(650) 210-1900
1235 Pear Avenue, Suite 111
Mountain View, CA 94043
SAEGIS
TRADEMARKSCAN
Scott Rutherford
Senior Marketing Communications Specialist
Scott.Rutherford@t-t.com
(617) 376-7667
Thomson & Thomson
500 Victory Road
North Quincy, MA 02171
Westlaw
Ruth Orrick
Senior Vice President, Corporate Communications
ruth.orrick@westgroup.com
(651) 687-4099
West Group
610 Opperman Drive
Eagan, MN 55123

Thomson Media
Litigation Stock Report
Paul E. McGowan
Editor-in-Chief
pmcgowan@lsrmail.com
(804) 282-7026
P.O. Box 18322
Richmond, VA 23226

U.S. Board of Governors, Federal Reserve System
Federal Reserve Board
Jennifer J. Johnson
Secretary
(202) 452-3000
20th Street and Constitution Avenue NW
Washington, DC 20551

U.S. Bureau of Economic Analysis
Bureau of Economic Analysis (BEA)
Larry R. Moran
Media contact
LARRY.MORAN@BEA.GOV
(202) 606-9691
1441 L Street NW
Washington, DC 20230

U.S. Bureau of Labor Statistics
Bureau of Labor Statistics
Katharine G. Abraham
Commissioner
blsdata_staff@bls.gov
(202) 606-7800
2 Massachusetts Avenue, NE
Washington, DC 20212

U.S. Bureau of the Public Debt
Bureau of the Public Debt online:
Treasury Bills, Notes, and Bonds
Van Zeck
Commissioner
OAdmin@bpd.treas.gov
Bureau of the Public Debt
200 3rd Street
Parkersburg, WV 26106

U.S. Census Bureau
Bureau of the Census
Stephen Buckner
Media contact
stephen.l.buckner@census.gov
(301) 763-2135
U.S. Census Bureau
Washington, DC 20233

U.S. Congressional Budget Office
Budget and Economic Outlook
William J. Gainer
Associate Director for
Management
(202) 226-2600
Ford House Office Building,
4th Floor
Second and D Streets SW
Washington, DC 20515

U.S. Consumer Product Safety Commission
U.S. Consumer Product Safety Commission
info@cpsc.gov
(301) 504-6816
4330 East-West Highway
Bethesda, MD 20814

U.S. Copyright Office, Library of Congress
U.S. Copyright Office
Marybeth Peters
Register of Copyrights
101 Independence Avenue, SE
Washington, DC 20559

U.S. Patent and Trademark Office
Trademark Applications and Registrations Retrieval (TARR)
Trademark Electronic Search System (TESS)
USPTO
James E. Rogan
Director
usptoinfo@uspto.gov
(800) 786-9199
Office of Electronic Information
Products
Crystal Plaza 3, Suite 441
Washington, DC 20231

U.S. Securities and Exchange Commission
U.S. Securities and Exchange Commission
Harvey L. Pitt
Chairman
help@sec.gov
(202) 942-7040
Office of Investor Education and
Assistance
450 Fifth Street, NW
Washington, DC 20549

USADATA, Inc.
USADATA
Dominic LeClaire
Director of Marketing
dleclaire@usadata.com
(212) 679-1411 x222
292 Madison Avenue, 3rd Floor
New York, NY 10017

Value Line
Value Line
David Henigson
dhenigson@valueline.com
(212) 907-1500
Institutional Services
220 E. 42nd Street
New York, NY 10017

Vault, Inc.
Vault
Mark Oldman
mark@vault.com
(212) 366-4212
150 West 22nd Street
New York, NY 10011

VersusLaw, Inc.
VersusLaw
Jim Corbett
Vice President, Business
Development
jcorbett@versuslaw.com
(888) 377-8752 x3024
2613 - 151st Place NE
Redmond, WA 98052

VNU eMedia

Adweek
Brandweek
Deborah Patton
Media Relations
Dpatton@vnubusinessmedia.com
(646) 654-5755
770 Broadway, 7th Floor
New York, NY 10003

White House, The

White House Economic Statistics
Briefing Room
feedback@whitehouse.gov
(202) 456-1414
1600 Pennsylvania Avenue, NW
Washington, DC 20500

Winthrop Corporation

CorporateInformation
Eugene Helm
EHelm@wisi.com
(800) 232-0013

Yahoo! Inc.

Yahoo! Bond Center
Yahoo! Finance
Chris Castro
Chief Communications Officer,
Senior Vice President
(408) 349-3300
701 First Avenue
Sunnyvale, CA 94089

Zacks Investment Research

Zacks
support@zacks.com
(800) 767-3771
155 N. Wacker Drive
Chicago, IL 60606

Table C.1. Data Source Ratings – Alphabetical by Data Source

DATA SOURCE	1. RELATIVE COST-TO-VALUE	2. RELATIVE TIMELINESS OF DATA	3. RELATIVE COMPREHENSIVENESS OF DATA	4. EASE OF USE	5. SEARCH OPTIONS AVAILABLE	6. LEVEL OF SUPPORT SERVICES	7. LEVEL OF TRAINING OFFERED	8. AMOUNT/ KINDS OF SPECIAL SERVICES OFFERED	TOTAL
10k Wizard	9	10	10	10	10	10	5	9	73
ABI/Inform	6	10	8	10	10	9	9	10	72
Accounting & Tax Database	5	8	8	4	6	7	7	7	52
Accurint	10	9	7	9	9	7	9	9	69
Adweek	7	10	10	5	3	5	5	3	48
AICPA	8	9	8	7	6	7	5	3	53
Alacra	8	8	8	7	7	8	7	7	60
BigCharts	10	10	8	9	5	5	1	2	50
Bloomberg Professional	8	10	9	6	10	10	10	9	72
Bondtrac	5	9	9	9	9	9	9	9	68
Brandweek	7	10	10	5	3	5	5	3	48
Briefing.com	8	10	8	9	7	8	8	8	66
Budget and Economic Outlook	10	10	10	10	5	5	5	5	60
Bureau of Economic Analysis (BEA)	10	10	10	8	5	7	6	8	64

Appendix C: Business Data Source Rating Survey

Table C.1. Data Source Ratings – Alphabetical by Data Source (cont.)

DATA SOURCE	1. RELATIVE COST-TO-VALUE	2. RELATIVE TIMELINESS OF DATA	3. RELATIVE COMPREHENSIVENESS OF DATA	4. EASE OF USE	5. SEARCH OPTIONS AVAILABLE	6. LEVEL OF SUPPORT SERVICES	7. LEVEL OF TRAINING OFFERED	8. AMOUNT/KINDS OF SPECIAL SERVICES OFFERED	TOTAL
Bureau of Labor Statistics	10	10	10	7	8	8	7	8	68
Bureau of the Census	10	10	10	6	7	8	8	8	67
Business & Industry	7	6	8	8	8	7	8	6	58
Business Dateline	5	9	8	9	9	8	7	6	61
Business Wire	5	10	5	7	5	5	5	5	47
CBS MarketWatch	10	9	9	9	8	8	8	8	69
CCH Tax Research Network	7	9	8	10	10	9	8	8	69
CEOExpress	9	9	8	9	8	9	9	8	69
Chilling Effects	9	6	7	8	8	7	5	9	59
CI Resource Index	10	8	8	9	8	5	5	7	60
Closed-End Fund Center	10	10	8	9	5	2	7	2	53
Competia	8	7	6	7	5	8	9	9	59
Corporate Affiliations	5	7	7	9	10	10	9	9	66
CorporateInformation	9	9	7	8	8	6	6	7	60
Country Data	10	10	10	8	8	10	6	10	72

Table C.1. Data Source Ratings – Alphabetical by Data Source (cont.)

DATA SOURCE	1. RELATIVE COST-TO-VALUE	2. RELATIVE TIMELINESS OF DATA	3. RELATIVE COMPREHENSIVENESS OF DATA	4. EASE OF USE	5. SEARCH OPTIONS AVAILABLE	6. LEVEL OF SUPPORT SERVICES	7. LEVEL OF TRAINING OFFERED	8. AMOUNT/KINDS OF SPECIAL SERVICES OFFERED	TOTAL
D&B—Dun's Electronic Business Directory	7	7	6	2	9	8	8	8	55
D&B—Dun's Financial Records Plus	7	7	6	2	9	8	8	8	55
D&B—Dun's Market Identifiers	7	7	6	2	9	8	8	8	55
D&B Key Business Ratios (KBR) on the Web	6	7	8	7	6	7	3	6	50
D&B Million Dollar Database	5	7	8	9	7	7	3	5	51
DailyStocks.com	8	6	8	4	3	5	5	1	40
Datamonitor Market Research	7	6	9	8	6	6	5	5	52
Dialog	8	9	9	7	10	10	9	8	70
Disclosure Database	7	8	9	9	7	7	5	7	59
Economic Indicators	7	8	6	5	3	4	5	5	43
Economy.com	8	10	8	9	7	8	8	8	66
EIU ViewsWire	8	9	9	10	9	9	9	8	71

Table C.1. Data Source Ratings – Alphabetical by Data Source (cont.)

DATA SOURCE	1. RELATIVE COST-TO-VALUE	2. RELATIVE TIMELINESS OF DATA	3. RELATIVE COMPRE-HENSIVENESS OF DATA	4. EASE OF USE	5. SEARCH OPTIONS AVAILABLE	6. LEVEL OF SUPPORT SERVICES	7. LEVEL OF TRAINING OFFERED	8. AMOUNT/KINDS OF SPECIAL SERVICES OFFERED	TOTAL
Encyclopedia of Associations (EA)	9	8	8	8	9	9	5	5	61
Epinions	10	10	10	9	8	6	6	7	66
EventLine	7	8	7	7	10	10	10	5	64
Experian Business Credit Profiles	3	8	5	6	6	7	6	9	50
Factiva	9	10	10	8	7	6	6	9	65
FactSet	7	10	10	7	5	8	8	8	63
Fastcase	7	7	6	7	8	9	5	6	55
Federal Reserve Board	10	10	8	10	10	6	5	10	69
Financial Accounting Research System (FARS)	9	8	9	6	7	4	4	5	52
Financial Accounting Standards Board (FASB)	10	10	8	10	5	8	5	3	59
Financial Forecast Center	10	10	8	10	5	8	5	8	64
Financial Times	8	10	6	7	7	2	5	5	50
FindLaw	10	8	10	7	8	2	5	7	57

Table C.1. Data Source Ratings – Alphabetical by Data Source (cont.)

DATA SOURCE	1. RELATIVE COST-TO-VALUE	2. RELATIVE TIMELINESS OF DATA	3. RELATIVE COMPREHENSIVENESS OF DATA	4. EASE OF USE	5. SEARCH OPTIONS AVAILABLE	6. LEVEL OF SUPPORT SERVICES	7. LEVEL OF TRAINING OFFERED	8. AMOUNT/KINDS OF SPECIAL SERVICES OFFERED	TOTAL
First Research	5	8	8	8	5	5	5	5	49
FreeEDGAR/EDGAR Online/EDGARpro	6	9	7	6	7	8	8	6	57
Gale Group Business A.R.T.S.	7	10	7	6	6	7	8	5	56
Gale Group New Product Announcements/Plus (NPA/Plus)	7	10	9	8	9	9	8	7	67
Gale Group Newsletter Database	7	8	7	6	6	8	9	9	60
Gale Group Trade & Industry Database	8	9	6	8	9	4	5	5	54
Global Financial Data	8	9	10	10	8	10	8	7	70
GPO Access	5	7	6	6	8	1	3	6	42
Hoover's Online	9	8	8	8	8	9	8	9	67
Internal Revenue Service: *The Digital Daily*	10	10	10	8	8	8	5	8	67

Table C.1. Data Source Ratings – Alphabetical by Data Source (cont.)

DATA SOURCE	1. RELATIVE COST-TO-VALUE	2. RELATIVE TIMELINESS OF DATA	3. RELATIVE COMPREHENSIVENESS OF DATA	4. EASE OF USE	5. SEARCH OPTIONS AVAILABLE	6. LEVEL OF SUPPORT SERVICES	7. LEVEL OF TRAINING OFFERED	8. AMOUNT/KINDS OF SPECIAL SERVICES OFFERED	TOTAL
International Accounting Standards Board	9	9	8	10	6	7	5	3	57
Investext	7	7	8	6	8	7	6	7	56
KnowX	5	7	6	8	5	5	2	4	42
Legal Information Institute (LII)	10	10	10	10	9	8	5	9	71
LexisNexis	9	10	9	7	9	8	8	10	70
LexisNexis (Public Records)	7	9	10	7	10	8	8	9	68
LexisNexis Statistical	7	8	8	7	9	7	9	8	63
lexisONE	5	7	4	5	7	1	2	5	36
Lipper Horizon	5	10	10	6	7	8	7	8	61
LIVEDGAR	9	9	9	8	9	8	9	9	70
LLRX.com	10	9	9	10	8	8	5	10	69
Loislaw	10	10	9	8	8	9	7	9	70
Market Share Reporter	10	5	10	10	10	10	8	10	73
MarketResearch.com	8	9	9	10	10	10	7	8	71
Markets & Industry Library on LexisNexis	8	10	10	7	8	10	10	10	73

Table C.1. Data Source Ratings – Alphabetical by Data Source (cont.)

DATA SOURCE	1. RELATIVE COST-TO-VALUE	2. RELATIVE TIMELINESS OF DATA	3. RELATIVE COMPREHENSIVENESS OF DATA	4. EASE OF USE	5. SEARCH OPTIONS AVAILABLE	6. LEVEL OF SUPPORT SERVICES	7. LEVEL OF TRAINING OFFERED	8. AMOUNT/ KINDS OF SPECIAL SERVICES OFFERED	TOTAL
MarkMonitor	10	10	10	10	9	9	9	10	77
Mergent Online	6	9	9	8	7	8	9	6	62
MindBranch	9	8	9	9	7	10	2	7	61
Morningstar	10	10	10	9	9	8	9	9	74
MSN Money	9	8	8	7	7	4	1	3	47
Multex Fundamentals	6	8	10	7	8	5	5	5	54
National Law Library	4	3	4	4	5	2	4	2	28
News on LexisNexis	8	8	7	7	8	7	6	8	59
OneSource	8	8	8	10	9	8	8	9	68
PlanetFeedback	10	8	7	9	8	8	7	8	65
Profound	9	10	9	9	9	9	10	10	75
PROMT	8	10	7	7	7	6	6	7	58
Reuters Business Insight	7	6	7	8	5	9	9	7	58
RMA's Annual Statement Studies	10	8	6	9	4	7	3	7	54
SEDAR	10	9	9	9	8	8	7	7	67
SmartMoney	7	10	8	6	7	5	5	6	54
Standard & Poor's NetAdvantage	8	10	8	7	8	7	6	8	62
TableBase	8	8	8	9	9	7	7	7	63

Table C.1. Data Source Ratings – Alphabetical by Data Source (cont.)

DATA SOURCE	1. RELATIVE COST-TO-VALUE	2. RELATIVE TIMELINESS OF DATA	3. RELATIVE COMPREHENSIVENESS OF DATA	4. EASE OF USE	5. SEARCH OPTIONS AVAILABLE	6. LEVEL OF SUPPORT SERVICES	7. LEVEL OF TRAINING OFFERED	8. AMOUNT/ KINDS OF SPECIAL SERVICES OFFERED	TOTAL
The Virtual Chase	10	9	9	8	9	7	9	9	70
The Wall Street Transcript	8	10	8	9	9	8	8	10	70
TheStreet.com	9	10	9	6	8	8	8	9	67
Thomas Register	10	8	9	9	7	10	2	10	65
Thomas: Legislative Information on the Internet	10	10	10	10	10	8	5	8	71
Thomson Research	5	10	10	7	8	6	5	8	59
Trademark	10	8	9	10	8	8	5	5	63
Trademark Applications and Registrations Retrieval (TARR)									
Trademark Electronic Search System (TESS)	9	8	9	9	10	7	8	5	65
Trademark.com	8	9	10	8	9	8	9	8	69
TRADEMARKSCAN (Dialog)	9	9	10	10	8	10	10	5	71
TRADEMARKSCAN (SAEGIS)	10	10	10	8	10	10	10	10	78

Table C.1. Data Source Ratings – Alphabetical by Data Source (cont.)

DATA SOURCE	1. RELATIVE COST-TO-VALUE	2. RELATIVE TIMELINESS OF DATA	3. RELATIVE COMPREHENSIVENESS OF DATA	4. EASE OF USE	5. SEARCH OPTIONS AVAILABLE	6. LEVEL OF SUPPORT SERVICES	7. LEVEL OF TRAINING OFFERED	8. AMOUNT/KINDS OF SPECIAL SERVICES OFFERED	TOTAL
U.S. Consumer Product Safety Commission	10	10	10	8	8	8	8	7	69
U.S. Copyright Office	9	10	9	7	7	1	5	10	58
U.S. Copyrights	10	9	9	9	8	10	10	1	66
U.S. Securities and Exchange Commission	10	10	8	9	5	6	2	2	52
USADATA	10	8	9	10	3	8	8	9	65
USPTO	10	10	10	7	9	8	7	10	71
Value Line	9	9	9	10	5	10	10	9	71
Vault	9	8	7	9	9	8	8	9	67
Westlaw	8	9	9	8	8	8	7	8	65
Yahoo! Finance	9	10	9	9	9	5	5	6	62
Zacks	10	9	9	10	10	5	5	10	68

Note: Reviewers were asked to rate each research data source on the basis of a "10" being the highest, most complimentary, rating and "1" being the lowest or least complimentary ("80" being a perfect score).

Table C.2. Data Source Ratings – Ranked by Overall Rating

DATA SOURCE	1. RELATIVE COST-TO-VALUE	2. RELATIVE TIMELINESS OF DATA	3. RELATIVE COMPREHENSIVENESS OF DATA	4. EASE OF USE	5. SEARCH OPTIONS AVAILABLE	6. LEVEL OF SUPPORT SERVICES	7. LEVEL OF TRAINING OFFERED	8. AMOUNT/KINDS OF SPECIAL SERVICES OFFERED	TOTAL
TRADEMARKSCAN (SAEGIS)	10	10	10	8	10	10	10	10	78
MarkMonitor	10	10	10	10	9	9	9	10	77
Profound	9	10	9	9	9	9	10	10	75
Morningstar	10	10	10	9	9	8	9	9	74
10k Wizard	9	10	10	10	10	10	5	9	73
Market Share Reporter	10	5	10	10	10	10	8	10	73
Markets & Industry Library on LexisNexis	8	10	10	7	8	10	10	10	73
ABI/Inform	6	10	8	10	10	9	9	10	72
Bloomberg Professional	8	10	9	6	10	10	10	9	72
Country Data	10	10	10	8	8	10	6	10	72
EIU ViewsWire	8	9	9	10	9	9	9	8	71
Legal Information Institute (LII)	10	10	10	10	9	8	5	9	71
MarketResearch.com	8	9	9	10	10	10	7	8	71

Table C.2. Data Source Ratings – Ranked by Overall Rating (cont.)

DATA SOURCE	1. RELATIVE COST-TO-VALUE	2. RELATIVE TIMELINESS OF DATA	3. RELATIVE COMPREHENSIVENESS OF DATA	4. EASE OF USE	5. SEARCH OPTIONS AVAILABLE	6. LEVEL OF SUPPORT SERVICES	7. LEVEL OF TRAINING OFFERED	8. AMOUNT/KINDS OF SPECIAL SERVICES OFFERED	TOTAL
Thomas: Legislative Information on the Internet	10	10	10	10	10	8	5	8	71
TRADEMARKSCAN (Dialog)	9	9	10	10	8	10	10	5	71
USPTO	10	10	10	7	9	8	7	10	71
Value Line	9	9	9	10	5	10	10	9	71
Dialog	8	9	9	7	10	10	9	8	70
Global Financial Data	8	9	10	10	8	10	8	7	70
LexisNexis	9	10	9	7	9	8	8	10	70
LIVEDGAR	9	9	9	8	9	8	9	9	70
Loislaw	10	10	9	8	8	9	7	9	70
The Virtual Chase	10	9	9	8	9	7	9	9	70
The Wall Street Transcript	8	10	8	9	9	8	8	10	70
Accurint	10	9	7	9	9	7	9	9	69
CBS MarketWatch	10	9	9	9	8	8	8	8	69
CCH Tax Research Network	7	9	8	10	10	9	8	8	69
CEOExpress	9	9	8	9	8	9	9	8	69

Table C.2. Data Source Ratings – Ranked by Overall Rating (cont.)

DATA SOURCE	1. RELATIVE COST-TO-VALUE	2. RELATIVE TIMELINESS OF DATA	3. RELATIVE COMPREHENSIVENESS OF DATA	4. EASE OF USE	5. SEARCH OPTIONS AVAILABLE	6. LEVEL OF SUPPORT SERVICES	7. LEVEL OF TRAINING OFFERED	8. AMOUNT/KINDS OF SPECIAL SERVICES OFFERED	TOTAL
Federal Reserve Board	10	10	8	10	10	6	5	10	69
LLRX.com	10	9	9	10	8	8	5	10	69
Trademark.com	8	9	10	8	9	8	9	8	69
U.S. Consumer Product Safety Commission	10	10	10	8	8	8	8	7	69
Bondtrac	5	9	9	9	9	9	9	9	68
Bureau of Labor Statistics	10	10	10	7	8	8	7	8	68
LexisNexis (Public Records)	7	9	10	7	10	8	8	9	68
OneSource	8	8	8	10	9	8	8	9	68
Zacks	10	9	9	10	10	5	5	10	68
Bureau of the Census	10	10	10	6	7	8	8	8	67
Gale Group New Product Announcements/Plus (NPA/Plus)	7	10	9	8	9	9	8	7	67
Hoover's Online	9	8	8	8	8	9	8	9	67

Table C.2. Data Source Ratings – Ranked by Overall Rating (cont.)

DATA SOURCE	1. RELATIVE COST-TO-VALUE	2. RELATIVE TIMELINESS OF DATA	3. RELATIVE COMPREHENSIVENESS OF DATA	4. EASE OF USE	5. SEARCH OPTIONS AVAILABLE	6. LEVEL OF SUPPORT SERVICES	7. LEVEL OF TRAINING OFFERED	8. AMOUNT/ KINDS OF SPECIAL SERVICES OFFERED	TOTAL
Internal Revenue Service: The Digital Daily	10	10	10	8	8	8	5	8	67
SEDAR	10	9	9	9	8	8	7	7	67
TheStreet.com	9	10	9	6	8	8	8	9	67
Vault	9	8	7	9	9	8	8	9	67
Briefing.com	8	10	8	9	7	8	8	8	66
Corporate Affiliations	5	7	7	9	10	10	9	9	66
Economy.com	8	10	8	9	7	8	8	8	66
Epinions	10	10	10	9	8	6	6	7	66
U.S. Copyrights	10	9	9	9	8	10	10	1	66
Factiva	9	10	10	8	7	6	6	9	65
PlanetFeedback	10	8	7	9	8	8	7	8	65
Thomas Register	10	8	9	9	7	10	2	10	65
Trademark Electronic Search System (TESS)	9	8	9	9	10	7	8	5	65
USADATA	10	8	9	10	3	8	8	9	65
Westlaw	8	9	9	8	8	8	7	8	65
Bureau of Economic Analysis (BEA)	10	10	10	8	5	7	6	8	64
EventLine	7	8	7	7	10	10	10	5	64

Table C.2. Data Source Ratings – Ranked by Overall Rating (cont.)

DATA SOURCE	1. RELATIVE COST-TO-VALUE	2. RELATIVE TIMELINESS OF DATA	3. RELATIVE COMPRE-HENSIVENESS OF DATA	4. EASE OF USE	5. SEARCH OPTIONS AVAILABLE	6. LEVEL OF SUPPORT SERVICES	7. LEVEL OF TRAINING OFFERED	8. AMOUNT/ KINDS OF SPECIAL SERVICES OFFERED	TOTAL
Financial Forecast Center	10	10	8	10	5	8	5	8	64
FactSet	7	10	10	7	5	8	8	8	63
LexisNexis Statistical	7	8	8	7	9	7	9	8	63
TableBase	8	8	8	9	9	7	7	7	63
Trademark Applications and Registrations Retrieval (TARR)	10	8	9	10	8	8	5	5	63
Mergent Online	6	9	9	8	7	8	9	6	62
Standard & Poor's NetAdvantage	8	10	8	7	8	7	6	8	62
Yahoo! Finance	9	10	9	9	9	5	5	6	62
Business Dateline	5	9	8	9	9	8	7	6	61
Encyclopedia of Associations (EA)	9	8	8	8	9	9	5	5	61
Lipper Horizon	5	10	10	6	7	8	7	8	61
MindBranch	9	8	9	9	7	10	2	7	61
Alacra	8	8	8	7	7	8	7	7	60
Budget and Economic Outlook	10	10	10	10	5	5	5	5	60

Table C.2. Data Source Ratings – Ranked by Overall Rating (cont.)

DATA SOURCE	1. RELATIVE COST-TO-VALUE	2. RELATIVE TIMELINESS OF DATA	3. RELATIVE COMPREHENSIVENESS OF DATA	4. EASE OF USE	5. SEARCH OPTIONS AVAILABLE	6. LEVEL OF SUPPORT SERVICES	7. LEVEL OF TRAINING OFFERED	8. AMOUNT/KINDS OF SPECIAL SERVICES OFFERED	TOTAL
CI Resource Index	10	8	8	9	8	5	5	7	60
CorporateInformation	9	9	7	8	8	6	6	7	60
Gale Group Newsletter Database	7	8	7	6	6	8	9	9	60
Chilling Effects	9	6	7	8	8	7	5	9	59
Competia	8	7	6	7	5	8	9	9	59
Disclosure Database	7	8	9	9	7	7	5	7	59
Financial Accounting Standards Board (FASB)	10	10	8	10	5	8	5	3	59
News on LexisNexis	8	8	7	7	8	7	6	8	59
Thomson Research	5	10	10	7	8	6	5	8	59
Business & Industry	7	6	8	8	8	7	8	6	58
PROMT	8	10	7	7	7	6	6	7	58
Reuters Business Insight	7	6	7	8	5	9	9	7	58
U.S. Copyright Office	9	10	9	7	7	1	5	10	58
FindLaw	10	8	10	7	8	2	5	7	57
FreeEDGAR/EDGAR Online/EDGARpro	6	9	7	6	7	8	8	6	57

Table C.2. Data Source Ratings – Ranked by Overall Rating (cont.)

DATA SOURCE	1. RELATIVE COST-TO-VALUE	2. RELATIVE TIMELINESS OF DATA	3. RELATIVE COMPRE-HENSIVENESS OF DATA	4. EASE OF USE	5. SEARCH OPTIONS AVAILABLE	6. LEVEL OF SUPPORT SERVICES	7. LEVEL OF TRAINING OFFERED	8. AMOUNT/ KINDS OF SPECIAL SERVICES OFFERED	TOTAL
International Accounting Standards Board	9	9	8	10	6	7	5	3	57
Gale Group Business A.R.T.S.	7	10	7	6	6	7	8	5	56
Investext	7	7	8	6	8	7	6	7	56
D&B—Dun's Electronic Business Directory	7	7	6	2	9	8	8	8	55
D&B—Dun's Financial Records Plus	7	7	6	2	9	8	8	8	55
D&B—Dun's Market Identifiers	7	7	6	2	9	8	8	8	55
Fastcase	7	7	6	7	8	9	5	6	55
Gale Group Trade & Industry Database	8	9	6	8	9	4	5	5	54
Multex Fundamentals	6	8	10	7	8	5	5	5	54
RMA's Annual Statement Studies	10	8	6	9	4	7	3	7	54
SmartMoney	7	10	8	6	7	5	5	6	54
AICPA	8	9	8	7	6	7	5	3	53

Table C.2. Data Source Ratings – Ranked by Overall Rating (cont.)

DATA SOURCE	1. RELATIVE COST-TO-VALUE	2. RELATIVE TIMELINESS OF DATA	3. RELATIVE COMPREHENSIVENESS OF DATA	4. EASE OF USE	5. SEARCH OPTIONS AVAILABLE	6. LEVEL OF SUPPORT SERVICES	7. LEVEL OF TRAINING OFFERED	8. AMOUNT/KINDS OF SPECIAL SERVICES OFFERED	TOTAL
Closed-End Fund Center	10	10	8	9	5	2	7	2	53
Accounting & Tax Database	5	8	8	4	6	7	7	7	52
Datamonitor Market Research	7	6	9	8	6	6	5	5	52
Financial Accounting Research System (FARS)	9	8	9	6	7	4	4	5	52
U.S. Securities and Exchange Commission	10	10	8	9	5	6	2	2	52
D&B Million Dollar Database	5	7	8	9	7	7	3	5	51
BigCharts	10	10	8	9	5	5	1	2	50
D&B Key Business Ratios (KBR) on the Web	6	7	8	7	6	7	3	6	50
Experian Business Credit Profiles	3	8	5	6	6	7	6	9	50
Financial Times	8	10	6	7	7	2	5	5	50

Table C.2. Data Source Ratings – Ranked by Overall Rating (cont.)

DATA SOURCE	1. RELATIVE COST-TO-VALUE	2. RELATIVE TIMELINESS OF DATA	3. RELATIVE COMPRE-HENSIVENESS OF DATA	4. EASE OF USE	5. SEARCH OPTIONS AVAILABLE	6. LEVEL OF SUPPORT SERVICES	7. LEVEL OF TRAINING OFFERED	8. AMOUNT/KINDS OF SPECIAL SERVICES OFFERED	TOTAL
First Research	5	8	8	8	5	5	5	5	49
Adweek	7	10	10	5	3	5	5	3	48
Brandweek	7	10	10	5	3	5	5	3	48
Business Wire	5	10	5	7	5	5	5	5	47
MSN Money	9	8	8	7	7	4	1	3	47
Economic Indicators	7	8	6	5	3	4	5	5	43
GPO Access	5	7	6	6	8	1	3	6	42
KnowX	5	7	6	8	5	5	2	4	42
DailyStocks.com	8	6	8	4	3	5	5	1	40
lexisONE	5	7	4	5	7	1	2	5	36
National Law Library	4	3	4	4	5	2	4	2	28

Note: Reviewers were asked to rate each research data source on the basis of a "10" being the highest, most complimentary, rating and "1" being the lowest or least complimentary ("80" being a perfect score).

Appendix D:
Contributor Biographies

Melissa Barr
Cuyahoga County Public Library

Melissa Barr is the legal resources specialist and reference librarian at the Maple Heights Regional Library, part of the Cuyahoga County Public Library system in northeast Ohio. She serves as a building steward for the Cuyahoga County Library Union (Service Employees International Union, District 1199) and as an SEIU/1199 delegate to the Cleveland Federation of Labor. She is a member of the Ohio Regional Association of Law Libraries, the American Association of Law Libraries (AALL), and two AALL Special Interest Sections: Research Instruction & Patron Services and Legal Information Services to the Public.

Barr earned a B.A. in English from Heidelberg College in Tiffin, Ohio (1977), a paralegal certificate from Ohio Paralegal Institute in Cleveland, Ohio (1982), and an M.L.S. from Kent State University (1997). She has also attended Baldwin Wallace College in Berea, Ohio; Central Texas College in Killeen, Texas; Bad Kreuznach, West Germany; Cuyahoga Community College in Parma, Ohio; and Cleveland State University, where her interests ranged from criminal justice to business communications, cultural anthropology, and Web page design.

After completing a tour of duty in the U.S. Army, Barr started out in the legal field as a file clerk for a law firm and then moved on to work as a paralegal, bankruptcy liaison clerk, legal secretary, recruiting coordinator, and law library assistant. She also worked as a research assistant for a consulting company that prepared economic damage claim reports for court cases. While attending graduate school at Kent State University, Barr was employed as the waste-tracking coordinator at a hazardous waste recycling plant. She joined the Cuyahoga County Public Library staff in 1999. Barr is the author of "Democracy in the Dark: Public Access Restrictions from Westlaw and LexisNexis," which appeared in the January 2003 edition of *Searcher: The Magazine for Database Professionals.*

Kathy Biehl
Independent Researcher

Attorney and freelance journalist Kathy Biehl is co-author of *The Lawyer's Guide to Internet Research* (Scarecrow Press[year?]). She has reviewed online legal research resources as a columnist for *LLRX.com, the Internet Legal Research Newsletter,* and *Pro2Net* (now Smart Pros). In addition to legal and Internet writing, she has contributed more than eight hundred articles on a spectrum of general interest topics to national and regional publications. She is the winner of the 2002 Lone Star Award in magazine column writing presented by the Houston Press Club. Biehl earned a B.A. from Southern Methodist University with highest honors and a J.D. from the University of Texas School of Law with honors. She taught business law at Rice University and legal research and writing at the University of Houston Law Center. A member of the State Bar of Texas, she maintained a private law practice for nineteen years before turning to full-time research and writing.

Polly D. Boruff-Jones
IUPUI University Library

Polly Boruff-Jones is an assistant librarian at University Library on the Indiana University Purdue University Indianapolis (IUPUI) campus, where she serves as the reference team leader and business subject specialist. She received both her B.A. and M.L.S. degrees from Indiana University–Bloomington.

Boruff-Jones's primary areas of research are integration and assessment of information literacy in the business school undergraduate curriculum and management of virtual reference services in academic libraries.

Meryl Brodsky
Consultant

Meryl Brodsky is working as an independent consultant after working as a librarian at Ernst & Young LLP for four years and Cornell University for ten years. She has an M.B.A. from the Business School at Cornell and an M.L.S. from Southern Connecticut State University. She specializes in the financial services industry and particularly likes to analyze and compare databases. She is a member of the Special Libraries Association and the American Library Association.

Helen P. Burwell
Burwell Enterprises

Author and online expert Helen Burwell is well known for providing consulting services to the information industry and international business community. Since 1984, as president of Burwell Enterprises, Inc., she has helped corporate clients develop successful strategies for electronic retrieval of competitive intelligence information.

Burwell is editor and publisher of *The Burwell World Directory of Information Brokers*, an annual annotated directory of nearly one thousand companies that provide information retrieval and consulting. Now in its fourteenth edition, *The Burwell Directory* is widely used by business and industry for outsourcing information research. The directory is also available on the Internet at *http://www.burwellinc.com*.

Burwell holds a master's degree from Louisiana State University's School of Library and Information Science, which named her its 1996 Outstanding Alumna for her contributions to the information profession. In 1998, the Association of Independent Information Professionals, an international organization comprising information consultants, online searchers, document delivery services, and other information professionals, presented Burwell with the President's Award for outstanding service to the profession.

In recent years Burwell has been an invited guest speaker both at the European Information Brokers Meeting in Frankfurt, Germany, and at the first Asian and Pacific Rim Conference and Exhibition on Electronic Commerce in Shanghai, China. Regular speaking engagements in the United States have included national conferences and large trade shows such as the National Online Meeting, Online World, and the Society of Competitive Intelligence Professionals.

Burwell is the author of *Online Competitive Intelligence*, published by Facts On Demand Press in 1999/2000. The second edition was released in January 2004.

Cindy Carlson
Fried, Frank, Harris, Shriver & Jacobson

Cindy Carlson is the electronic resources librarian for the Washington, D.C., office of the law firm of Fried, Frank, Harris, Shriver & Jacobson and has more than fifteen years of experience working in libraries. She writes a monthly column, "Notes from the Technology Trenches," on electronic research, training, and legal information technology for *LLRX.com, the Law Library Resource Exchange.* An occasional contributor to other publications covering information research, she has also spoken at several conferences concerning Internet resources in business and legal research. She leads the Legal Research Training Focus Group of the Law Librarians' Society of the District of Columbia.

Elena Carvajal
Ernst & Young

Elena Carvajal is an information professional at Ernst & Young's Center for Business Knowledge. She has more than twenty years of experience as a librarian, researcher, analyst, and communications specialist. Before joining Ernst & Young, Carvajal worked at EDS in a variety of roles, including research analyst for the corporate library and market analyst and industry relations/public relations specialist for the travel and transportation industry. She also served as marketing communication specialist for the Executive Communications Group at EDS.

Carvajal earned her B.A. in English and her M.L.S. from the University of North Texas. She has served on a number of committees and programs for the American Library Association, where her contributions include editing *COGnotes*, the conference newsletter, and presenting a workshop titled "Wrestling with the Future" at an ALA LITA Pre-Conference. She is a member of the Special Library Association.

Donna Cavallini
Kilpatrick Stockton LLP

Donna F. Cavallini has more than fifteen years' experience in the legal profession in a wide variety of settings, including academic and governmental, and in both large and small law firms. She serves the attorneys of the law firm of Kilpatrick Stockton LLP as manager of competitive knowledge, a position that combines the disciplines of knowledge management and competitive intelligence and focuses on the practice areas of corporate/securities, intellectual property, and technology law. Before joining the firm in 1996, Cavallini was library program administrator for the Florida Attorney General's Office, and before working for the state of Florida, she was solo librarian for a medium-sized firm in Tallahassee. She is a regular contributor to information professional Listservs and newsletters, including *LLRX* and the *Virtual Chase,* and she has been a speaker for professional groups both large and small. Cavallini received a B.A. in classics from Washington University and a J.D. from St. Louis University.

Dudee Chiang
Amgen, Inc.

Dudee Chiang works as the library business analyst at Amgen, Inc., the world's largest biotechnology company. Before her current position, she worked as the database information consultant at Amgen Library and held various positions at the Norris Medical Library and Leavey Library at the University of Southern California. She holds an M.S. degree and a certificate of advanced studies in library and information science from the University of Illinois at Urbana-Champaign, and she has an M.B.A. degree from Pepperdine University. She is an experienced professional in information retrieval, end user training, and resource evaluation; in recent years, she has taken on project management responsibilities for implementing technologies within the library environment, including Web and portals. She is always looking for new challenges in her work

Wes Edens
Thunderbird School of International Management

Wes Edens is on the faculty of the International Business Information Centre at Thunderbird, the American Graduate School of International Management, in Glendale, Arizona. In addition to duties as a full-time international business researcher, Wes evaluates and selects electronic resources for Thunderbird, ranked number one in the world for international business by *US News & World Report* and the *Wall Street Journal.* He holds a B.S. in business administration and an M.L.S. degree, both from the University of Arizona, and is an M.B.A. candidate at Arizona State University.

Before coming to Thunderbird, Edens was business librarian/bibliographer for the University of North Dakota in Grand Forks. He has also worked as a reference librarian for Pima Community College in Tucson, Arizona.

Edens's publications include "An International Information Gateway: Thunderbird's Intranet for Teaching, Learning and Research" (with Carol Hammond, Ann Tolzman, and Cate Cebrowski) in *Advances in Library Administration and Organization,* October 1997; and "World Database of Business Information Sources on the Web," a review for the November/December 1998 issue of *Business Information Alert.* In addition, he was interviewed by Mary Ellen Bates in the 2001 book *Super Searchers Cover the World: The Online Secrets of International Business Researchers,* published by Eight Bit Books.

He is a member of the Special Libraries Association and the Arizona Libraries Association. He is married with three children, and is an avid reader, stargazer, and amateur radio operator.

David Ernsthausen
Kenan-Flagler Business School

Since 1997 David Ernsthausen has been the faculty teaching and research support librarian of the University of North Carolina–Chapel Hill's Kenan-Flagler Business School. He consults with faculty and students about which resources are most likely to provide useful answers for their research. He also presents guest lectures for classes in the M.B.A. and bachelor's degree programs. Before 1997 he worked for seven years as a reference librarian at Wake Forest University, working mainly with the undergraduate business students and faculty. He has an M.B.A. from the Babcock Graduate School of Management at Wake Forest University and an M.L.S. degree from Indiana University.

Michelle Fennimore
Competitive Insights

Michelle Fennimore is the principal of Competitive Insights, a market research company specializing in competitive intelligence, company, and industry research. Its services range from online research and one-on-one interviews to custom-designed market research studies, including mail and telephone surveys. Fennimore's work focuses primarily on marketing and advertising issues, as well as business development and expansion. Before founding Competitive Insights, she spent nine years in New York City, marketing national brands for global advertising agencies, including J. Walter Thompson, Saatchi & Saatchi, and Grey Advertising.

James Harrington
Fujitsu Network Communications

Jim Harrington earned his M.L.S. from the State University of New York at Buffalo. He began his career assisting libraries in the setup and implementation of a variety of automated services for both staff and end users, primarily dealing with system design and training. For the past four years, he has worked as the corporate librarian for Fujitsu Network Communications, providing library services primarily for the marketing and sales organizations.

Tanja Harrison
Acadia University

Tanja Harrison is an academic librarian at Acadia University. She is the liaison librarian to the School of Recreation Management and Kinesiology and the Vaughan Memorial Library's information literacy coordinator. Her responsibilities include teaching, assisting faculty and students with research requests, and collection development. She has also been the business and education librarian at Acadia and has four years' experience as the business and economics librarian at Dalhousie University. She has been an instructor with the Acadia University Division of Continuing and Distance Education and a part-time lecturer at the School of Library and Information Studies (SLIS), Dalhousie University, and has worked on government projects for Environment Canada.

Harrison graduated on the dean's list with her B.A. from Bishop's University in 1993. She earned her M.L.I.S. in 1996, graduating with Beta Phi Mu standing, and was awarded the Special Libraries Association (SLA—Eastern Canada Chapter) prize. She has been an active member of several professional associations, including the Canadian Library Association, the Atlantic Provinces Library Association, and the Nova Scotia Library Association. She has recently joined the Association of College and Research Libraries of the American Library Association. She is currently the chairwoman of the Dalhousie SLIS Associated Alumni. Her research interests include the effects of information literacy as core curriculum in higher education.

Michelle Hartstrom
Columbia Financial Advisors, Inc.

Michelle Hartstrom is a financial analyst with more than ten years of experience in the valuation of closely held business interests. In her analysis of client companies, she researches economic and industry information, financial market data, public company information, and merger and acquisition data. She performs financial analysis for clients for a variety of purposes, including ESOP, litigation, gift and estate tax, and management planning. In addition to the financial analysis aspect of her work, verbal and written communication is an integral part of each project she performs.

Before joining Columbia Financial Advisors, Inc., Hartstrom worked for Willamette Management Associates in its Portland, Oregon, office. She has earned accreditation as a senior appraiser in business valuation from the American Society of Appraisers and a certification in financial management from the Institute of Management Accountants. She earned a B.S. in business administration with high scholarship from Oregon State University. Her concentrations of study were financial management and international business, and she minored in behavioral science.

Jean M. Heilig
Jones International University

Jean M. Heilig is the director of the online library at Jones International University (JIU), the first completely online university to achieve regional accreditation. Heilig has been working full time for the university since January 2003. Before that, she worked part time for the university and part time for Jones e-global library (a licensed product), where she was the senior director of research and information. At both Jones e-global library and the JIU library she has been involved with resource development and review as well as the selection and evaluation of database vendors and content providers. She participates in client (student, faculty, and staff) outreach, support, and training and also monitors copyright issues, national and international digital library initiatives, advances in electronic publishing, and similar issues that affect the competitive environment of e-global library. Before joining Jones in 1999 she was the program coordinator for the Library and Information

Services graduate program at the University of Denver (DU), where she managed all program logistics, budget, personnel, and student advising.

Heilig obtained her master's degree in library and information services from the University of Denver (1999), and her master's degree in business administration from the University of Colorado–Denver (1992). She also holds a certificate in competitive intelligence from Drexel University (2002). In addition to her work with JIU, she is an adjunct faculty member in the Library and Information Science master's degree program at DU.

Karl Kasca
Kasca & Associates

Five years agoKarl Kasca formed his own company, Kasca & Associates, which provides top-level information research results to business and legal decision makers. His company specializes in business research and competitive intelligence, as well as market, product, and industry trends and due diligence—information useful to businesses and attorneys in making decisions and acting on them.

Kasca was formerly with a Fortune 500 company with more than sixteen years' experience performing operational and financial internal audits as well as vendor and conflict-of-interest/fraud examinations in diverse business situations. As a result, he has become very experienced at finding creative approaches and solutions to problems/questions as well as performing insightful analyses of results.

Wendy S. Katz
Factscope LLC

Wendy Katz owns Factscope LLC, a research consulting firm based in Lexington, Kentucky. Katz received her B.S. in conservation of natural resources, with highest honors, from the University of California–Berkeley in 1977. She has seventeen years of laboratory experience in biomedical research and has published research papers and literature reviews in Cell and other peer-reviewed journals. She earned her Ph.D. in biology from the Massachusetts Institute of Technology in 1989, where her research focused on structure-function analysis of proteins. Her postdoctoral research at the California Institute of

Technology used tools of molecular genetics to study how cells in a developing animal know where they are. Katz joined the Department of Biochemistry in the University of Kentucky College of Medicine in 1995 and both continued her research and taught graduate biochemistry there from 1995 to 2000. She has a long-standing interest in animal training and behavior modification and in her free time teaches dog obedience classes.

Hal P. Kirkwood, Jr.
Purdue University

Hal P. Kirkwood is an assistant professor of library science at the Management & Economics Library at Purdue University. He acts as the instruction coordinator for the Management & Economics Library, conducting workshops and class sessions on the multitude of business databases available. He has written extensively in publications such as *Online, Journal of Business & Finance Librarianship, FreePint,* and the *Bulletin* of the Business & Finance Division of Special Libraries Association. Kirkwood has presented at Online World, Internet Librarian, and the Special Libraries Association's annual conference. His research interests are in teaching business information to people with M.B.A.s, Web design and usability, and concept mapping.

Jan Knight
Bancroft Information Services

Jan Knight is owner of Bancroft Information Services. As an independent research consultant, she provides a variety of business intelligence and market research services to a diverse list of companies, including publishers, corporate trainers, software companies, biotechnology firms, marketing strategists, and sales consultants. Much of her work involves providing industry profiles, market studies, and competitor profile reports. Clients often commission her services when working on initial business plans, marketing strategies, or new product development.

Originally from England, Knight has a professional background in advertising, marketing, and publishing. She holds an M.A. in information resources and library science from the University of Arizona and a B.A. in humanities/renaissance studies from the University of California–Berkeley. She regularly attends local business events and has spoken to various business groups on the topic of "Jump-Starting Your Own Market

Research via the Internet." Her Web site provides more information on services as well as client testimonials. It can be found at *http://www.bancroftinfo.com.*

Margery A. Mackie
Mackie Research LLC

Margery A. Mackie is an independent business researcher in Portland, Oregon. Her firm, Mackie Research LLC, specializes in online industry research and overview writing. Other services include regional economic profile research and writing, environmental research, and specialized industry data searches. Mackie is also a contributor to *The CyberSkeptic's Guide to Internet Research,* a monthly newsletter. Before launching her business, Mackie worked in a variety of private sector, nonprofit, and government settings, always enjoying the research and reporting aspects of her work the most. She is a member of the Association of Independent Information Professionals and the National Association for the Self-Employed, and holds an environmental planning degree from Stanford University.

Matthew J. McBride
Information Consultant

Matthew J. McBride is the president and principal information consultant of CInC, Inc. He holds an M.S. in plant pathology from the University of Minnesota and a B.S. in molecular biology from Purdue University. McBride is completing his M.L.S. degree at Drexel University. He has worked as a biological research scientist for a major chemical company and as an information consultant for The Dialog Corporation. He has more than seven years of experience searching commercial systems and databases for scientific, technical, and intellectual property information.

Karin Mohtadi
KZM LLC

Karin Mohtadi has participated in business valuations and business research during the last eight years. She researches economic and industry information, public company information, and merger and acquisition data. As a financial analyst conducting business valuations and other analysis, she worked for clients for a variety of purposes, including buy-sell agreements, damages and lost profits analyses, economic damage analysis, enhanced earnings, employee stock ownership plans, litigation support, and gift and estate tax.

Before forming KZM LLC, Mohtadi worked for Veber Partners LLC, an investment bank in Portland, Oregon. Before that she worked for Willamette Management Associates in its Portland, Oregon, office. She holds an M.S. in economics as well as a B.A. in both economics and French from Portland State University.

Rita W. Moss
University of North Carolina—Chapel Hill

Rita Moss's education includes a B.A. from the University College of North Wales, Bangor, U.K, with a double major in social theory and institutions and history, an M.Ed. from the same institution, and an M.L.S. from the University of North Carolina–Chapel Hill, received in 1988. She has worked since 1991 as a business and economics librarian at the University of North Carolina–Chapel Hill. For the past twelve years she has also conducted workshops on business information resources for the Southeastern Library Network and for North Carolina Libraries for Virtual Education, as well as giving several presentations at workshops offered by the North Carolina Library Association.

Moss recently finished revising the second edition of the *Handbook of Business Information* for Libraries Unlimited.

Robin Neidorf
Electric Muse

Robin Neidorf has provided research, writing, and consulting services through her company, Electric Muse, since 1996. She works with clients in the fields of nonprofit management, health care, business consulting, law, investment services, public policy, education, and market research to help them find and use information to communicate more effectively in print, electronic formats, and face to face. Neidorf holds a master's degree in nonfiction writing from the Bennington Writing Seminars and teaches research, writing, and public relations through the University of Minnesota's Compleat Scholar program. Her articles and essays have appeared regionally and nationally in such publications as *Ms.* magazine, *Minnesota Law & Politics*, *Corporate Report*, and *Ventures* magazine, and she is the co-author of *e-Merchant: Retail Strategies for e-Commerce* (Addison Wesley, 2001). Neidorf often speaks to groups on market research, communications, public relations, life-work balance, and other topics. She is a member of the Association of Independent Information Professionals and Business/ Professional Women USA.

Judith M. Nixon
Purdue University

Judith Nixon has worked at the Purdue University Libraries since 1984, first as a consumer and family sciences librarian and since 1993 as a management and economics librarian. Before that she worked as a reference librarian at the University of Wisconsin–Platteville and at the Cedar Rapids Public Library.

Nixon is widely published in the field. Her works include *Industry and Company Information*, which she co-authored with Craig A. Hawbaker (Ann Arbor, Mich.: Pierian Press, 1991), and *Lodging and Restaurant Index*, a quarterly periodical index (West Lafayette, Ind.: RHIMI, Purdue University, 1985–1993), as well as numerous journal articles. Her awards include the John H. Moriarity Award for Excellence in Library Service to the Faculty and Students of Purdue University (1989) and the Gale Research Award for Excellence in Business Librarianship (1994).

Nixon has a master's degree in library science from the University of Iowa (1974) and a B.S. in education from Valparaiso University (1967). She is a member of the American Library Association, the Reference and User Services Association, and the Business Reference and Services Section.

Judith Parvez
Tax Analysts

Judy Parvez is a senior information specialist at Tax Analysts. Before that, she was employed as a tax librarian and tax knowledge manager for several professional services firms. She is a member of the Special Libraries Association and has served as moderator of the Tax Roundtable–Legal Division.

Parvez received a bachelor of administration/library science degree from the University of Wisconsin–Eau Claire.

Marcy M. Phelps
Phelps Research

Marcy Phelps is the founder and president of Phelps Research, in Denver, Colorado. Her company offers business and market research to management, marketing, and financial services professionals. Phelps specializes in providing clients with industry profile reports and has particular expertise in online database searching. Phelps Research also offers company profiles, competitive intelligence, litigation support, regional economic overviews, comparable company research, and merger and acquisition research. Phelps has a master's degree in library and information services from the University of Denver as well as a degree in mathematics from the State University of New York at New Paltz. She holds memberships in the Association of Independent Information Professionals, the Business Marketing Association, and the Metro Denver Chamber of Commerce. A first-degree black belt in Taekwondo, Phelps enjoys golf and mountain biking in her spare time.

Brenda Reeb
University of Rochester

A native of rural southern Illinois, Brenda Reeb earned her B.A. in history from Loyola University of Chicago in 1987. During her senior year in college she wrote her first paper on a microcomputer, using MS DOS and WordPerfect. She earned her M.L.S. from Simmons College in Boston in 1991. In 1993 Reeb relocated to Rochester, New York, to serve as the management librarian at the University of Rochester. With no previous business background, she was hired primarily for her computer skills. Now the director of the Management Library, she manages a staff of three, serving the William E. Simon School of Business and the economics department at the university.

After nearly a decade of business library reference work, Reeb remains fascinated by the ways students engage business sources, particularly in an online environment. She coordinates several Web interface design projects in the library and maintains a private consulting practice in user-centered design. She is a member of the American Library Association and the Association for Women in Computing.

While living in Boston, Reeb became an avid bicycle commuter, which she continues to this day, although she no longer rides in the winter.

Jennifer Richard
Acadia University

Jennifer Richard is an academic librarian at Acadia University. She is the liaison librarian for a number of the science departments. Her responsibilities include teaching, reference, assisting faculty and students with research requests, and collection development. She also headed up the implementation of an electronic theses project at the university.

Richard is an elected councillor-at-large on the executive council of the Canadian Library Association and a board member of the Annapolis Valley Regional Library Board. She is very involved in professional conference planning. She has been the program convenor for the Atlantic Provinces Library Association Conference 2000, the local arrangements coordinator of the Canadian Library Association Conference 2002, a co-chair of the Library Boards Association of Nova Scotia Conference 2004, and the program chair of ACCESS 2004. Her research interests include leadership in libraries, digital initiatives, and the evaluation of Web resources.

Richard graduated with a B.Sc. from St. Francis Xavier University in 1990 and then received her master's of library and information studies from Dalhousie in 1994. Before coming to Acadia in 1997, Richard was international projects information officer at Dalhousie University's School of Resource and Environmental Sciences. She is married and the mother of two young boys.

Jan Rivers
Dorsey & Whitney LLP

Jan Rivers is reference/electronic services librarian for Dorsey & Whitney LLP. Before joining Dorsey, Rivers worked for Arthur Andersen LLP, where she was a manager in the Risk Management Services Group, as well as a project manager and team leader for Andersen's AskNetwork e-Products Consulting Team and a regional leader in the firm's Business Information Network. She managed projects relating to the firm's intranet and Internet sites, and she developed databases and electronic information products for groups within the firm. She also conducted in-depth research and analysis for firm personnel and leadership worldwide. Before joining Arthur Andersen, Rivers worked for the Hennepin County Public Library System. She has also presented at Intranets 2000 and at Computers in Libraries and has been published in *Searcher* and *Intranet Professional.*

Mary Rumsey
University of Minnesota Law School

Mary Rumsey is the foreign, comparative, and international law librarian at the University of Minnesota Law Library. She received a B.A. in philosophy and political science, Phi Beta Kappa, from the University of Wisconsin, and a J.D. from the University of Chicago Law School. Rumsey practiced law for two years and then worked for West Group in its Westlaw Research and Development department. In 1998, she received an M.L.I.S. from Dominican University.

Rumsey worked for the William Mitchell College of Law as its electronic services librarian before joining the University of Minnesota Law Library in June 2000. She teaches a law school seminar on foreign and international legal research, lectures frequently on research to other groups, and has published several articles on legal research. Her article "Libraries Confront the Challenges of Accommodating Disabled Users" in *AALL Spectrum,* April 2002, received the 2003 AALL Spectrum Article of the Year Award.

Roger V. Skalbeck
George Mason University School of Law

Roger Skalbeck is the technology librarian at George Mason University School of Law. Skalbeck has worked in law libraries for almost a decade, including work in five law firms in three jurisdictions. Skalbeck has analyzed and reviewed numerous legal resources and technologies, and he frequently participates in conferences focused on law libraries and legal technology. He received his B.A. from Macalester College and his M.L.I.S. from Dominican University, and he is pursuing a J.D. at George Mason University School of Law.

Jen Venable
Purdue University

Jen Venable is the assistant management and economics librarian and an assistant professor at Purdue University. She holds a B.A. in news-editorial from Oklahoma State University (1994) and an M.L.I.S. from the University of Texas at Austin (1997).

Venable has been working in libraries in the academic, public, and private sectors since the age of nineteen. She began her professional career as a reference librarian for Queens Borough Public Library (QBPL) system in New York City. After working in the branch libraries, she became a business reference librarian and later assistant manager of the business research department for QBPL. After three years in New York, she moved back to Austin as the solo librarian for Hoover's, Inc., a business information database company. Venable worked for a year in the dot-com industry; she then accepted a position at the Management and Economics Library at Purdue University, where she works today.

Patricia A. Watkins
Thunderbird School of International Management

Patricia Watkins is a business information service and resources librarian in the International Business Information Centre at Thunderbird, the American Graduate School of International Management in Glendale, Arizona. In her position she consults regularly with executives from a variety of fields worldwide to help find solutions to their business intelligence needs. Before her current position, she was manager of Information Resources at MORPACE International, a Michigan-based market research firm partnering with the automotive industry.

Raised in Dearborn, Michigan, Watkins now lives in Phoenix. Before relocating to Arizona in 2001, she spent a career in advertising, marketing, and market research within the automotive industry. She was founding partner and senior project director with Creative Marketing Consultants, a Southfield, Michigan–based primary market research company whose clientele included General Motors Corporation. Before that, she worked with the Polk Company, Campbell-Ewald Advertising, and Ward's Automotive Research. In 2000, Watkins earned a master's degree in library and information science from Wayne State University in Detroit. Her undergraduate degree is in political science from the University of Michigan.

Watkins served on the board and is a past president of Women in Communications of Detroit. She is active in several information and library organizations: the Society of Competitive Intelligence, Arizona Women in International Trade, the American Library Association, the Arizona Library Association, the Mountain Plains Library Association (MPLA), and the Special Libraries Association. She was recently chosen to attend the inaugural MPLA Leadership Institute in Abiquiu, New Mexico. She is involved with research on the history and economic effect of immigration between Arizona and Mexico.

Susan F. Weiler
Weiler Information Services

Susan F. Weiler is the owner of Weiler Information Services (WIS), an information brokerage business that since 1989 has provided customized business research to companies that do not have in-house libraries or information centers. Weiler Information Services provides customized business research services to a variety of organizations, including executive recruiting firms, consulting firms, financial services firms, telecommunications equipment and service firms, and manufacturers of consumer packaged goods.

Weiler holds a master's degree in library and information sciences from Simmons College and has extensive experience as an information specialist and corporate reference librarian. Before founding WIS, she was employed by Bain & Company, an international strategic management consulting firm. Weiler is a frequent writer and speaker on topics relating to the library and information industry.

Weiler is a member of the Association of Independent Information Professionals (AIIP), New England Online Users Group, and the Special Libraries Association. She serves as a trustee of the Walpole Public Library in Walpole, Massachusetts, a member of The Dialog Corporation's Customer Advisory Board (2001–2003), and served as a director-at-large and vendor relations chairwoman of the AIIP Board (1999–2002).

Samuel Werberg
FIND/SVP, Inc.

Sam Werberg joined FIND/SVP, Inc. as a research consultant in the Technology, Information and Communications Group in August 2000, after serving as an information specialist in Morocco for three years with the U.S. Peace Corps. Before that he worked for an information broker in Austin, Texas, where he covered the semiconductor and telecom industries.

For FIND/SVP, Werberg covers artificial intelligence, consumer and business Internet usage patterns, enterprise content management, information services, knowledge management, semiconductors, and wireless technologies and communications. Werberg has also worked in academic libraries in Texas and New York and volunteers in the Queens Public Library in Astoria, New York.

Werberg received a B.S. in sociology from Hamilton College and an M.L.I.S. from the Graduate School of Library and Information Science at the University of Texas at Austin.

Kim Whalen
Emory University

Kim Whalen is a business librarian at Emory University's Goizueta Business School. She has a B.A. in business administration with a major in marketing from the Illinois Institute of Technology (1990) and an M.L.I.S. from the University of Pittsburgh's School of Information Sciences (2002).

In addition to her responsibilities within the Goizueta Business Library, Whalen is the liaison to Goizueta's Career Management Center. Through the development of Web research tools, group instructional sessions, and one-on-one consultations, she assists job-seeking students with their research of companies, industries, and geographic areas.

Before earning her master's degree, Whalen spent more than eleven years in Chicago's nonprofit sector. Positions with the University of Chicago Graduate School of Business, Illinois Institute of Technology, Advocate Health Care Foundation, and the City of Chicago developed her nonprofit marketing, public relations, and program administration experience. She is an active member of the Special Libraries Association and the American Library Association and serves on the SLA Georgia Chapter Membership Committee.

INDEX